Mad Dogs

Number Twenty-six:
The Louise Lindsey Merrick Natural Environment Series

Mad Dogs

THE NEW RABIES PLAGUE

 Don Finley

Texas A&M University Press
College Station

The paper used in this book meets the minimum requirements
of the American National Standard for Permanence
of Paper for Printed Library Materials, Z39.48-1984.
Binding materials have been chosen for durability.

Library of Congress Cataloging-in-Publication Data

Finley, Don, 1956–

Mad dogs : the new rabies plague / Don Finley. — 1st ed.

p.   cm.— (The Louise Lindsey Merrick natural environment series ;
no. 26)

Includes bibliographical references and index.

ISBN 0-89096-804-7 (cloth : alk. paper). — ISBN 0-89096-822-5 (paper
: alk. paper)

1. Rabies—Texas—Epidemiology. 2. Rabies vaccines. I. Title.

RA644.R3F54   1998

614.5′63′09764—dc21   97-34672

                                                       CIP

To my mother,
MYRTLE FINLEY,
and to the memory of my stepfather,
ROBERT E. FINLEY, SR.

The coyote said to us,
Passing over to the State of Texas,
"Here I knocked over the honey jar,
There I leave you with the bees."

—*"Corrido Del Coyote"*

CONTENTS

ILLUSTRATIONS

Along the Texas-Mexico border, the coyotes have begun acting strangely. The normally timid animals are suddenly fearless, challenging ranch dogs twice their size, attacking a toddler on her front porch, menacing oil field workers. In a nation where human deaths from rabies are rare, three people living within an hour's drive of one another are dead, the youngest a fourteen-year-old boy.

The most dangerous outbreak of rabies in America in decades has swept through coyotes—and most ominously, domestic dogs—in South Texas and threatens to push into the nation's ninth largest city and beyond. And in another outbreak stretching from Florida to New York, it is the toylike and benign raccoon that has turned vicious, attacking people and pets without provocation.

The United States has been helpless to deal with these outbreaks. Although Canada and most of Europe have nearly eliminated rabies in wild animals, health officials in this country have yet to cross the scientific, regulatory, and economic hurdles obstructing an oral rabies vaccination strategy here. Unlike the rest of the world, the United States considers rabies a local health problem, despite the fact that the virus is blind to state lines and international boundaries.

This book is really two stories: the first is of the canine rabies outbreak, which, since its birth in 1988, has inflicted considerable human suffering in Texas; the second tells of the long and curious struggle to develop an effective oral rabies vaccination program in the United States—an effort that has seen its share of politics and side issues over the past three decades.

Both stories are also about strong personalities and professional feuds—oddly enough, often between scientists and public health officials who share far more in common than one would immediately discern, given the heat of the debate that continues to rage around rabies in North America. Science, politics, economics, and personalities are woven inextricably within this tale of one of the most ancient and feared diseases ever faced by man and the contemporary battle to vanquish it.

ACKNOWLEDGMENTS

This book grew out of news stories that have appeared in the *San Antonio Express-News,* where I have worked since 1980, and I am most grateful to my editors for their encouragement and support. Thanks to Publisher W. Lawrence Walker Jr., Assistant Managing Editor Raul Reyes, City Editor Craig Thomason, and my current editor, Ron Wilson. Most of all, I wish to thank Executive Editor Robert Rivard, who offered me advice and encouragement from the very beginning of the book—even steering me toward the Texas A&M University Press; and Patrick Williams, who edited the original newspaper series, and was kind enough to read and offer many good suggestions for this much expanded work.

The other person who deserves much credit (and no blame) for these pages is John Herbold at the San Antonio branch of the University of Texas School of Public Health, whose letter to me back in 1994 sparked my interest in rabies, and who also read and offered sage advice on the manuscript.

Many, many others—too many to name them all—have gone out of their way to be helpful for this project. Keith Clark, Gayne Fearneyhough, and the rest of the crew at the Zoonosis Control Branch of the Texas Department of Health have tolerated far more pestering from me than any humans should have to endure. Keith in particular has been so helpful and encouraging—even allowing me into his home when his medical condition gave him every excuse not to—that a large part of the credit for this work should go to him.

Charles Rupprecht, the father of V-RG and the head of rabies programs for the Centers for Disease Control and Prevention, was generous enough to clear the better part of a day from his busy schedule to share with me the fascinating story of V-RG, and to make his staff available when I visited there. His recollections were clear, colorful, and forthright, and added immensely to this book.

Others who deserve special thanks include Jack Berg and the scientists and staff at Rhone Merieux in Athens, Georgia; Jean Smith at CDC; Charles MacInnes with the Ontario Ministry of Natural Resources, and his former colleague, Dave Johnston; Cathleen Hanlon with the New York State Department of Health; Faye Sorhage with the New Jersey State Department of Health; Douglas Roscoe with the New Jersey Division of Fish, Game and Wildlife; Kerry Ann Pflugh with the New Jersey Department of Environmental Protection; Robert Miller at USDA; Fernando Guerra, Ned Lammers, and Anna Crowder at the San Antonio Metropolitan Health District; former Texas Commissioner of Health David Smith; George McKirahan, Oscar Tamez, and Laura Robinson with the Harlingen office of the Texas Department of Health; Margot Martinez with the Rabies Center of Excellence in Laredo; Barry Truitt with the Nature Conservancy; Jane Rissler with the Union of Concerned Scientists; John Brown with the South Carolina Department of Health; Bill Johnston with the Alabama State Department of Health and Environmental Control; Billy Howard with Pinellas County Animal Services; and Barbara French and Janet Tyburec with Bat Conservation International.

Thanks also to George Baer, Hilary Koprowski, Sam Patton, David Heard, Fred Knowlton, Keith Jones, Denny Constantine, Roberto Margo, Sue and Monte Smith, and the other residents of South Texas who shared their stories with me. In particular I wish to thank the families, friends, and physicians of the three South Texans who lost their lives to rabies: Manuel Riojas, San Juanita Barrera, and Rolando Bazan.

I am very grateful to my agent, Elizabeth Frost Knappman at New England Publishing Associates, who showed remarkable patience and encouragement to this freshman author, and to the editors and staff of the Texas A&M University Press.

Finally, I am indebted beyond measure to my wife, Gloria Padilla, who not only provided wise criticism of this book as it developed, but also has shouldered far more than her share of household duties during the two years I have been preoccupied with it—particularly in regard to our eighteen-month-old daughter, Hannah. I'm still trying to figure out a way to pay that one off in installments.

Mad Dogs

Madness begins with a brief but furious scuffle in the cool dry minutes before dawn, two gray-brown shapes locked together in a single rolling blur, obscured within a cloud of dust rising among the huisache, mesquite, and prickly pear. Perhaps this combat was trumpeted by the famous howl, as familiar as the rooster's crowing to the farmers and ranchers throughout these South Texas plains. Only this time, the howl is a bit different, the pitch higher with an odd and somehow unnerving trill. A change in voice is a frequent symptom of rabies in animals; health workers sometimes can follow the sound to locate a sick animal. But the coyote's song is unique, and has always held different meanings to different listeners. To some, it inspires feelings of comfort and curiosity, and even awe; to others—particularly those whose livelihood depends on the survival of the young sheep and goats often lost to hungry coyotes—the reaction is more hostile. The Plains Indians, who considered them holy, imitated the yelps of coyotes in their songs. Cowboys humorously called them the prairie tenors. But regardless of its effect on humans, the coyote's cry has always been directed at other coyotes, and their language has yet to be deciphered by man.

A fierce and sudden encounter between two coyotes is not unexpected. Coyotes are territorial and will challenge trespassers, particularly during seasons of mating and whelping. The family's homestead is often marked by natural or manmade boundaries like creeks or roads. Frederick F. Knowlton, a wildlife biologist with the Denver Wildlife Research Center in Logan, Utah, who has spent a lifetime studying coyotes, observes that although the animals will fight each other, more often their confrontations are mutual attempts at intimidation. "Where you normally see it is at the borders of the territories. And when you do see it, it's a remarkable display. You'll see a group of coyotes on each side of the border, sitting there and flagging their tails—putting their tails straight up and flagging them slowly back and forth—scratching and kicking up dirt. They may howl. Each group doing it on their own side of the border.

"That doesn't mean they don't try to trespass from time to time. They'll go right up to the border, and if nobody's around, they may go over to explore. But if the territory owners show up, they pull back."

Not that strangers are never accepted into new families. Each fall, some of the adolescent coyotes—and those whose ranking has somehow fallen within the coyote social hierarchy—will set out on their own; most will die, but a few will find a new group and live on the fringes, slowly working their way inside. These are the rules, understood by most coyotes. But a rabid coyote loses awareness of the rules, and despite his cleverness—having outwitted the best attempts by man to eradicate him, having outlived his fiercest natural enemy, the timber wolf—loses the natural wariness of danger that has permitted him to survive and prosper.

As the coyote whose territory has been invaded stands his ground, he feels the intruder's fangs sink into the highly sensitive flesh around his narrow muzzle. With a yelp, he frees himself and backs away, snarling in fear and anger. Perhaps the stranger continues the battle for a time—or, in his delirium, may forget the encounter almost immediately and stagger back into the brush. In any case, the contact has been made, the infection passed along. Rabies, which typically is spread through the saliva of an infected animal through a break in the skin from a bite or scratch, is unique among diseases in that it causes changes in behavior that help the virus to spread. In other words, the unthinking fury of a rabid animal ensures it will infect another.

Under an electron microscope, the rabies virus resembles a bullet with outer spikes of glycoprotein that attach to receptors on nerve cells. Rabies is a single-strand RNA (or ribonucleic acid) virus that uses the nerve cell's own internal mechanisms to reproduce. Once infection has set in, the virus travels along the neural network, the long axons of nerve cells, through the nervous system to the brain. The virus favors specific parts of the brain, particularly the limbic system—a region at the center of the brain that controls the emotions. The preference by the rabies virus for that particular region was first identified by Dutch physician Herman Boerhaave in 1715. Boerhaave observed that people who died after a bite by a rabid animal had marked inflammation in the limbic system.

Despite the encephalitis or inflammation that causes the trademark madness and aggression, rabies induces very little overt destruction in the brain. Within nerve cells, particles first identified by Adelchi Negri in 1903, called Negri bodies, are present in rabies and are part of the pathologic identification of the disease. Still, "nobody really knows what happens in the brain," says Jean Smith, who heads the rabies laboratory at the Centers for Disease Control and Prevention. "There really aren't that many changes in neuronal function associated with the infection. There are some, but not what you might anticipate. It's not like poliomyelitis, or measles encephalitis, where you actually get destruction of neurons. It's much quieter."

At the height of infection in the brain, the virus jumps to the peripheral nerves and travels back to highly innervated areas of the body such as the cornea, the skin (particularly at the head and neck), and the salivary glands. With insidious timing, the virus multiplies in the saliva glands in concert with the changes in the brain that cause the aggression and biting behavior. Part of those brain changes may be partly due to the body's own natural defenses trying vainly to repel the virus. Some studies have shown that when you weaken a rabid animal's immune system, their symptoms improve. "In animals you can almost suppress all of the clinical signs, and other than the fact that they become very thin during the process, they will eat and live for months while they have massive amounts of virus in their central nervous system," Smith says. "If at some point you decide to end the experiment, you can just give them immune serum or immune cells and they will die within two or three days."

The speed with which the disease progresses from bite to brain varies, depending in part on where the bite occurred; in dogs, the incubation period is typically between three and twelve weeks. Bites to the head and neck cause the most rapid progression of rabies. One of the most dramatic accounts of this phenomenon occurred at the turn of the century, when Nathaniel Garland Keirle, the medical examiner of the city of Baltimore, and founder of one of the earliest Pasteur Institutes (centers established around the country where those bitten by rabid animals could travel to receive Pasteur's new rabies vaccine), wrote of eight local boys ranging in age between eight and eighteen, bitten by a large, rabid Saint Bernard–mastiff cross. All were treated within three days.

Of the eight boys, four died. Those who died were bitten on the face and neck. Of the four who survived, three were bitten on the arm, and one on the ear through an ear warmer. Describing those who died, Keirle wrote, "all these were treated by this method with a result as disastrous as if they had not been treated at all." Of course, as Smith points out, the earliest Pasteur vaccine was made from nerve cells—rabbit spinal cords, ground, and processed. Adverse reactions to those nerve cells, particularly a nerve protein called myelin, were frequent and terrible; many people died from the vaccine itself. Later vaccines were grown from suckling mouse and then duck embryo—which were less likely to cause neurological side effects than vaccines from adult animals—and finally from human cell lines.

Keirle described one young victim:

> The little fellow was semi-recumbent on the couch and complained that opening the doors annoyed him, and the air hurt his head and face. He had been delirious but spoke with clearness. He would have a clonic convulsion during which he seemed to be struggling with someone, but he was conscious all the way through. If you sat opposite him he talked to you until the convulsion came on, when his attention was altogether distracted. His pupils were dilated and the anterior chamber rather deep. He had another symptom that was almost pathognomonic, that is, sputation. He would spit saliva in little pools on the carpet and apologize to his mother for soiling the room. When these convulsions passed off he would get up, put on his clothing, walk to the window, and then would come back to the couch and have another convulsion. It was about 11 o'clock that I saw him, and he died that night. He would not have impressed anyone at the time as being so ill as to die in such a short time.

Rabies, described by ancient Egyptians, is one of the oldest diseases known to humanity; yet there are many things about the virus that scientists still do not understand. One of those is the extent to which the infection is maintained sublethally in wildlife populations. Some animals recover from rabies. "You know, rabies isn't a fatal disease," Don Hildebrand, president of the vaccine manufacturer Rhone Merieux, told me during a visit to the company's headquarters in Athens, Georgia. He had never been vaccinated against rabies, he said, and yet his years of working with the virus had left him with detectable blood levels of rabies neutralizing antibodies.

The coyote, or *canis latrans,* whose name is derived from the Aztec word *coyotl,* is perhaps the most widely distributed and best-adapted wild animal in North America. Once limited to the open plains and grasslands in the southwestern United States and Mexico, they now are found in every U.S. state except Hawaii. "And I facetiously say there are at least three swimming that direction right now," Knowlton says. Coyotes have traversed north into northern Canada, and south to Panama. Despite three centuries of efforts by humanity to wipe them out, they have tenaciously survived and thrived, largely because of their adaptability. They can survive on meat or vegetation; on rabbits in the brush or on restaurant scraps from trash cans in the alleys of Chicago. Biologists examining coyote stomachs have found them unfussy eaters, with a diet that includes rats and watermelon, sheep and lizards, deer and crickets, grass and belt buckles.

Knowlton provided the earliest research that showed there were more coyotes in South Texas, mile for mile, than anywhere else—between four and six per square mile in the fall. The irony in this is that the war between the federal government and coyotes began in Texas in 1914, when Texas members of Congress, acting on behalf of sheep ranchers, appropriated special funds for coyote eradication. Those in other parts of America tend to think of Texas as cattle country, but for many years the state was the biggest sheep and goat producer in the nation. Millions of coyotes in Texas have been killed, to little effect. Charles L. Cadieux, who led coyote eradication efforts in Texas, Nebraska, and the Dakotas in the 1950s and 1960s, wrote of the futility of the campaign in his book, *Coyotes: Predators & Survivors:* "Biology teaches us that when a pressure is exerted downward on a species, that species reacts with an equal and upward pressure. After centuries of persecution, coyotes survive very easily and have become amazingly adaptable. When it appeared that the poison 1080 was reducing coyote numbers over much of the west, upward resistance became strong. When 1080 was banned in 1972, the upward resistance faced little pressure and the coyote numbers increased."

That tenacious adaptability is demonstrated in how coyotes survive the feast-or-famine conditions in the wild. Researchers such as Knowlton, studying the availability of food sources such as rats and rabbits on coyote population, have found a somewhat complicated relationship. While studies show that an increase in an important food source such as jackrabbits is followed by an increase in coyote numbers, some research suggests the reverse is not the case—when food sources disappear, coyote populations may not decline. Other studies have indicated the availability of food may have an indirect effect on coyote populations: when food is plentiful, female coyotes have more pups. When it scarce, the death rate among young coyotes soars.

Others argue the fairly recent decline in fur prices has also caused coyote numbers to increase. In the early 1980s, Cadieux writes, coyote pelts sold for more than one hundred dollars apiece. Political correctness, among other factors, led to a collapse in the fur market. The same farm and ranch interests that have spearheaded the coyote war also eliminated the coyote's one nonhuman natural enemy, the timber wolf, from the West. Meanwhile, human settlements have expanded, squeezing against open lands that traditionally have offered up coyote habitat. Increased numbers, sharpened adaptation, ever increasing proximity to humans—all these ingredients come together in an increasingly risky recipe where rabies is concerned.

The coyote first feels a burning and itching sensation on his muzzle where the trespasser bit him. He rubs at the wound furiously with his paw—even rubs it in the dirt, reopening the scab—but to no relief. Gradually he withdraws from the other animals in the pack, preferring to rest in dark, isolated spots. But sleep is elusive; he cannot stay down for long, preferring to pace and wander. Sometimes he impulsively picks up a stone or a twig and moves it a short distance; other times he swallows such objects, vomiting them up later.

Rabies has three distinct phases after an incubation period: first is the prodromal stage, characterized by behavioral changes, followed by the furious stage, and finally paralysis and death. As the hours bleed into days, he becomes more irritable and agitated, wandering farther and farther from his territory, barely aware of his surroundings. He snaps at almost anything that enters his line of vision.

John Spruell, a Laredo veterinarian who has decapitated dozens of coyote carcasses to send for testing, said that often he can smell a rabid coyote before it's brought through his door. "A coyote in it's right mind won't mess with a skunk," Spruell said. "When they pull that animal control truck up and I go walking out there and can smell a skunk, I know they're positive every time." Coyotes are free-ranging; during the dispersal of adolescents and outcasts, coyotes have been known to travel more than a hundred miles.

South Texas geography is vast and unfriendly, awash in shrub and cactus. For centuries it has largely been left to the coyotes and a few sturdy ranchers. No longer. Cities like Laredo and McAllen along the Texas-Mexico border are among the fastest-growing in the nation. Development between San Antonio and the border has been steady over the past two decades. Margot Martinez, a veterinarian with the Texas Department of Health, recalls driving back from college to her native Eagle Pass and rarely seeing a service station. "Now they're everywhere," she says. With more people around, a coyote doesn't have to wander far before stumbling into one. Under normal conditions, of course, coyotes will avoid at all costs contact with humans, who have been trying fervently to wipe them out for centuries. But rabies scrambles the intelligence coyotes have developed to stay alive.

Somewhere in the fevered vision of the coyote is a fence line and a house. Somewhere in his range of acute hearing are dogs barking furiously, having picked up his scent from a distance. The coyote moves towards the noise, oblivious to all but the rage that propels him forward. The noise is angry, and the coyote is angry. In a few minutes the anger will merge in a white-hot burst, and perhaps there will be satisfaction.

CHAPTER ONE

Birth of a Plague

Sue Smith's feet dangled from the open rear door of the family Suburban as she read aloud from the assembly instructions to the brand new lawnmower beside her in the truck. Her husband, Monte, stood outside the truck facing her, studying the parts in the fading late afternoon light. They had ordered the mower weeks before, and Sue had picked it up in town earlier in the day. It was the beginning of a three-day weekend, the Saturday before Labor Day 1988, and the pace on the farm was a bit slower than usual. Sue read from the instructions "badly, so as to annoy him," she joked later. They were practically newlyweds, having married shortly before moving to the desolate brushlands of eastern Starr County in May. The house sat like an island on an expanse of pasture attached to the farm Monte Smith had been hired to oversee. The nearest town was Rincon—which was barely a town, more of a wide spot in the road. But the solitude pleased them. "We're both country people," Sue explained.

From beneath the house, where the dogs took refuge from the brutal South Texas sun, came excited barking. The couple didn't even look up; the dogs were always scrambling after an errant jackrabbit or squirrel, or even an occasional rattlesnake. "Go get 'em," Monte said absently, and soon the dogs quieted.

But a few minutes later, the dogs sounded again. This time there was a commotion in the yard, and Sue glanced up from the instruction booklet to see the coyote standing only about fifteen feet away. This was unsettling enough; coyotes are plentiful around Starr County, but they always kept their distance. This animal was angry and appeared ready to attack Monte. But the two dogs intervened: Buckwheat, a four-year-old female Labrador, and Sheiba, a year-old, female Lab-wolf cross, fought with the coyote as Monte and Sue ran back to the house. Monte grabbed the loaded rifle they kept near the back door and returned. The smaller coyote was winning the battle with the dogs—even whipping Sheiba, who was half wolf—as Monte took aim and fired. The coyote dropped.

Flushed with adrenaline, the couple stood over the dead animal for several minutes and speculated.

"Well, it looks healthy."

"But they don't come up in the daytime."

"Well, maybe he was coming up for a drink of water."

"Well, one of the dogs is in heat, maybe it was coming up for something else."

Inside the house, they telephoned their veterinarian in McAllen, but his office was closed. They left a message on his answering machine. The possibility of rabies occurred to them, and somehow they got the idea to pack the coyote in ice until Tuesday, after the holiday, when they could deliver it to the vet for testing.

They did succeed in reaching Dr. Roberto Margo, the only veterinarian in Starr County, by telephone. Margo told them to sever the coyote head and freeze it until it could be tested. Sue, who would soon return to school at age forty-four to become a registered nurse, insisted on gloves and goggles. Monty stood over the animal and decapitated it with a machete. They wrapped the head several times in plastic. The vet in McAllen finally returned their call and told them not to bother freezing it; packing it in ice would be fine.

On Tuesday, Sue Smith put the plastic-wrapped coyote head in the back of the Suburban and drove to McAllen, where the vet repacked it in dry ice and shipped it to the Texas Department of Health laboratories in Austin.

Texas maintains one of the best public health laboratories in the country, where nearly four hundred employees process tests for everything from influenza to water pollutants to inherited diseases in newborns. Added duties over time have long overwhelmed the 68,000 square feet of lab space, most of it built in the 1950s—with some spillover contained in adjacent temporary buildings. On one edge of the laboratory complex is a small, well-lit autopsy room where rabies testing begins. The most interesting feature in the otherwise unremarkable room is a powerful vent looming over the metal autopsy table, designed to suck from the air any aerosolized virus that might be unleashed during cutting. Dropping from the vent like a curtain is a Plexiglas shield, resembling the sneeze guard at a restaurant salad bar.

The process is the same for any animal. The head is unwrapped and placed on the table. Working with his arms beneath the Plexiglas shield, a technician grasps the head with steel forceps and makes an incision with a scalpel across the top, from muzzle to behind the ears, exposing the skull. The skin is then peeled back, and an electric circular saw, its blade the size of a half-dollar, splits the bony skull. The technician cracks the skull and removes the brain. Discarding the head for incineration, the technician moves to another table a few feet away, where small samples are removed from the cerebellum, the hippocampus, and the stem. "You can find rabies in other parts of the brain, but it will be in highest concentration in those three areas," says Susan Neill, supervisor of medical virology for the health department.

Each brain sample is smeared upon different parts of a single glass slide, which is then routed to another room for processing. There it is fixed with acetone for three hours before being treated with an antibody reagent—an antibody that attaches to rabies virus, spliced with a substance that will fluoresce green under an ultraviolet-source microscope. The reagent is allowed to work for thirty minutes before excess brain matter is washed away. In a third room, this one darkened, the slide is examined in turn by two different technicians. "We always have two people look at every specimen," Neill says. "We don't want to miss a weak positive. A strong positive is very easy to see." Under the microscope, a positive slide resembles a galaxy of eerie green stars.

When a rabies test is positive, lab personnel return to the original brain sample, which is stored in a small tin. All brain samples are routinely saved in a household chest freezer for six months to permit follow-up tests. In the early 1990s, the lab gained the technology to determine the strain of rabies virus using a panel of nineteen different monoclonal antibodies. That test, however, cannot distinguish between dog and fox rabies. It wasn't until the beginning of 1995 that the lab was able to make such fine distinctions using a method known as polymerase chain reaction. Prior to those two advances, Texas had to rely on the rabies laboratory headed by Jean Smith at the Centers for Disease Control and Prevention in Atlanta. It was in Atlanta that the strain from the coyote in Monte and Sue Smith's yard ultimately was matched with a strain closely related to one obtained from rabid dogs in Mexico City in 1978 and 1991, and reported sporadically along the border. From then on, the strain of canine rabies that began sweeping northward through South Texas was described as Mexican Urban Dog.

When the call from McAllen came two weeks later, the Smiths had other things besides rabies on their minds. Hurricane Gilbert had slammed into northern Mexico, and "it was blowing and going" along the border, Sue recalls. Later, much later, she would read in the newspaper speculation that the rabies outbreak began with the hurricane somehow causing coyotes to cross the Rio Grande from Mexico. Baloney, Sue Smith said. Their coyote showed up two weeks before the hurricane.

The veterinarian started the conversation with, "Remember the coyote head?"

With rabies confirmed, the Smiths' next call was from Oscar Tamez, a veteran rabies technician from the state health department's regional office in Harlingen. Tamez asked Sue a few questions about the incident, then recommended that Buckwheat and Sheiba be put to sleep.

But the dogs were current on their rabies vaccinations, she protested. Years later, as he described the history of the canine rabies outbreak in talks to groups, Keith Clark, the state health department's chief of zoonosis control, would joke that Buckwheat and Sheiba were the only two vaccinated dogs in Starr County.

But Tamez stuck with his recommendation. Sometimes the vaccine doesn't take, he said. Best to be safe.

"We told him the dogs saved us," Sue said later. "We are going to keep the dogs chained for forty-five days, and we will watch them carefully, but we're not killing them," Sue said. "And we were satisfied we hadn't touched the coyote, and weren't interested in any follow-up."

That might have been the end of it, but suddenly it seemed sick-looking coyotes were popping up all over the area. "I don't know how many my husband killed out in the field. The other ranchers, the company he works for—everybody was on the lookout for coyotes. One day I was driving into town and one staggered out into the road. I thought, well, there goes the alignment. It was obviously salivating and slobbering. We had more dumb rabies than we had the vicious rabies. You would just see them staggering, stumbling across the road."

The couple tried to spread the word, first warning oil rig workers to beware of strays. "We would stop and tell the guys, if a nice puppy comes up here don't pet it. We tried to get the newspapers to write something because it was hunting season, and the newspapers ignored us. We went to the TV stations, and they basically ignored us too."

Soon, of course, no one would be ignoring the problem—particularly after it moved into more populated areas. But at the time it was scary to the Smiths, who had learned to live with a few scary things since moving to the farm.

"It's like rattlesnakes," Sue Smith says. "We live out here with the biggest damn rattlesnakes you ever saw in your life. You are always aware that there could be a rattlesnake, so you try not to do anything stupid. We would never live without dogs here because the dogs are your first line of defense. Against rattlesnakes, too."

Except for an occasional bat, no rabies case had been reported in Starr or surrounding counties during the previous eighteen years, until the Smiths' coyote came along. Further west along the border, in Laredo and Eagle Pass, occasional outbreaks had arisen in dogs over the years, usually coinciding with outbreaks in sister cities on the other side of the Rio Grande. In those instances, the communities had mobilized, sponsored pet vaccination clinics, redoubled efforts to pick up strays—the traditional public health tools of rabies control. They had always been successful—at least for a while. In 1976, Laredo suddenly found itself with an outbreak of rabid dogs after having been free of rabies since the mid-1950s. "We were kind of like living in a bubble," John Spruell, a Laredo veterinarian, recalls. "When it broke— bang, there were fifty-six cases in two months. The community really came out. We started vaccinating dogs, giving the shots for a dollar. Then one of the Chevrolet dealers jumped up and said he'd buy all the vaccine. McDonald's got into it, saying everybody that gets their dog vaccinated, we'll give them a Big Mac and a Coke.

"Free shots, plus they got a Big Mac and a Coke, and we got to about 90 percent" of pet dogs in Laredo vaccinated, Spruell says. After the crisis, the vaccination rate dropped again.

Like Laredo in 1976, Starr and other counties in the region known as the Lower Rio Grande Valley had been rabies free for so long, few if anyone considered the disease a serious threat. That meant few bothered vaccinating their animals. The low vaccination rates, along with other factors, made it seem almost as though rabies had deliberately singled out the most vulnerable spot in the nation to launch an explosive outbreak. "These are communities that are in a rural-to-urban transition," says Margot Martinez, a veterinarian and lifelong border resident, later recruited by the state health department to head a border rabies command post in Laredo. "We still hold onto many of the old practices, where we have the dream of holding onto our little plot of land and bringing as many animals as God will provide us." Starr was listed in census records as being the second poorest county in the nation—a ranking viewed with some skepticism by observers who note the census takers generally fail to include income derived from the county's thriving drug trafficking industry. Nevertheless, most residents *are* poor and struggling—a fact apparent by even the most casual inspection. Starr had one part-time veterinarian, Roberto Margo, and one animal control officer. Throughout the Valley, rapid growth had overwhelmed local services, and poverty often placed the family pet at the bottom of any list of priorities.

As if the socioeconomics hadn't already created a rabies tinderbox, the weather had also lent a hand. Drought conditions over the past year had dried up creeks and caused normal food supplies to dwindle. Small animals, like mice and rabbits, and the coyotes that fed on them, concentrated around fewer water sources such as stock tanks and reservoirs. One study had demonstrated that during normal years, South Texas had the highest known coyote population density of any part of the country, with somewhere between four and six animals per square mile after breeding season in the fall. As the coyote density increased with the dry weather, so did the opportunity for territorial squabbles, and the spread of disease. The Valley's long reprieve from rabies was about to end.

Less than a month after the first case, at a ranch about ten miles north of the Smiths' house, a coyote attacked three unvaccinated dogs around midday. The owner shot the coyote, and was instructed by his veterinarian in Raymondville to bring the head in for testing. Four days later, the results came back from the state laboratory: positive. The three dogs—all six years old, black-and-white mixed-breeds from the same litter—were destroyed, as was a fourth dog that the owner thought might also have tangled with the coyote. No humans were exposed.

On November 3, 1988, rabies came to Rio Grande City, the county seat and largest town in Starr County, with a population of about ten thousand.

Raymond Munsell, a Department of Public Safety trooper, had just completed his shift and was pulling into the driveway at his home when he saw his neighbor approaching, an odd look on his face. As Munsell stepped out of the car, the neighbor pointed to a tan-colored shape visible in the grass. Instinctively, Munsell grabbed his rifle. "When he got up out of the grass, you could tell he was a coyote," Munsell says. "The animal didn't look scared or anything. A coyote doesn't do that."

Munsell had some familiarity with coyotes, having lived in Starr County all his life. Although they tended to give humans a wide berth, they frequently could be spotted moving through the brush in the early morning. They weren't something to worry about, as a rule, unless they were sick—as this one appeared to be.

As Munsell approached it, the coyote backed away—perhaps a vestige of its normal survival instinct penetrating its foggy senses. It moved slowly across the street, with Munsell following at a safe distance. The animal went behind another house, but was startled by a group of men working on a pipeline and backtracked toward the street. By this time, a small crowd of curious neighbors had gathered to watch the spectacle. Munsell had seen enough. He raised his rifle, took aim and fired, dropping the coyote.

Munsell telephoned Roberto Margo, the county's only veterinarian, who maintained a part-time practice at his ranch on the outskirts of Rio Grande City. Margo told Munsell to bring the animal to his office, a detached portable building about fifty yards from the front door of his ranch-style home. Results of the positive test came back November 9. The coyote, it turned out, had fought with three dogs in the neighborhood—a black male mixed-breed, a male German shepherd cross, and a brown and black Pekingese cross. All three were destroyed the same day the positive results came back, along with an Angora cat suspected also to have been exposed.

On the same day Munsell shot the coyote, a family in rural Abram, in Hidalgo County, to the east of Starr—heard noises outside about five A.M. They found that their seven-week-old Chihuahua puppy, Dooty, had been attacked and dragged several yards away to a nearby canal. The family took Dooty to the veterinarian, who treated her for a broken jaw and apparent bite wounds, and sent her home. Twelve days later the family returned with Dooty, complaining she was sick and appeared to have reinjured her jaw. The vet suspected rabies and asked the family's permission to put the dog to sleep. The state lab confirmed rabies November 21. Eighty-four days after the Smiths' coyote, the first rabid dog of the South Texas rabies epizootic—the term for epidemic in animals—had been confirmed. Hidalgo County would prove to be the exception to the normal pattern as the epizootic spread: first, a rabid coyote would appear in a county, then, two to four months later, the first rabid dog or cat would appear. In the days that followed Dooty's lab results, twenty-one people received postexposure shots —including the owners, their three adult children, eight family friends ranging in age from nine to thirty, and eight employees of the veterinary clinic. Except for the veterinary workers, none of those receiving shots had been bitten; all said they had handled the puppy or hand-fed it since it had a broken jaw. Afterward, state health officials organized a rabies vaccination clinic in Abram, and fifty-eight pet dogs were vaccinated.

By mid-October, George McKirahan had completed his six weeks of training at Yoakum in the fine art of meat inspection and was in place as veterinarian at the Texas Department of Health's regional office in Harlingen. The duties of the regional veterinarian at the time were divided between overseeing the inspection of slaughterhouses and zoonosis—the control of animal diseases that can infect humans. Oscar Tamez, the region's zoonosis technician, later joked that McKirahan had brought the rabies with him. McKirahan, who for the past eleven years had operated a private veterinary practice in the small town of Smithville, about forty miles west of Austin, had gone to work for the state health department September 1 for what was then the Bureau of Veterinary Public Health. Later, the rabies outbreak— among other factors—would prompt the state to separate those two functions, meat inspection and zoonosis control. McKirahan would wind up on the meat inspection side. But almost as soon as he arrived in Harlingen, rabies occupied the vast majority of his time in two of the twenty-seven counties under his responsibility.

As the end of the year approached, rabid dogs and coyotes, it seemed, were turning up everywhere. A sixty-five-year-old store owner near Mission, in Hidalgo County, was bitten by Bow, his son's dog, as he tried to untangle Bow's chain. The year-old, female Doberman cross, which was unvaccinated, died two hours later that day, November 19. David Heflin, the family's veterinarian, found a wound on the dog's groin the owners were unable to explain. The family later said the dog's bark seemed to have changed. When rabies was confirmed four days later, another community rabies vaccination clinic was quickly organized.

On the same day the store owner was bitten, in a neighborhood not far away, a neighbor's Doberman got loose and entered a yard, biting a four-year-old boy on the eye and fighting with other dogs. The family called the Hidalgo County sheriff's department, and an officer advised them to tie up the dog. But the following day, on a Sunday, the dog got loose and was struck and killed by a pickup truck. The owner took the dog to Heflin, who sent the head to Austin. It was rabid. The boy who was bitten began postexposure treatment in Mission. The dog's owner instead took her two daughters to Mexico for treatment. She later told Tamez the dog was a stray the family had adopted. It had displayed no suspicious symptoms she had noticed.

Shortly afterward, a seven-month-old, male Boston terrier–Chihuahua mix, died at its home outside Rio Grande City. The owner took the animal to Dr. Margo, who asked her if it had tangled with any other animals recently. She recalled seeing a small coyote approach their chain-link fence November 5. After she shooed away the coyote, she noticed the puppy had quite a bit of saliva on its nose. When the state lab confirmed rabies November 28, five people ranging in age from six to thirty-five underwent postexposure treatments.

A Rio Grande City physician had inherited Angel, an eleven-year-old Labrador, from a neighbor. Although his other dog was vaccinated, he had never considered Angel's vaccination status. It was only after the dog's rapid change in temperament on November 26 that it became an issue. Suddenly the dog appeared to have difficulty maintaining its balance and drooled excessively. It also looked as though Angel was uncomfortable swallowing. The doctor took the dog to Margo, who put it down and sent the head to the state lab. Six people required rabies shots, including the doctor, his wife, and three children, ages three through eight. The youngest child, in particular, had been slobbered on by the dog. Margo recommended a booster shot for the other dog and placing it in quarantine for forty-five days, just to be sure. He also asked the doctor to help him spread the word in the community about the sudden and frightening explosion of rabies cases.

A plumber working near an abandoned house inside Rio Grande City shot a rabid coyote December 2. Health department records fail to note why the plumber was armed. In the town of Abram near Mission, where two other rabies cases had been confirmed, a dog named Polomo turned vicious, killing one cat and fighting with several neighborhood dogs. As the owner tried to load it into a truck, it bit him and escaped. Two days later, the dog returned home and the man shot it. Health officials repeatedly urged a neighbor whose dog scuffled with the animal to have it euthanized. The neighbor refused.

Nearby, on December 6, a stray wandered into a yard and fought with the family's dog, which was tied up. As the stray was leaving, it stumbled into a deep pit on the property. The family called the sheriff's department, which came to investigate two days later. The animal, which was already dead, tested positive. The same day, in nearby Palm View, a two-year-old boy was bitten on the finger by a neighbor's dog. His father captured the nine-month-old animal, named Paloma, with the help of another neighbor, and delivered it to a veterinarian. The vet advised them to return home and tie the dog up for observation. It died the following day. Another dog Paloma had tangled with was also tied up for observation on the advice of a Palm View police officer. State health officials recommended the dog be destroyed and issued rabies guidelines to the Palm View Police Department.

In Alto, near Mission, a Chihuahua was struck by sudden paralysis, trembling, a drooped jaw, and broken teeth. The dog tested positive. The owner said she was nursing five pups, and had been in a fight three or four days earlier. Five pups and six adult cats were destroyed by the Upper Valley Humane Society. When the health department recommended the family spread the word throughout the neighborhood about rabies, they were told about a neighbor whose two dogs tethered outside his home appeared sick, staggering, and slobbering. When Tamez inquired, the owner of the two dogs shot them.

Back in Starr County, the problem continued to be coyotes. A rancher north of Alto Bonito, near Rio Grande City, spotted a coyote beneath a mesquite tree December 22. He crept within fifteen yards and fired with his rifle, but the shot went wide. The coyote retreated slowly. The rancher got off another shot and killed the coyote, which later tested positive. In Rio Grande City the following day, a coyote came into a yard and attacked five puppies. The sheriff picked up four, which were euthanized. Another was never found. The owner, the sheriff said, had dumped the wounded animal in a remote area off a dirt road.

Seven miles west of Mission, a man who had found a dog at a levee near his house six weeks earlier reported it was foaming at the mouth, running in circles, staggering, and refusing to eat or drink. The dog, who the man had named Foxy, was euthanized at the Mid Valley Humane Society. In nearby Alton, a male beagle who had been attacked and bitten on the front left leg by another dog two weeks earlier began acting sick, biting at the air, refusing to sit or take food. Two children ages ten and thirteen were exposed and underwent postexposure treatment. The beagle, whose name does not appear in case records, was the final positive rabies case in South Texas in 1988, the first year of the canine rabies epizootic.

Between September 3—when the first rabid coyote wandered into Monte and Sue Smith's yard—and the end of the year, seventeen laboratory-confirmed rabies cases had been reported in Starr and Hidalgo counties. Eleven were in dogs, six were in coyotes. All the rabid coyotes had been discovered in Starr. Other domestic dogs were suspected, and, of course, most sick-looking coyotes weren't even reported, so the total was certainly much higher.

For McKirahan, the problem was nearly overwhelming. Not only were traditional rabies control methods almost impossible to implement here—with maybe 80 percent or more of domestic dogs unvaccinated, and almost no animal control infrastructure to pick up strays—but there were no public health tools at all to deal with this new element of rabid coyotes. Still, he and Tamez focused on what they felt was possible: briefing local politicians, holding town meetings, speaking to school children, and organizing vaccination drives. A briefing to the Starr County commissioner's court in December led the court to declare the county an emergency rabies quarantine area—allowing them to implement any measures they felt were necessary to control the outbreak. To McKirahan's disappointment, the county took no significant action following that declaration.

"A lot of people wanted to rely on the state, but the state had limited resources, limited manpower—me and Oscar Tamez," McKirahan says. "Certainly we were there more to offer assistance in the way of training, education—more or less as advisers. We saw it as a community problem, and we thought the community should get together. They knew their community better than we did. They could get things moving better than we could. That was our feeling, and it kind of did work like that in some areas, and didn't in others." They urged county officials to hire animal control officers, and promised to train them. Although they made little headway in Starr, Hidalgo County, which had a somewhat richer tax base, did step up animal control measures. The two men organized town meetings, even going house to house in neighborhoods badly hit by rabies, handing out notices. At one meeting, twenty-eight people showed up—nearly all of them with state agencies or the media. "Where were all those community people we felt should be there?" McKirahan wondered. "It was their people, their families, their neighbors, and friends. Maybe it's apathy. Maybe it's: 'Not my dog, he's been vaccinated.' Or, 'Not my kid.' It's always somebody else's kids that gets bit. Human nature being what it is, that was probably a lot of the problem."

Setting Up Defenses

A man in LaJoya, in West Hidalgo County, returned home from a brief trip about 1 A.M. January 2, 1989, and was surprised when his three-month-old puppy, Brownie, attacked him viciously. He later told Oscar Tamez he had left the animal alone for several days. The attack marked a definite change in the animal's behavior—which included unusual aggressiveness, a change in bark, and excitability. He took Brownie to the vet three days later. The dog died that afternoon. Seven people required postexposure treatment.

From that first case of 1989 to the end of the year, another forty-three rabid animals were reported in Starr and Hidalgo counties, including thirty-four dogs, six coyotes, and spillover of the canine rabies strain into two raccoons and a cat. The previous year, all six rabid coyotes had been in Starr. The six reported during 1989 included five in Starr and one in Hidalgo. The main problem during 1989 were dogs, making the risk to humans acute. Hundreds of people required postexposure treatments.

At first, it appeared as though Starr County might get a reprieve. Except for a rabid coyote in February, the county remained rabies free during the first half of the year. Then, in mid-July, a rabid dog and a rabid coyote were reported within a two-day period. Three weeks later, two more cases of rabies were confirmed in dogs, followed by a dozen more through the end of the year. In November and December 1989, three more rabid coyotes were reported in Starr. Hidalgo had nineteen rabid dogs and one rabid coyote during 1989. But county and city officials in Hidalgo—with a few notable exceptions—took the threat seriously, and invested in animal control officers and *vacunas,* or vaccination clinics. That investment paid off. The following year, Hidalgo had no reported rabies cases, while cases in Starr nearly doubled.

Again, there were plenty of dramatic and frightening stories that made the headlines and evening news broadcasts. In February, the health department was called to the Rio Grande Children's Home in Mission. A stray— one of many tolerated around the orphanage—had undergone a change of personality. Witnesses said the "cowdog," which was white with black-and-gray spots, and one blue eye, continually barked, even when no one was around. She snapped at children who approached to pet her. She seemed to develop tremors. When a worker tied her to the back of a truck, she snapped at the gooseneck ball on the hitch. County authorities took the dog to Heflin, who said she had developed an aversion to water, a symptom common to rabies in humans. She had cuts and scrapes on her ears that had scabbed over. By the time McKirahan and Tamez had completed their investigation, they found that seventy-one people had been exposed, including fifty-six children. The administrator promised to try to discourage strays from the property.

In Mission, a man noticed a wound on the muzzle of his two-year-old male German shepherd about three weeks before the dog became ill. The dog developed a strange, high-pitched bark, staggered and fell frequently, had difficulty closing its jaws, and produced a thick, clear discharge from his mouth. Shortly after the dog was admitted to a veterinary clinic, he chewed at the cage door so frantically that most of his teeth were torn out.

A Rio Grande City woman reported that a strange dog attacked her two-month-old puppy. Three weeks later the puppy bit her, as well as her fifteen-year-old son. The following day, the dog attacked her daughter, her nephew, an older son, and again the fifteen-year-old. Margo was called, and he picked up the dog in person. Oscar Tamez advised them "not to get any more dogs until the rabies epizootic is over."

In October, a McAllen woman called Roman Garza, a local veterinarian, when a sick-looking black Labrador wandered into her yard. After examining the dog, Garza suspected rabies and suggested she call the county animal control officer. According to reports, the animal control officer argued with Garza, saying he wasn't going to have it tested because the county didn't have the money, and he didn't take his orders from veterinarians. He did, however, deliver it to the Upper Valley Humane Society, where it was euthanized and tested. When McKirahan was notified of the positive result, he was struck by the fact the animal was described as having had a collar and leash. "That meant there had to be an owner," McKirahan recalls. "We put it on TV that night—a rabid dog, black Labrador with a blue collar and leash. That night, a guy called up frantically and said the dog had been in his yard. He tried to shoo him off the porch, and the dog bit him on the arm." McKirahan and Oscar Tamez canvassed the caller's neighborhood and located the owner, living in a mobile home a few blocks away. The owner, who had two small daughters, said the dog disappeared

Saturday, three days before it had been taken to the Upper Valley Humane Society. The day he disappeared, he had been ill, refusing to eat, and biting at the air. Ultimately, nine people underwent postexposure treatment. McKirahan is convinced most of them would never have sought treatment if they hadn't been tracked down and notified.

The Case of Manuel Riojas

On April 13, 1990, Manuel Riojas, a twenty-two-year-old phlebotomist with an area blood bank, was having a drink with friends in an Hidalgo County tavern when a bat flew through a broken window, causing a minor commotion. Riojas helped capture the creature. Friends said he was waving it around the room, particularly at female patrons, playfully trying to frighten them, when the animal bit him on the right index finger. Although coworkers at the blood bank urged him to seek treatment, he refused. On May 22, Riojas—a regular donor at his place of employment—donated a unit of blood. Platelets isolated from the blood were transfused into a patient. Eight days later, Riojas began complaining of weakness in his right hand. The weakness and tingling spread up his arm, and relatives reported he had brief spells of blankness and unresponsiveness lasting up to fifteen seconds or so.

Josie Rodriguez, a coworker at the blood bank, recalled seeing him one Saturday, a busy day for donors at a blood bank. Riojas walked in from the parking lot

> looking half-dead. I thought to myself, he was probably out partying last night. I hadn't heard anything about him feeling sick, because he had been feeling sick a couple of days already. He walked in, and he was interviewing donors. Then he went to my desk to ask for aspirin. They all knew I kept the bottle. I said, 'What's the matter?' He was shaking and looked terrible. He said, 'I don't know. I'm feeling bad. I'm completely out of it. I've been feeling like this a couple of days.' I think he said a fish had bitten him a couple of days ago. People were beginning to tell him that maybe that was what was wrong with him, and he mentioned the technical director had urged him to see a doctor, but he hadn't yet. He looked so bad, I said, 'I don't think you should be around donors like that.' Because was shaking and he looked very bad. I said, 'Call your supervisor and tell him how bad you are, so you can go home.' The following Monday he was in the hospital.

McKirahan later said he was told by a coworker that Riojas claimed his symptoms were a result of an ex-girlfriend placing a hex on him. Regardless, he became concerned enough to seek treatment in Mexico, where a doctor gave him some medication investigators were later unable to trace. He sought additional care at an emergency room for pain in his hand, which was becoming severe. Apparently he had forgotten, or discounted, the bat bite; he attributed the pain to being stuck recently by a barb from a catfish. An emergency room doctor gave him a tetanus shot and an oral antibiotic.

He returned to the emergency room June 3. According to McKirahan, a doctor there told Riojas he might be having a nervous breakdown, and the young man returned home. But once at home, he began experiencing hallucinations; relatives said he had episodes of stiffness and difficulty swallowing, holding his breath for extended periods. "He had a fear of fans and wind drafts. The fan couldn't be going, he couldn't have the air conditioning on, he couldn't have the window up," McKirahan said. That same evening he was admitted to a larger hospital, Valley Baptist Medical Center in Harlingen. His mouth and face jerked in constant, spastic movements, his breathing was fast and labored, and he spoke in a stutter. Doctors guessed he had either tetanus or a form of encephalitis.

The following day, Riojas remained obviously disoriented. A battery of tests showed slightly elevated levels of protein in his cerebrospinal fluid and slightly elevated glucose. An electroencephalogram was abnormal. His drooling was so profuse he was intubated, to allow him to breath, and his temperature shot up to 107°F. That night, his supervisor told doctors about the bat bite, and rabies was immediately suspected. Cerebrospinal fluid and a skin biopsy from the nape of his neck were sent to CDC. On June 5, the next morning, Riojas lapsed into a coma and died. Sixty-seven family members, friends, coworkers and medical personnel were started on postexposure treatment. The remainder of the blood products Riojas had donated were destroyed after being tested for rabies. The test results were negative. Still, the patient who received the platelets was also given postexposure treatment as a precaution.

McKirahan had just driven home from a meeting of the Binational Border Health Association in Saltillo, Mexico, when his office called, informing him of the rabies death. Certain that it was the canine strain, McKirahan felt sick. "I felt like we had made a good effort, and put a lot of time and effort in those areas, and here he comes down with rabies from a dog." Compounding the unpleasantness, McKirahan and Tamez had to interview the family the day of the funeral. "We needed to talk to the family because we weren't sure of the exposures, and wanted to make sure there were no other family members or associates that might have been exposed. We were in the situation of having to interview family who were already distressed, already saddened by his death. It was kind of a do-we-or-don't-we situation."

When results of the monoclonal antibody typing identified the rabies variant was that of Mexican free-tailed bat, McKirahan was almost relieved. He was also disturbed by the needlessness of Riojas's death. "He was educated, he was a phlebotomist, worked for the blood bank. His coworkers told him to go get a shot. His opinion was that he was too strong, and a little rabies virus wasn't going to hurt him. Had we known about it, we maybe could have talked him into it. But we didn't get all that history until after he died."

CHAPTER TWO

The Scientist

Perhaps a raccoon or two had awakened to the sound of the outboard motor cutting through the dense fog and blackness in the predawn hours of August 20, 1990. More likely they were awake anyway, foraging for food along the shore of one of the barrier islands dotting the Eastern Shore of Virginia. In any case, had their night vision somehow penetrated the darkness, they might have been rewarded with an odd sight: two men in a small boat—one at the stern, steering an outboard motor, the other at the bow, aiming a flashlight at the unfamiliar waters ahead—cruising a bit too fast, a quiet discussion under way regarding the correct route. Between the two men were several ten-gallon buckets. Each bucket was plastered with a label identifying its contents both by text and international symbol as a biohazardous substance.

While both were tense, the pilot of the boat, Ray Buchanan, was perhaps more eager than anxious; his main responsibility at the moment was simply transporting the buckets the five miles or so from Wachapreague, the village where the research team was headquartered, to Parramore Island, a deserted wildlife refuge owned and managed by the Nature Conservancy. The man in front, Charles Rupprecht, had more reason to worry. Not only had he spent much of the past decade developing the contents of the buckets, he was minutes away from launching an historic experiment: the first release on U.S. soil of a genetically engineered vaccine, a self-replicating virus intended for consumption by wildlife. The fact that field trials had already taken place in Belgium and France did not lessen the importance of the event. Back at Wachapreague, waiting to follow, were visiting scientists from across the United States, as well as Canada, Germany, Switzerland, and China. And although he had successfully anticipated a thousand small details, Rupprecht had failed to plan for this one: how to navigate these waters in complete darkness without navigational equipment. The island had been simple enough to find in the daytime.

Suddenly, his flashlight illuminated landfall ahead—too close, and coming closer entirely too fast. It was an island, but it wasn't *their* island. Buchanan, who was fairly nearsighted, but disliked wearing glasses, threw the motor in reverse as the pair felt the jolt of land beneath them. Rupprecht quickly inspected the buckets; his mind racing with visions of them tumbling into the waves, their precious contents feeding the fish, rather than the raccoons for which they were intended. "It could have all ended there," Rupprecht recalled later with a smile. "Our small boat overturned, and all of our baits washed out to sea." Catastrophe was averted, and a short time later they delivered their cargo to its intended destination.

Rupprecht might have been forgiven for wondering if the project was jinxed. The night before, a student on the team had collapsed while mixing a vat of the special sauce they had cooked up to attract raccoons. The recipe consisted of sugar, egg yolks, vegetable oil, and fermented blue crab parts, the last of these scavenged from the Dumpsters of Philadelphia-area seafood restaurants. The concoction was potent—an early batch left fermenting over one weekend back at Rupprecht's laboratory had exploded, bewildering the nervous biosafety engineers who came to investigate the putrid odor. Here, in the sweltering seaside heat of August, the aroma of the greenish-brown goo proved too much for the student laboring in the kitchen of the small, rented house. The other researchers suspected the young man had volunteered for the job because he was trying to impress one of his classmates, an attractive female student. Someone noticed he was hyperventilating and sweating heavily and tried to get his attention: "Ken? Ken! Stop what you're doing." But Ken didn't even look up, and finally he collapsed in a dead faint. Someone fetched a physician member of the research team from a nearby hotel, the only hotel in Wachapreague, where she had been getting ready for bed. She came running down the village's main street, clad only in a tight-fitting leotard, adding to the circus-like feel the project had attained not only for the researchers, but also the fifty or so astonished full-time residents of the quaint seaside town. An ambulance had delivered the student to a hospital for observation, and he later rejoined the project.

But now, Rupprecht and Buchanan were unloading their cargo in the darkness on Parramore, described by some as the crown jewel of Virginia's barrier islands. Eight miles long and a little over a mile wide at its widest point, Parramore consisted of upland pine forest—some of the trees soaring to eighty feet—scrub thicket, salt marshes, and open dunes. The only human inhabitants were a handful of people assigned to a small Coast Guard station on the northern end of the island; otherwise, unauthorized visitors were forbidden by its stewards. As to its aesthetic qualities, opinions varied according to whom you asked: some found the island a bit bleak, others breathtakingly beautiful. For Rupprecht and the others, Parramore's charms were measured by somewhat different criteria: the thousands of raccoons that lived there, and the surrounding sea that contained them. A short time after Rupprecht and Buchanan unloaded their cargo, the entire international team of two dozen or so researchers followed on a flotilla of similar small boats and Boston whalers. The experiment was under way.

When Rupprecht Met Rabies

Charles E. Rupprecht came upon the field of rabies via bats. While pursuing a master's degree in biology at the University of Wisconsin, the native of Trenton, New Jersey, had accepted a Smithsonian fellowship, traveling to Panama as part of that scientific organization's long-term programs of ecological monitoring. There, he studied Neotropical bats, particularly the *Trachops cirrhosus,* known as the amazing frog-eating bat. A photograph of a specimen he captured appeared on the cover of the journal *Science.* Although the work was enjoyable, he felt the need to expand his horizons in more practical ways. "That was the time of Reaganomics, and an awful lot of my colleagues who were Ph.D.s weren't exactly getting jobs. I had met a veterinarian in Balboa who was working on night monkeys as a model for malaria. I thought, that would be neat to go to veterinary school and use that as a basis for studying infectious diseases and wildlife diseases."

He chose the veterinary college at the University of Pennsylvania. Each day, walking to class, he would pass the Wistar Institute, which was on the university grounds. "It had at that time a peculiar collection of human oddities, and was thought of more as a museum—although a lot of basic research was going on." While in veterinary school, Rupprecht met Tadeusz Wiktor, who directed Wistar's rabies unit. Rupprecht told Wiktor of his work with bats, and Wiktor, the virologist, said, "Ah, yes. Bats. How do you grow them?" As if they were some kind of virus. Rupprecht saw the chance to work at Wistar as an opportunity to develop new skills, bringing his own knowledge of bats to one of the premier rabies research programs in the country. He became a volunteer in 1982 and signed on as a research associate the following year.

Wistar was the oldest independent research institution in the United States, citing its founding in 1892. Caspar Wistar, a physician and professor who succeeded Thomas Jefferson as president of the nation's premier scholarly organization, the American Philosophical Society, commissioned a remarkable collection of wooden models of human anatomical features before his death in 1818. The collection became known as the Wistar and Horner Museum (Horner being the custodian appointed by Wistar to oversee the pieces). By 1890, the museum was badly neglected. Caspar Wistar's great-nephew, Isaac Wistar, led an effort to restore the collection and create an institute of scientific research around it. Although founded in 1892, the Wistar Institute of Anatomy and Biology officially opened its doors two years later, according to a history of the institution published on its centennial anniversary in 1994.

In 1957, Wistar hired Dr. Hilary Koprowski as its director. Koprowski—a cosmopolitan scientist who spoke eight languages, read literature voraciously, and played the piano with considerable skill—brought the institute its greatest acclaim. The Polish-born physician had studied both medicine and music at Warsaw, continued musical training in Italy, and had emigrated to Brazil before going to work for Lederle Laboratories in New York. But rabies was his lifelong interest, which began on the ocean voyage from Brazil to New York in November 1944. During a brief stop in Trinidad, Koprowski arranged a meeting with a doctor whose expertise was rabies.

"He told me also about the fact he saw a furious fight between a vampire bat and an insect-eating bat, and he was absolutely sure it (the vampire bat) had infected the insect-eating bat—and that it may prove quite a menace to the United States." The United States was too far north to be habitat for any vampire bats but had lots of insectivorous ones. "This was 1944, and in 1953, the first bat rabies case was observed in Florida. So in a way, he was prophetic," Koprowski says.

"That raised my interest. I was in general interested in rabies, not only from the point of view of science, but also from the point of view of bizarre diseases. This really was one of the oldest diseases of mankind, and the fear was so great from rabies." Later, Harold Johnson, a virologist with the Rockefeller Foundation, gave him a sample of a rabies strain called Flury, launching his vaccine research at Lederle. Johnson, himself a prominent figure in rabies research, known for his work with bat rabies in Latin America, was later crippled by a mysterious neurotropical disease. In a 1991 oral history published by the University of California at Berkeley's Bancroft Library, Johnson expressed suspicion he had been infected by, and recovered from, rabies itself.

As head of Wistar, Koprowski gave special attention to the rabies program, arguably the leading rabies laboratory in the nation. Koprowski's interest, Rupprecht later said, gave the rabies researchers considerable latitude in pursuing their goal of an oral rabies vaccine.

The Development of V-RG

V-RG, or vaccinia-recombinant glycoprotein, was born at the beginning of the 1980s, a time when the promise of biotechnology to radically alter both medicine and agriculture was beginning to be felt, both by scientists and the public alike, with equal measures of excitement and trepidation. By 1980, the gene that forms the spiky outer glycoprotein coat of the bullet-shaped rabies virus had been identified and cloned by researchers at the Wistar Institute in Philadelphia. At the same time, researchers such as Bernard Moss at the National Institutes of Health were looking at vaccinia as the basis for a number of bioengineered vaccines. Vaccinia was one of the best-studied viruses on earth, having been used as a vaccine for two centuries to successfully wipe out the scourge of smallpox around the world.

Moss and Wistar researchers came together to produce a genetically engineered rabies vaccine. Their first efforts to splice the rabies glycoprotein gene to vaccinia were unsuccessful; the new virus did not properly express the rabies glycoprotein needed to produce an immune response. They turned to Transgene, a small biotech firm in Strasbourg, France. Transgene partially removed the thymidine kinase gene, which seemed to have a role in its virulence, from the vaccinia virus, and replaced it with the rabies gene. That construction not only led to healthy expression of the glycoprotein gene, but made the vaccinia itself safer, it was believed.

Vaccinia had been around for so long, in fact, that its exact origins in history had been lost since Edward Jenner first introduced it in 1796. Various scientists speculated vaccinia had evolved from cowpox, or from horsepox, or even from smallpox itself. A number of strains were out there; the researchers had obtained a particularly stable virus, called the Copenhagen strain, from New York virologist Enzo Paoletti. He had thoroughly characterized the Copenhagen vaccinia, sequencing its genome to 191,636 base pairs. The Copenhagen strain had been used as a smallpox vaccine for a time in Europe, but its use was halted because of excessive and occasionally fatal side effects, ranging from skin lesions to encephalitis. Still, its initial choice for V-RG was strictly one of bioengineering.

At the beginning, V-RG was considered by many at Wistar to be more of a laboratory tool to study gene expression. Rupprecht believed it had real potential as a third-generation rabies vaccine. In this he was encouraged by his boss and mentor, Tad Wiktor, who had posed his favorite question to Rupprecht: "What does it cost you?" To try, that is. Of course, the Wistar group was always thinking about a better rabies vaccine. They had made the first significant improvement upon Pasteur's original vaccine, which despite its enormous benefit to mankind was at times capable of causing serious and even fatal reactions. "In 1947 and '48 in Florida, there was not a single case of human rabies. But there were two cases of paralytic reaction to the rabies vaccine," says Koprowski, who now heads the Center for Neurovirology at Thomas Jefferson University in Philadelphia. Wistar's human diploid cell rabies vaccine had been created using a human cell line also developed at Wistar. In December 1971, when Wiktor finally had the new rabies vaccine ready for testing, the first three human subjects were himself, Koprowski, and Stanley Plotkin, another Wistar scientist. None suffered any adverse effects, and several years of human trials ensued. The vaccine was first licensed for human use in France in 1977 and in the United States in 1980. With the new human diploid cell vaccine, the long and painful series of fourteen to twenty-one shots in the abdomen were replaced by five injections in the arm, administered over twenty-eight days, plus a single injection of rabies immune globulin at the site of the bite on the first day, to provide immediate immune protection.

The raccoon rabies epizootic that eventually blanketed the East Coast, described by the CDC as the most *intense* outbreak of wildlife rabies ever to occur in the United States, had been present in the southeastern states for decades, but jumped to the Mid-Atlantic in the mid-1970s with the help of hunters importing wild raccoons to restock game preserves. The outbreak crossed the Virginia border in the late 1970s and into Maryland in the early 1980s. And in the spring of 1982, raccoon rabies moved into Pennsylvania—and the backyard of the Wistar Institute. "So not only did we have the ability at Wistar to say, yes, raccoon rabies has crossed the front now and is here, but at the same time, now that it's here, what can we do about it?" Rupprecht said.

In 1984, Rupprecht inoculated rats and rabbits with V-RG and found it produced powerful immunity when injected both intramuscularly and just beneath the skin. Almost accidentally, he also found it also worked when given orally. That was a major surprise, although Rupprecht later found some early research suggesting vaccinia might be used orally for small-pox. Although it conferred some immunity, "it just never worked well. And of course it never gave you the identifying mark to show you had received primary vaccination." So with raccoon rabies exploding around them, and a potential new oral vaccine in hand, Rupprecht tested it next in raccoons. It worked beautifully. That was important, because earlier re-search had demonstrated that the existing vaccines, which were weakened, or attenuated, live viruses, did not work orally in raccoons. A research collaboration was formed, with Rhone Merieux of Lyon, France, a major inter-national manufacturer of rabies vaccine, coming aboard largely because of the relationship with Transgene in France.

Parramore Island

For Cathleen Hanlon, the odd group of researchers scrambling all over her island felt something like an invasion. For two years, beginning in October 1987, the young veterinarian had been working alone on Parramore; the only footsteps on the sand when she arrived each morning were hers from the previous day. She would sail her Boston whaler the five miles or so from Wachapreague, a fishing village on the Virginia Eastern Shore where she had rented a tiny house, to the island when weather permitted. Sloshing through the salt marsh and tall scrub-pine forest, she would take careful field notes of the animal and plant life, trapping and ear-tagging raccoons to determine their density (a tedious job that required endless trapping and retrapping to see how many previously tagged animals were among the day's catch—a process that eventually would lead to a rough estimate of the density of the raccoon population).

The fact that Parramore was thought to have an extremely high rac-coon density, at least anecdotally, had brought them here in the first place. To some of the raccoons she would attach radio collars to determine if somehow they swam from Parramore to other, nearby barrier islands (they did not). The most exciting moment had been discovering the first known naturally occurring cleft palate in a raccoon cub. Later, she said she was grateful she had found it before the experiment—otherwise, it would surely have been blamed on the recombinant vaccine.

Having moved from busy Philadelphia to this village that seemed almost frozen in some earlier time, her two years here had been a time for introspection. The residents, she knew, were amused by her work; although she might go weeks without speaking to another human being, she had been accepted by them to the extent that they would notify the Coast Guard if she were late returning to dock. She enjoyed the close-knit life on Wachapreague, where people waved to one another on the street, and everyone knew everyone on a first-name basis. Later, when it came time for the public hearings required for approval to launch the experiment, the folks in Wachapreague were among its biggest supporters. Rupprecht gave Hanlon a lot of credit for overall acceptance of the project among residents along the Eastern Shore. Others disagreed, saying the same traits that gave Wachapreague and the rest of the Eastern Shore its charm also made it insular and suspicious of outsiders, a category of humans defined broadly: "Everybody who ever moved here in their lifetime is referred to as a Come-here for the rest of their life," said one observer.

After the two years were up, Hanlon returned to graduate school while waiting for the project to be approved. A year later that approval came, and now they were here. Hanlon grimly noted it was exactly the wrong time of year to be doing this kind of arduous field work; the August heat was oppressive, the humidity intense, and the ticks and mosquitoes were particularly aggressive. Rupprecht marveled at the wide range of fashions the researchers sported. Bernard Dietzchold, a German scientist from Wistar and an avid skier, was dressed for the slopes, while the Chinese appeared in typically utilitarian attire. Few of them had any real experience in field work, so their clothing was mostly ill-suited to the job at hand. Hanlon did her best to protect them from the bugs by sealing their sleeves and pant legs with duct tape, and covering them with mosquito netting, but that only made the heat and humidity worse.

Still, they were motivated by importance of this experiment. Much was riding on its success, and so they trudged dutifully through the marshes in small teams, placing the 3,120 vaccine-laden baits by hand in a grid pattern, more or less, in six study areas. The baits were fishmeal-polymer cylinders containing a wax ampoule filled with the V-RG vaccine. The cylinders were sealed in numbered plastic bags with printed warnings (the language provided by the U.S. Department of Agriculture, the regulatory agency overseeing the experiment) and covered with a dollop of the sugar-crab slurry that had cost the group its first casualty the night before. The slurry also contained a tetracycline biomarker, so that the researchers could easily tell later whether an animal had eaten a bait, regardless of its immune status. Numbered flags were placed next to each bait; for the next two weeks, the group would return each day and check by each flag to see if the bait was missing or disturbed. If it was missing, they would search up to ten feet away. If any pieces of the bait or its contents were still around, they would make careful note of its appearance and location. Near some of the baits, sand pits were constructed so that animal tracks could be recorded and identified. Although the baits had been designed to appeal to raccoons and not to other creatures, it was important to know if the baits were in fact taken by raccoons, or by the other primary carnivore present on Parramore, the red fox. White-tailed deer and rodents also lived on the island, along with a wide variety of shore birds.

By the time the exhausted researchers finished their work, it was already dark. Rupprecht realized he faced the same problem as that morning, only multiplied. "How do you get exhausted people in the dark off of this island, and safely back? There were a lot of arguments between boats about, 'Is this the right way to go, or is it this way?' until one boat went one way and one went that way. Who knows what could have happened?"

When they arrived back in the village, they realized in their exhaustion they had left someone behind on Parramore—the young woman Ken had been trying to impress. She had been assigned to stand watch at the southern tip of the island in case any uninvited tourists from the mainland decided impulsively to land. State game commission officers also patrolled from boats to prevent unauthorized visitors. A group returned to find the young woman fairly distraught. "As it got dark, she began trudging up the good coastline along the shore—because at least you always knew where you were when you were on the shoreline," Hanlon said. "As we were crossing the island along the main road, we saw her approaching us. This was her first time on the island, and to be left alone and completely out of communications, thinking she was totally forgotten, was distressing."

Later, the same unlucky woman caused additional excitement when she was bitten on the index finger by a trapped raccoon she was trying to sedate. The animal had recently eaten one of the vaccine baits, and the researchers immediately launched an emergency protocol they had developed for just such an accident: she was rushed back to the mainland to be examined by a physician in case she developed a reaction to the vaccinia construct. Blood was drawn to see if the vaccine had boosted her immunity from her earlier rabies vaccination, since humans were among the few mammals Rupprecht hadn't tested V-RG on. It did not.

But back in town that first night, Rupprecht, who is described as occasionally abrasive even by his admirers, was in no mood for subtlety. He telephoned Warren Cheston, the deputy director of Wistar, and demanded a decent boat. When Cheston protested, Rupprecht described the day's events and pointed out the potential liability issues involved, particularly with the visiting scientists participating. "There's no way we're going to do this ragtag anymore," Rupprecht said. "We need a boat. We need a new boat. We need a new boat ASAP."

By the end of the week, the Wistar Institute—the nation's oldest independent biomedical research institution since its founding in 1892, located in Philadelphia, many miles from an ocean—had acquired a boat. "A very nice boat," Rupprecht concedes. It had navigational equipment on board. More importantly, it arrived in time for a VIP visit. The visitors included Wistar director Hilary Koprowski, a legendary figure in rabies research; Konrad Bögel, the head of rabies programs for the World Health Organization; Bögel's wife; and Anna Wiktor, the widow of Tadeusz Wiktor—who, until his death in 1986, had been Rupprecht's chief at Wistar.

A celebratory lunch was planned. The VIP delegation was waiting at the dock, waving as the new boat arrived from Parramore. As most of the scientists scurried off for a quick shower and change of clothes before lunch, the visitors told Rupprecht they wanted to see Parramore. Fine, he said. With one foot on the dock and one foot inside the boat, Rupprecht helped first Mrs. Wiktor, then Mrs. Bögel, down the dock ladder and onboard, when suddenly "the dock and boat moved in opposite directions. And unfortunately, Mrs. Bögel fell into the water. She was very nicely attired for lunch." As he looked around for help, Rupprecht spotted Konrad Bögel on the dock, filming the spectacle. Mrs. Bögel maintained both her poise and her sense of humor on the ride to Parramore, removing some of her soggy garments to dry, so that they resembled a sort of nautical flag in the sea breeze.

Developing the Bait

Cathleen Hanlon had first met Charles Rupprecht when she was a veterinary student at the University of Pennsylvania, looking for a summer research job. She was immediately impressed by his intensity and his ideas about widescale vaccination of wildlife. Hanlon already had some laboratory research experience, but this was an opportunity to participate in research that extended from the lab bench to the field. And it was the field that Rupprecht offered Hanlon, sending her off to Pennsylvania state gamelands to trap raccoons, take blood samples and ear-tag the animals as the rabies epizootic approached. It was a totally foreign experience to the twenty-five-year-old Hanlon, who worked out of her compact car that summer, with Rupprecht's office making arrangements for her to live on area college campuses.

Meanwhile, Rupprecht was trying to come up with a bait. At first he had borrowed a method used early on when George Baer had begun his pioneering work on an oral rabies vaccine in the 1960s: hollowing a Slim Jim-like sausage and inserting a straw filled with the vaccine. They weren't very popular with his laboratory raccoons. Nor were hard-boiled eggs, another early bait idea. Meanwhile, Canada was moving ahead on a parallel track to develop an oral rabies vaccine program for red foxes, an effort spurred by the death of a twelve-year-old girl there a decade earlier. Dave Johnston at the Ontario Ministry of Natural Resources had telephoned Rupprecht when he heard V-RG looked as though it might work. The Canadians were using a modified live-virus vaccine, something U.S. researchers considered unsafe, and knew was ineffective against raccoons. Still, the Canadians were further along with their bait development, and Johnston came down and spent a year at Wistar, bringing along a wax sponge bait he had developed.

Rupprecht quickly launched placebo baiting studies using the Canadian baits. The cubes were sealed in small plastic bags and covered with sauces designed to appeal to raccoons. Rupprecht then underwent a quick education in homespun manufacturing techniques, since thousands of baits required assembling by hand. "We didn't have any funding for this in the early days. It was all, go to the hardware store, go to the supermarket. Halloween and Easter were great times. Finding what was out there, how it was packaged." Soon a production line was in place. "We had a little device whereby you could buy these baggies attached to one another on long rolls, and we had a crank mechanism where the baggies would come through it and be perforated with these spikes, and they'd come out the end and we would stamp them with a rubber stamper we got at some ink place that said what this thing was, and somebody then would rip them off and hand them to somebody else who would put the cubes of vaccine in them, who would go ahead and put different overlays of attractants on top of them." They tested a stomach-turning range of attractants, including turkey gravy, fish oil, feta cheese, and grape jelly.

They received permission to drop the vaccine-less baits in Pennsylvania state gamelands. First they hired a small plane, whose good-natured pilot didn't mind them taping bizarre-looking ducts from the cargo door as bait chutes. Dave Johnston was the navigator and Rupprecht dropped the baits. Other members of the team delivered additional supplies of baits at predetermined reloading sites in cars. They started at the Maryland border, flying north along the Susquehanna River, often circling the mountainous terrain. "It was like being on a very peculiar amusement ride that I did not appreciate. Dave's advice to me was to have a good carbohydrate breakfast, to keep your spine straight, and keep your eye on the horizon. That might be easy for the navigator, but not when you're in the backseat of a small plane getting thrown around, and at the sound of a metronome had to make sure you were throwing these things into the chute. I got deathly ill." Cathleen Hanlon, whose father was a pilot, didn't last long either. "I was totally useless," she recalls. And so, as so often happens with unpleasant tasks required by scientific research, the actual job of dropping baits was handed off to a graduate student.

But the wax sponge baits that Canadian red foxes found irresistible were less successful with raccoons. The baits finally selected by Rupprecht were hollow fishmeal-polymer cylinders, not much bigger than a large spool of thread, manufactured by a subsidiary of Dupont and originally designed for use in crawfish traps. The baits proved spectacularly effective in attracting raccoons, but how they came to the attention of the Wistar researchers remains a bit cloudy. Charles MacInnes, who heads the oral rabies vaccination program for foxes in Canada, claims to have steered the company to Rupprecht. For his part, Rupprecht—who finds a number of points on which to disagree with the Canadians—discounts this one as well.

"In a very strange, historical way, I'm the father of this bait," MacInnes says. "As supervisor of wildlife research (for the Ontario Ministry of Natural Resources), a salesman for Dupont, based in Guelph, Ontario, came into my office one day. At this time, Dave Johnston was on a year's leave paid for by the Canadian International Development Fund, working with Rupprecht to develop a better raccoon bait. This guy from Dupont came into my office with this thing that was developed to bait crawfish traps in Louisiana. Fishermen wanted a bait that would stay together at least a week underwater, and maintain its attractiveness to crawfish. He had been given the job of trying to sell the bait to lobster fishermen on the East Coast and to fur trappers. He came to me to get some contacts with fur trappers, and I said, 'I can think of a lot of reasons why the fur trappers won't be interested. But there's a guy down in Philadelphia who I think will find this interesting.' I gave him Rupprecht's phone number. And that's my whole involvement."

"MacInnes alleges that's what happened," Rupprecht replies, all humor draining from his voice. "He may have sent the salesman to us, but the first call we got wasn't about a bait. The first call we got was because they knew we were working on raccoons and baiting. They had problems with raccoons breaking into their warehouse, and they wanted to know if we had any advice to offer them to keep the raccoons from coming in, because they were being attracted to this bait. This was a great boon to us, because they were attracted to it. Then we got another call, which must have been Charlie MacInnes's salesperson. So the salesman, who was looking at how to sell their product, may have come via hearing about the baiting. But the first call came in as raccoons being a problem. I don't how many times we have to go over this issue to set the record straight as far as people's memories go."

That issue aside, Rupprecht and his team found the baiting studies fun and exciting, but they were being undertaken on a shoestring budget. The state of Pennsylvania, which was facing the arrival of raccoon rabies, provided some early funding. And the fact that Hilary Koprowski was not only the head of Wistar, but wore a second hat as head of the rabies research group, gave Rupprecht and his team a little extra room to play. But with each success, the stakes grew higher. "This is fun," Wiktor told him, "but if you want this to go somewhere, you've got to find a way to pay for it." To get some serious backing, they needed to take the next step: seeking approval from the Department of Agriculture for licensure.

Testing V-RG

Robert Miller first heard about Wistar's plans to test an oral rabies vaccine in the United States at a rabies conference sponsored by the Pan American Health Organization in Washington in 1985. Rupprecht spoke to the group about potential rabies vaccines that might be used to halt the rapid spread of raccoon rabies. One was an attenuated rabies oral vaccine developed in Germany and being used in parts of Europe. The other, of course, was V-RG, constructed by Transgene in France. Miller, head of the biologics section of the USDA, introduced himself to Rupprecht after the speech, and told him that "before he proceeded with any of those trials or brought the viruses into the country, he had to come through Agriculture."

The approval process for V-RG proved to be a thorny problem for USDA. "We had had some vaccines that had been recombinantly derived before that, but those were either killed viruses or simple gene deletions." The agency had decided earlier that genetically inactivated viruses used in vaccines or other products "would be evaluated just as any standard product was, because there was no replication, no threat to the environment." In addition, those other vaccines were injected into one animal at a time. That made the question of environmental impact simply a matter of whether the animal injected shed the virus after it was administered.

But V-RG was a genetically engineered live virus, derived from a vaccine that had caused many side effects in humans including encephalitis and death, designed to infect a host animal and multiply countless times over in order to induce an immune response. It was to be cast into the environment where any number of animals, or humans, might come in contact with it. The Copenhagen strain used in the vaccine was "hotter" than the smallpox vaccine that had been used in the United States. Cloning the vaccine had weakened it, however, and elimination of the TK gene had further reduced its virulence. Still, the main concern was risk to humans. But how do you test the risk of an animal vaccine to people?

Miller consulted with a vaccine advisory committee of scientists organized by the Department of Health and Human Services. "They all agreed it would not be appropriate to test an animal vaccine in humans." And because the risks of side effects were so low, "you'd have to put it in so many people to even have the probability of detecting one adverse event, that it was probably not warranted." Instead, the risk to people would be minimized through warnings and public education where the vaccine was distributed. And although Wistar did test the vaccine in non-human primates, the question of human risk continued to shadow the project for many years.

Any risk would have been from the vaccinia, since the glycoprotein gene alone was not enough to risk developing rabies. The origin and behavior of the Copenhagen vaccinia strain, used in V-RG, became important, since different vaccinia strains used for smallpox control had varying complication rates. A study in the Netherlands found one case of postvaccination encephalitis per four thousand doses of Copenhagen vaccinia. In the

United States, the complication rate for its smallpox vaccine was between two and six per million, which included both skin lesions and encephalitis. The Copenhagen strain was believed to be more virulent than the strains used in the United States, and it gradually had been abandoned as a vaccine. But those complications had been the result of high concentrations of vaccinia given by injection. By getting rid of the TK gene, the researchers believed, they had further attenuated, or weakened, the virus.

Rupprecht was struck by the impression that they were breaking new regulatory ground as they went along.

> In veterinary medicine, you never want to be the last to do anything, but you damn sure never want to be the first. Which we found out the hard way with the regulatory agency. We initially proposed that the way to proceed was to test at least one major species representative of each major mammalian family that would or could be contacted or at risk of this vaccine. Because we were primarily interested in safety. Nobody told us this was what you had to do. This is what seemed reasonable to us. USDA acknowledged—and if they ever doubt it, I'll dig out the letters that show them—that we really were creating the rules as we went along.

Wistar proceeded to test V-RG on a virtual Noah's ark of species, nearly every creature that might possibly come in contact with the vaccine in the wild. That posed some logistical problems, since Wistar was not equipped to house all these animals. There was a celebrated incident with an otter, which managed to escape during a Wistar Christmas party, resulting in a small army of researchers in various levels of drunkenness chasing the frightened creature around the building.

Another memorable incident involved the bears. State parks officials volunteered to turn over quietly to Rupprecht some bears that had been particularly troublesome to tourists in the Poconos. The handoff was done quietly because, with all the controversy regarding bioengineering, Wistar took pains to keep the animal tests quiet. The parks people arranged a clandestine meeting in, of all places, the parking lot of a nearby McDonald's. As Rupprecht and Hanlon arrived in a Wistar truck, one of the parks workers mentioned that some reporters had gotten wind of the handoff, and were asking questions. "You're with the University of Pennsylvania?" the parks worker asked. Wistar is located on the university's campus, but maintains a proud independence from its neighbor, despite the fact that many of Wistar's faculty, including Rupprecht, hold joint appointments. "Yes," Rupprecht said, which wasn't *really* a lie, and stepped in front of the Wistar logo on the side of the truck.

Actually, the bears *were* headed for the university, where Rupprecht had made covert arrangements for them to be housed in the dental school. The researchers loaded the cage carrying the sedated bears, covered with a tarp, onto a small elevator. The researchers were dismayed when the elevator stopped before it got to their floor, and people squeezed onboard. On the endless ride up, Rupprecht and Hanlon affected a casual expression as the sleeping bears's heavy breathing penetrated the silence of the elevator through the heavy tarp. "We didn't volunteer any information," Rupprecht said later, "and the people looked at us like you'd expect in some movie. They got off at the next floor."

A good deal of space for the animals was found around the university. But for a few species, Wistar turned to others for help. Nonhuman primates were tested at a facility in New Mexico. The Canadians volunteered to test skunks, as well as some deer obtained from Albany. New York State refused to allow V-RG to be tested within its borders, and some complicated negotiations were needed to transport the animals to Canada. "It was basically an international transfer of animals just so we could put vaccine in them," Hanlon recalls.

Ultimately, V-RG was studied for safety and efficacy in fifty-nine species of animals and birds, including opossum, red fox, gray fox, dog, coyote, bobcat, domestic cat, skunk, river otter, mink, ferret, European badger, black bear, cattle, sheep, wild boar, white-tailed deer, European rabbit, house mouse, porcupine, groundhog, gray squirrel, cotton rat, marsh rice rat, Syrian hamster, several species of voles and mice, and birds, including red-tailed hawk, kestrel, carrion crow, common buzzard, ringbill gull, great horned owl, magpie, and jay. It was also tested in squirrel monkeys and chimpanzees to approximate human exposure. None of the primates suffered any adverse symptoms or lesions. No vaccinia virus was recovered from oral or fecal swabs, except for one chimpanzee which had suffered from bacterial dermatitis and developed an infection and fever. Some virus was isolated from the mouth of that particular animal. Antibiotics were administered, and the animal improved. No more virus was recovered from subsequent samples.

The Argentina Affair

With the earliest papers published on V-RG, considerable interest was generated outside the United States, where rabies remained a major health problem. The Pan American Health Organization (PAHO) operated an experimental station in Azul, Argentina, and Mario Fernandez, director of veterinary public health at PAHO, arranged a collaboration with Wistar to test V-RG in cattle there. Bovine rabies cost Argentine ranchers an estimated fifty million dollars a year. Rupprecht and Koprowski both say that Fernandez's was not the first inquiry from Argentina, that government health officials had contacted them before that.

In any case, in July 1986, twenty Argentine cows were vaccinated with V-RG and were allowed to mingle with twenty unvaccinated cows in a shed, in part to see if vaccinia lesions on the vaccinated cows might somehow infect or inoculate the unvaccinated animals. Four Argentine handlers previously had been immunized with a vaccinia virus against smallpox. For the Wistar researchers, who continued with their studies of V-RG on a wide range of animal species, any additional information was welcomed.

The Wistar group, led by Koprowski, held weekly meetings in the staff lounge to discuss the ongoing work, and any problems. For Rupprecht, those staff meetings were among his happiest times at Wistar; smart people brainstorming about rabies, arguing, cajoling, kidding around. At one of those meetings, an Argentine postdoctorate fellow working in another lab, who was friendly with a graduate student working for Rupprecht, overheard some details of the PAHO study and notified authorities back home.

To the Argentines, news of the experiment came as a shock. Neither Wistar nor PAHO, apparently, had bothered to inform them. In Buenos Aires, the testing of a genetically engineered substance, developed by U.S. scientists, on Argentine soil became a major scandal. Outraged government officials halted the experiment, then appointed a commission to investigate. The commission criticized the experiment as "a violation of ethical principles." Members were particularly unhappy with what they saw as a risk to the farmworkers, and the practice of allowing the milk from the inoculated cows to be sold.

The Argentines protested to the U.S. government, which expressed surprise and embarrassment over the matter. It didn't help that the United States had four years earlier taken Great Britain's side in the war over the Falkland Islands, known as the Malvinas to the Argentines. The NIH launched its own investigation, particularly to see if $1.4 million in federal grant funds provided to Wistar were used to pay for the study. "We want to know how this field study was paid for," Dr. Bernard Talbot, deputy director of the National Institute of Allergy and Infectious Diseases, told the *New York Times*. "If NIH gave Wistar a grant specifically for this field test, and we did not know about it, then they are apparently in violation of the [federal] guidelines." Under the Reagan administration, new rules were implemented requiring any research institution receiving federal funds to undergo an approval process before releasing genetically engineered substances in the United States, or abroad if the experiments were paid for by federal funds.

Response was fast and furious. Letters in the journals *Science* and *Nature* debated the propriety and the merits of the experiment, and how it was conducted. Dr. David Kingsbury with the National Science Foundation, who helped develop the new biotech regulations, told the *New York Times:* "I am not bothered by the idea of United States research institutes and companies going abroad for the testing. But I am appalled that they did it without the knowledge of that country. Given the volatility and concern on this issue, you just don't do things like that." An editorial in the *Times* was equally critical: "The Wistar Institute in Philadelphia has long been a pioneer in developing new vaccines. But when it went to Argentina to test a new, genetically engineered vaccine against rabies in collaboration with the Pan American Health Organization, it neglected to insure that Argentina was informed. The authorities there had understandable cause, when they learned of it, to stop the experiment. They called it a 'violation of ethical principles.' It is at the very least a poor way to do science, let alone win friends."

Wistar and PAHO argued that because Argentina had no regulations dealing with bioengineered substances, the researchers had no responsibility to notify them. Kaprowski fired back in a letter in the *Times* that the trials were not undertaken to avoid U.S. regulations, but rather in response to Argentina's bovine rabies problems. "The campaign to attack the trial *ex post facto* was initiated by an Argentine trainee working at the Wistar Institute who had no scientific knowledge about vaccinia virus and its effects on humans and cattle. Nor did he confirm his interpretation with anyone knowledgeable about the experiment before writing a denunciatory letter to the Argentine Government," Koprowski wrote, adding: "The reaction within Argentina and the U.S. has been tantamount to a campaign of vilification of the Wistar Institute and the Pan American Health Organization, in whose facilities the trial was conducted." However, Daniel Epstein, a spokesman for PAHO in Washington, told *Science* that "in retrospect, it would have been advisable for us to have informed Argentine officials of the experiment, and not treat it as a routine matter." And Wistar associate director Warren Cheston told *Science:* "We were a little naive, as I think scientists frequently are."

Rupprecht argued the experiment wasn't a secret, at least not in scientific circles. An article about it had appeared in the NIH *Reporter,* and it had been mentioned at a meeting at Cold Springs Harbor. But for the Wistar team, working to get approval for their oral vaccine, "it really set us back. There were charges of guinea pig-ism, all these peculiar allegations of wrongdoing—that this was really biowarfare, the CIA looking at the health effects of this on workers. It was just a tremendous nightmare. The [Argentine] government came in and the experiment was stopped, the freezers were chained, the samples were sealed, the animals were slaughtered and buried in lime pits."

Several years later, the World Health Organization conducted an investigation of the controversy. Seals were broken, blood samples were tested. The only workers with antibodies were those who had been traditionally vaccinated. The only cows with antibodies were those who received V-RG. From the Wistar researchers, feeling the sting of scientific and political criticism over the incident, there were whispers that the whole ugly controversy was stirred by Cold War interests. "Draw your own conclusion about who wouldn't have profited by U.S. biotechnology getting too large," Rupprecht said later.

European Testing of V-RG

While the Americans were busy with issues of safety and geopolitics, the Europeans were moving ahead with their own tests of V-RG. Europe already had considerable experience with using an attenuated live rabies oral vaccine to control rabies in red foxes. On September 23, 1987, the Belgium Ministry of Public Health authorized the first limited field trial of V-RG, which took place October 17 on an isolated military base in the Ardennes province, an area where fox rabies was endemic. Into 250 chicken heads were inserted a capsule containing the vaccine and a tetracycline marker. Of 145 small mammals trapped in the area over the next three months, only four had signs of tetracycline on their teeth. None suffered any detectable adverse effects.

The following year, Belgium launched a second, much larger trial, again in the Ardennes region. On October 24, 1988, six thousand vaccine-laden baits were hand-distributed over 450 square kilometers. This time, the baits were a fishmeal polymer with a small plastic bag inside containing the vaccine and marker. By the end of thirty days, more than 94 percent of the baits were disturbed, and 54 percent of foxes captured had eaten one or more baits as determined by tetracycline marker.

A full-scale launch using helicopters to drop the baits began the following year, involving twenty-four contiguous districts over twenty-two hundred square kilometers. Between October 1989 and November 1990, some 230,000 fishmeal polymer baits were dropped. While fox densities remained about the same during the trial, the incidence of rabies dropped significantly.

About the same time, the French were performing their own tests. The French Commission for Biomolecular Engineering, part of the Ministry of Agriculture, authorized a small trial on a military field at Mars le Tour, which began in November 1988. One-hundred-seventy-four baits similar to the fishmeal polymer used by the Belgians were manually distributed; 90 percent disappeared within fifteen days. A second drop of 6,400 baits occurred in October 1989. And in March 1990, the largest trial to date took place: six hundred thousand baits dropped in the regions of Liege, Luxembourg, and Namur.

In none of the European trials were any reduction in animal species noted, nor any pox-like lesions observed. No adverse effects were noted in people, either those participating in the project nor those living nearby the research areas.

Choosing the U.S. Test Site

With all the extraordinary concern about safety and V-RG, the idea of using islands for the initial field trials was a logical one. Wistar enlisted researchers with the Southeastern Cooperative Wildlife Disease Study in Georgia to look for candidates. They narrowed the selection to ten islands located from Louisiana to Maryland. "Like Goldilocks, either they were too big or too small," Rupprecht says, "or they didn't have enough raccoons on them, or they had endangered species, or reintroduction programs, or people." Finally, two candidates emerged: a pair of islands near Columbia, South Carolina, and Parramore. Rupprecht sent one team member, Chip Hable, to South Carolina to collect data, while Cathy Hanlon went to Parramore.

South Carolina received the initial attention. Anticipating fear and opposition to the idea of the release, Wistar hired a high-powered public relations firm from Washington, D.C., which helped orchestrate the campaign for public support, rehearsing the scientists in videotaped exchanges with reporters. It didn't help. John Brown, a veterinarian and toxicologist with the South Carolina Department of Health and Environmental Control, headed a local committee to consider Wistar's request for a field trial. Wistar paraded before the committee a host of experts, even flying in Frank Fenner from Australia, who was the world's expert on vaccinia and a key figure in the global eradication of smallpox. Brown was unimpressed. "Basically everybody decided this was the greatest thing since sliced bread," Brown told me later. "All of the federal science agencies said great, it's perfectly safe."

South Carolina politicians and public health officials were already skittish. There had been ongoing discussions about consolidating a number of plutonium processing plants for America's nuclear arsenal at the Savannah River Nuclear Plant in South Carolina, a facility built in the 1950s that had existing environmental problems. Local opposition was strong. "I think they just thought this was another dump-on-South Carolina sort of thing, just because they had one of the few islands amenable to being able to isolate this test," Robert Miller says. In any case, the committee headed by Brown turned down the request. In their report, dated June 7, 1989, they cited concerns about the Copenhagen strain:

> *A primary health concern of the Committee majority deals with the questionable human safety of the bioengineered Copenhagen strain of vaccinia virus used as a carrier of the rabies virus glycoprotein. There was no question of safety relative to the rabies virus glycoprotein component of the vaccine. While the Wistar testing of the bioengineered vaccinia virus indicated a reduced level of pathogenicity over the unaltered vaccinia virus (in the tested animals), no data of human or primate testing was presented to validate an assumption of reduced pathogenicity in man. In January 1963, the Copenhagen strain of vaccinia virus used for smallpox immunization in Denmark was replaced with the less pathogenic Elstree vaccinia strain with a subsequent reduction of infant vaccination complications. . . .*

The report went on to express concern that, since the elimination of universal smallpox vaccination in the United States, there were some twenty million citizens unvaccinated against the disease, mostly infants and children. Because various forms of encephalitis and meningitis of mostly undetermined origin were common along the South Carolina coast, there existed the potential for legal liability. And while the committee's vote was close—four to three for turning the proposal down—all seven members had problems with provisions of the contract dealing with protecting the state from legal liability.

Both the researchers and the USDA officials were angry at the committee, particularly its chairman. Most of all, the Wistar group was unhappy with what they felt was the committee's poor treatment of Fenner during his testimony before the committee. "They didn't hear many South Carolina accents" among the experts, Rupprecht remarked later. "So it was the NIMBY (Not In My Backyard)-ism—to which Fenner later remarked that it was a very interesting exercise in democracy, whereby it was not only the experts but the common person in the street whose advice was equally recognized." Hanlon, too, was embarrassed for Fenner, whom she described as representing "the gentleman scientist of an era that's almost gone by." To add insult to injury, Fenner later injured his leg on a boat ride to tour Parramore. "He got a tremendous bruise on his shin for his efforts to try and come out to help us," Rupprecht said.

The Choice is Made

Parramore Island had been suggested to Rupprecht by Suzanne Jenkens, a veterinarian with the Virginia Department of Health. Parramore was one of fourteen barrier islands that are part of the Virginia Coast Preserve, probably the last intact, naturally functioning system of barrier islands on the Atlantic Coast. The preserve is owned and managed by the Nature Conservancy, a group dedicated to maintaining the nation's diverse ecosystems. Barry Truitt, the director of science and stewardship for the preserve, was given the responsibility of evaluating Rupprecht's proposal. For Truitt, the decision was the biggest headache of his career. "I had many nights where I was tossing and turning all night long, especially when I first got into this. I didn't know anything about vaccinia viruses and recombinations and all that stuff."

Truitt was particularly unhappy with what he felt was a lack of scrutiny by the state, and even the USDA. "To me, it was basically rubber-stamped. It came down to the Conservancy here, and myself, having to decide whether it was something we were going to allow. Then, when they lost the South Carolina site, it doubled the pressure." Truitt studied everything he could find on the subject of vaccinia, telephoning Fenner in Australia and experts in South Africa and across the United States. He also turned to environmental groups that opposed biotechnology projects, particularly the National Wildlife Federation in Washington. D.C. Jane Rissler, a plant biologist with the group, was one of the most persistent critics, following V-RG for years, even after moving to the Union of Concerned Scientists, where she produced a newsletter called *The Gene Exchange*. "We wanted to make sure the product was reviewed carefully," Rissler said. "We didn't feel USDA, which had oversight, was giving a careful enough review. Part of our argument at the time was, we really didn't know what the risks were, but someone needed to figure out the potential problems and analyze them carefully."

Finally, Truitt said, he insisted the study's protocols be changed to collect more data on nontarget species and environmental impact. That did not sit well with Rupprecht, he recalls. "He's probably a brilliant guy, but his social skills are totally lacking. And he'd probably be the first person to admit that. It got pretty heated. Particularly when they were sitting there with their hands out for the permit, and at that point we said: 'Hey, you're going to have to redesign these protocols.'" Rupprecht said he doesn't recall any changes to the protocol, but rather a request from the Nature Conservancy to include in the project a scientist with whom they had worked before, to keep an eye on their interests.

As the Wistar group negotiated with Truitt, he reluctantly became the project's advocate among the Nature Conservancy's own diverse constituency. He argued for it before the group's Board of Governors, which had final say over the project. "It's not the mission of the Nature Conservancy to do this sort of stuff. But the decision was made fairly early that if it is a benefit to mankind, which apparently it's going to be, then it's a legitimate use of our property." As for Rupprecht, he acknowledges the courage it took for the group to allow the experiment on its land. "To their credit, they allowed us to participate on an island under their management, with relatively little to gain and potentially a lot to lose."

With efficacy tests on dozens of species completed, and a site in hand, Wistar submitted their final request for permission to release V-RG. In the summer of 1990, at a meeting in Berlin, Rupprecht received word of USDA approval.

The Parramore Experiment Begins

By the fifth day of the experiment on Parramore, 90 percent of the baits had been disturbed by animals. At the end of one month, 92 percent of raccoons captured within baiting areas and tested showed evidence of having eaten one or more baits. The only nervous moment came when the graduate student who had been left behind that first night was bitten while trying to sedate a captured raccoon. Tracks from the tracking pits indicated that only the raccoons and foxes—the vast majority of them raccoons—had taken the baits. Hundreds of raccoons were captured, sedated, and examined for any signs of vaccine-related symptoms, including abnormal behavior, lesions, or weight loss. Only one raccoon had anything remotely resembling vaccinia lesions, some bumps on its paws that on pathological examination were determined to be papaloma virus. Hanlon says the researchers were almost disappointed nothing out of the ordinary was found. "We were really like vultures waiting for something interesting scientifically to happen. We almost wanted it to happen. It was the best kind of research. It was almost boring to find nothing. It wasn't a bias of ignoring something, not doing enough research."

By the second week, four of seventeen captured raccoons had vaccine neutralizing antibodies to rabies detected in their blood, a sign they had been successfully immunized. By January 31, more than four months after the initial bait placement, about half the raccoons tested had detectable rabies antibodies.

The Parramore Island study, designed to determine whether V-RG could be safely released in the field with no harmful impact to the environment or non-target species, had gone a long way toward answering those questions. In 1991, with the worst fears about V-RG allayed, Rupprecht extended the safety trials to a mainland site, choosing Pennsylvania State Game Land 13, in Sullivan and Lycoming counties. The wooded, 49,527-acre site in north central Pennsylvania had restricted public access and a large raccoon population. Pennsylvania had provided some of the earliest funding for the oral vaccine research. Five thousand baits, covered in the same shellfish-egg slurry, were distributed along two stream valleys. As on Parramore, the baits were flagged, and tracking pits were dug to determine which animals were eating the baits. Over the next year, no pox lesions were discovered on any animal.

Rabies virus neutralizing antibodies, which the researchers felt were difficult to measure accurately, had been detected in only five of twenty-eight raccoons tested during the first six months of the trial. It was clear the results inland were not as good as on Parramore. Dave Johnston believed it was the bait, particularly the seafood slurry attractant, which remained unchanged from Parramore. "When we worked on Parramore Island with raccoons, they were associated with the seacoast. Things that worked very well there, like the seafood attractant, we took that into the interior of the country and it didn't work very well at all."

That was an important lesson: how critical the baits were, and the research required to understand the target species' habits and tastes. "There's no such thing, as everyone keeps talking about, as a universal bait," Johnston said. "You probably will get a certain percentage of animals eating something under certain conditions, but if you want to optimize for your cost benefit, then you're into looking at optimizing that bait through testing."

With good preliminary information on the effectiveness V-RG demonstrated in the laboratory, and with safety trials completed in the field, it looked as though oral vaccination of wildlife might finally be a viable option in the United States. But as Robert Miller at the USDA realized, studying a vaccine scattered in the field would never be as precise as studying it in the laboratory, where every condition could be carefully controlled. Some questions would certainly remain unanswered for a while. That, Miller says, is "the difficult thing about this vaccine, and the thing that kept me awake at night worrying about it." While you could demonstrate effectiveness of the vaccine, and make the bait attractive to the target species, in the end, "the people putting them out have to do an effective job of that so that all animals have a chance at getting to a bait, and getting the vaccine into them. Bait distribution is one thing we absolutely can't control. It worries me a lot."

CHAPTER THREE

A Plague Spreads

From his office in Austin, three hundred miles from the outbreak, Keith Clark would gaze at the map illustrating the spread of rabies, study the growing stack of case reports sent up from the field, and feel the kind of headache only someone with a disaster on his hands can feel. Clark, the head of the Zoonosis Control Division at the Texas Department of Health, was the person ultimately responsible for controlling the outbreak of canine rabies along the border. But it was a responsibility he was beginning to feel attached to his back like a big, fat bull's-eye.

Clark, whose quick grin and Texas drawl might not immediately point to a former academic career and a Ph.D. in veterinary pathology, knew about rabies. He had been a coauthor with George Baer, Jean Smith, and several others of a paper in the *Journal of Clinical Microbiology* back in 1986, adding to the weight of evidence that rabies was not a single disease, but rather a variety of distinct strains. "Some of us had believed on the basis of field observations and epidemiology that there were different strains, but a lot of the leading experts at the time just laughed at us—and even insulted us." That discovery was made possible with the arrival of monoclonal antibody testing. Monoclonal antibodies, which have a wide range of uses in medicine and research, can be engineered in the laboratory to identify antigens such as viruses with a high degree of specificity. Prior to that advance, many experts believed that rabies was the same virus in dogs, bats, skunks, and foxes. The advance brought by monoclonal antibody testing was the understanding that fox rabies, for example, would spread from

Keith Clark (far right). Courtesy Texas Department of Health

fox to fox, and occasionally spill over into dogs or other animals. But that spillover rarely spread beyond a case or two in non-host species.

This business of free-ranging coyotes carrying rabies far and wide, occasionally stopping long enough to start an outbreak in domestic dogs, was altogether new. And Clark knew there was nothing that could stop coyotes; South Texas ranchers had been trying to wipe them out for generations with little success. "During the '70s and '80s, we had incursions of canine rabies along the U.S.-Mexico border. It was mostly in Texas, but New Mexico, Arizona, and California all experienced some. We were always able to go in using the conventional rabies control methods of vaccination and law enforcement—picking up stray animals, educating the public—and get it under control. But it was real clear in late '88 that that strategy wasn't going to work with these coyotes. You can't just round them up and vaccinate them."

But Clark's problem extended even to the traditional rabies control methods. That was more a function of the health department's odd bureaucracy than anything else. At the time, the Zoonosis Control Division was a small part of the state's Bureau of Veterinary Public Health. The main function of the bureau was inspection of the state's slaughterhouses. James Weedon, Clark's counterpart in meat inspection, had tried to implement some reforms in the process, changes that had proven somewhat unpopular with some of the health department's regional medical directors. That was particularly true in Region 8, which included Starr and Hidalgo. The medical director there had been at odds with Weedon, and it had gotten so bad that Weedon had been ordered not to set foot in Region 8. Clark was caught in the fallout of the medical director's wrath, and thus had little influence over the region's veterinarian, George McKirahan, who worked for the local director and spearheaded the rabies efforts there. "We were absolutely powerless to do anything except worry a lot," Clark says.

Worry he did. Although his influence over the rabies effort was limited, he still carried the ultimate responsibility for its execution. If the canine rabies epizootic continued and spread—and all indications were that it would—he would feel the heat for failing to stop it. People would ask, why didn't the health department do something about it when it was still a small outbreak and easy to contain? "It was pretty obvious to me, having a background in wildlife diseases, that when it got into coyotes it was a whole new ball game," Clark says. "As soon as we saw it get into Rio Grande City and just go into those dogs like that. . . . If there was any doubt, as soon as it moved upriver to Roma and infected one coyote there—bingo, we had fifteen rabid dogs."

Clark came to the health department after a career that already had included stints as a U.S. Air Force scientist, a university professor, and a practicing veterinarian. He was born in Quitaque (pronounced Kit-a-quay), a town of about five hundred people in sparsely populated Briscoe County, northeast of Lubbock, and a short drive from the rugged splendor of Palo Duro Canyon. After earning a veterinary degree at Texas A&M University, he joined the Air Force and supervised animal research programs, first at Brooks Air Force Base in San Antonio, then at the U.S. Naval Aerospace Medical Institute at Pensacola, Florida. After his discharge, he returned to A&M and taught while working on a doctoral degree in veterinary pathology. There, he published a host of papers on wildlife diseases, particularly on malignant catarrhal fever, a deadly disease in Texas white-tailed deer populations. After earning his Ph.D., he opened a private veterinary clinic in Marble Falls, a scenic, lakeside town in the Texas Hill Country, west of Austin, where he had graduated high school. Two other items of note stood out on his *curriculum vitae:* he served as a colonel in the U.S. Army Reserve Veterinary Corps and he was an expert rifleman, earning the President's Hundred designation in marksmanship.

He came to the health department in 1978, the year after a fairly serious canine rabies outbreak had swept through Laredo. He had studied the Laredo outbreak and published an analysis in the *Texas Veterinary Medical Journal*. That outbreak, in which fifty-four dogs were infected and fifty-eight people exposed, had cost $137,000 to contain. It had also cost Laredo an estimated two million dollars in lost revenues from business and tourism because of the publicity.

But with the current outbreak, traditional rabies control methods were clearly inadequate. "It was clear we had a serious problem and no tools to do anything," Clark says. Sheep and goat raisers began hollering for de-regulation of 1080, a coyote-killing poison banned by the EPA. "We came under a lot of pressure to support poison or killing them all. I personally wouldn't have had any problem with killing them all if I thought it was possible or effective. But since World War II, they've been trying to control rabies by killing red foxes in Europe, in a situation where they had much better control of land use. And it didn't work."

Clark had been following the progress of oral rabies vaccination since the early Swiss trials, and was aware of Rupprecht's work with V-RG. He vaguely thought it might be a possible weapon against the South Texas epizootic. But it was more of a wistful fantasy than a realistic strategy, particularly given the lumbering bureaucracy of the health department. Zoonosis Control languished in the shadows of the meat inspection program. Although his bureau chief, Bill Rosser, was supportive, Clark grew frustrated when the two men would meet with their associate commissioner to discuss a zoonosis problem, and within minutes the conversation would veer to meat inspection. And Clark was certain the project would never sail past the state's commissioner of health, Robert Bernstein, an imposing, slow-talking retired Army general and physician, who had a reputation of trying to carry every program personally before the Texas Legislature, often unsuccessfully.

Clark confided to his closest friends he thought he would be made a scapegoat for the inevitable spread of the outbreak. His frustration led him to apply for the job as head of rabies programs at the Centers for Disease Control in Atlanta. George Baer was stepping down after thirty years at the agency. Clark was selected as a finalist for the job, along with another applicant: Charles Rupprecht, who had taken Baer's dream of oral vaccination of wildlife against rabies and proved it could work in the United States. In the end, it was Rupprecht who would win the job as head of the nation's rabies research and control efforts. But Rupprecht's recombinant vaccine would prove the answer to Clark's long, frustrating search for a tool to combat the South Texas rabies problem. And so the two very different men, who held very similar interests, would find their paths crossing once again.

1990: A Limited Engagement

In 1990, the year before it exploded northward, the South Texas canine rabies epizootic limited its assault to Starr County, the place where it was born. Hidalgo County that year had no cases, a fact that was attributed by health officials to aggressive pet vaccination clinics and elimination of strays. All told that year, thirty-one dogs, three coyotes, and three cats were confirmed with rabies. The cases were largely in and around populated areas, with Rio Grande City reporting fifteen dogs and all of the coyotes and cats. Roma, to the west, had dealt with sixteen rabid dogs between March 31 and June 12. In the first case of 1990, a Rio Grande City family's six-month-old male dog returned home January 29 after a few days' absence, acting sick and vicious. After it attacked and killed a neighbor's puppy, the neighbor beat it senseless with a board until the animal control officer could be summoned.

Again, the terrifying incidents—almost familiar now—continued: an eleven-year-old Rio Grande City boy was riding his bike in an alley when he was attacked by someone's pet. In Roma, police shot a dog that was foaming at the mouth. The dog had been vaccinated three weeks earlier. Another Roma dog became ill about a week after being vaccinated. The health department investigators, who were criticized for recommending routinely that vaccinated dogs be destroyed, pressed on: "Our first recommendation was euthanasia whether you vaccinate or not, unless there's a good enough reason not to euthanize the animal," McKirahan says. "That reason could just be, 'Well, we love our pet.' Or it could be he's a breeding stock show dog." If the dog was currently vaccinated and the owners insisted on keeping it, the health department would recommend a rabies booster, followed by a short confinement for observation. Privately, health officials noted the rabies scare had prompted many people to vaccinate their dogs, even if the animals were considered more of an inexpensive alarm system than a pet. Those dogs that were malnourished or sick with mange had weakened immune systems and probably were not going to get proper immunity from the vaccine.

As for the coyotes, the first case of 1990 occurred May 27 at a ranch near Rio Grande City. As in the Smiths' case, a couple heard their dogs fighting with a coyote. While the man ran in the house for a gun, the coyote tried to attack a ranchhand, who beat it with a two-by-four. The rancher returned and shot the unconscious animal. In September, another coyote attacked a litter of puppies. The mother, an unvaccinated boxer–pit bull mix, fought off the coyote, which ran away. A few days later, the mother became ill with rabies, and was destroyed, along with the five puppies she had fought to protect. Because the coyote disappeared, it was not included in the year's statistics. Nor were two others that fought with a German shepherd on a ranch about twelve miles west of La Gloria in November. A month later, the dog began foaming at the mouth.

Making Progress

What changed for Clark was the retirement of Bernstein, and the arrival of David Smith. Bernstein and Smith were perhaps as diverse in style and manner as is possible for two humans to be. Smith was a young and handsome pediatrician, with a firebrand style of public speaking, who would travel across the state making fiery pronouncements about the "biblical diseases" raging through Texas—tuberculosis, rabies, bubonic plague, and even leprosy. Smith, formerly senior vice president of Parkland Memorial Hospital in Dallas, who had studied at Cornell and Johns Hopkins universities among others, liked to talk about his public health awakening while serving a stint in Brownsville, the state's southmost border city, during a *Northern Exposure*-type commitment fresh out of medical school. The experience made him see the importance of medicine as patient-oriented, he said, rather than the disease-oriented approach taught in medical schools. Without taking into consideration the other elements of a patient's life and culture, Smith says, then treating the disease is only a temporary fix.

Clark, who had followed Rupprecht's progress with V-RG, in late 1992 drew up a proposal asking to study the feasibility of using the oral vaccine to contain the growing canine epizootic. With permission from his bureau chief, he sent the proposal up to the new commissioner and asked for an appointment. Smith, who was still learning his way around the massive state bureaucracy, was able to squeeze in a meeting with the two veterinarians near quitting time. Clark was impressed with Smith; the insight behind the questions he asked suggested he had studied the proposal thoroughly. One of the major concerns was whether Texans would have qualms about dropping a genetically engineered substance onto their property. But unlike the northern states that had to wrestle with that issue, Texas had had good experience with the screwworm fly eradication program in the 1960s.

For decades, screwworm flies had cost Texas ranchers millions of dollars in livestock losses each year, and caused disease in humans as well. Entomologists learned how to sterilize male flies using X-rays; the first success occurred at what is now Brooke Army Medical Center in San Antonio, where the commander allowed the researchers to borrow the hospital's radiation oncology unit after regular patient hours. A huge production facility was built in Mission, along the border, which produced as many as 175 million sterilized flies a week. The flies were dropped from airplanes in infested areas, and by the mid-1960s the state was largely free of screwworms. The program then moved into Mexico, eliminating the pest there, and then further south into Central and South America, where it continues today. Robert Miller, the USDA official overseeing the V-RG trials, also was part of that historic project.

"We decided," Clark says, "we could tie it (V-RG) to the public's memory of the screwworm program. The government flew over our lands, dropped packages out of airplanes, and good things happened." And at the close of the late afternoon meeting, Clark told the commissioner: "What I'm looking for here is for you to tell me to go ahead or forget it." Smith replied, "Let's go for it."

The Wave Rises

Although everyone expected it to happen, when the epizootic finally broke loose from two index counties and spread northward, health officials were dismayed. Nothing they could do, no public health tools they currently possessed, could keep this thing from expanding. The break occurred March 6, 1991, in Falfurrias, a town of about six thousand people in northern Brooks County, whose southern border touched both Starr and Hidalgo. About noon, a woman heard her dogs barking and growling beneath her house. When she went out to investigate, she saw a coyote in the yard. She called two neighbors, who clubbed the coyote to death. They placed a leash around its neck, and dragged it out of the yard. Eight adult dogs and fifteen puppies suspected of having contact with the coyote were destroyed.

The outbreak continued speeding north. In Jim Wells County—an irregular-shaped county, north of Brooks, that on a map resembles a pistol with the barrel pointing south—a man was driving his pickup on a road about ten miles northwest of Premont on April 26 when he saw a coyote with a puppy in its jaws. He veered and ran the coyote over. In Concepcion, to the west of Premont in Duval County, a man shot and killed a coyote that had been fighting with a female collie protecting its newborn pups. On investigation, the man found the coyote had eaten one puppy's head and had started eating another.

Not that rabies had left Starr entirely behind. Instead, the epicenter of the outbreak had shifted to the northern part of the county, which previously had been spared. In San Isidro, in northern Starr, the parish priest had taken ill, and his dog abandoned for more than a month. On May 15, the priest's dog attacked several other dogs, and the local constable shot it and took it to Roberto Margo in Rio Grande City for testing. Two days later, one of the dogs attacked by the priest's dog began foaming at the mouth. It, along with several others, were destroyed.

And as if to remind everyone that rabies was not confined to dogs and coyotes, a teacher at Benevides Elementary School in Sullivan City, in far western Hidalgo County, saw a bunch of children huddled on the playground. When she approached, she saw they were playing with a dead bat. By the time school and health authorities finished their investigation, they determined that thirty-two children may have touched the creature. The boy who first discovered the bat and had picked it up told conflicting stories on repeated questioning about whether it was alive or dead when he found it. All received postexposure treatment.

Hebbronville

Residents of Hebbronville, in Jim Hogg County, north of Starr and west of Brooks, knew by September 1991 that the rabid coyotes had arrived. The first was reported by a woman who said one coyote had taken to showing up on her porch each night. The animal liked to snap at bugs attracted by her porch light, until she came out to shoo it away. When it got to the point the coyote wouldn't be shooed, she called authorities, who shot it.

The next coyote incident in Hebbronville was not so benign. Marisda Molina, a three-year-old girl, was playing alone on the family's front porch about 5:40 P.M. on September 28, when she was attacked from behind by a coyote. She screamed, a sound that sent her mother and brother scrambling outside to investigate. They were shocked to find the child's back covered in blood, and a coyote standing a few feet away. They chased the animal off, and it was later shot by a family member. The child was taken to Mercy Hospital in Laredo for treatment. When a deputy was summoned, an aunt told him she did not know how the coyote could have entered the well-fenced yard, according to an account in the local newspaper, the *Jim Hogg County Enterprise*. Although the town had organized a rabies clinic that summer when more than a hundred pets were vaccinated, another was quickly held. The sheriff warned residents not to allow children to play unattended, and to keep them indoors as much as possible "until this epidemic is stopped."

Encino

It almost had to happen sooner or later. On October 18, a ranch hand shot a rabid coyote trying to enter the main gate of the El Coyote Ranch, near Encino. According to the case report, there were no human or known animal exposures. It was unclear if the coyote was seeking refuge.

Home Remedies

Understandably, the epizootic brought with it different degrees of fear. Some people set traps for strays. A man who trapped a stray cat at a trailer park in Edinburg took it upon himself to kill the animal. He did this by squeezing its head—to suffocate it, he later told authorities. The cat, understandably, fought for survival and scratched and bit him badly. This made the man angry, and he put the animal back it its cage and ran the whole thing over with a tractor. He then went to his doctor to get his wounds treated. The physician recommended testing what was left of the cat for rabies. It was positive.

During 1991, the epizootic moved one hundred miles to the north. Ten counties, including the original two, reported forty-two rabid coyotes and twenty-five dogs. It was also the first year that rabid coyotes had outnumbered rabid dogs, a trend that has remained constant throughout the epizootic. Health officials attributed that to increased education and mass vaccination clinics. Other animals infected with the canine strain included a raccoon, a skunk, a cow, and the positive cat in Edinburg.

The Case of San Juanita Barrera

In August 1991, the canine outbreak of rabies claimed its first human victim, in El Sauz, a village of about four hundred people, twenty-five miles northwest of Rio Grande City. San Juanita Barrera, a fifty-five-year-old grandmother, complained to her family of feeling nervous, of increasing shortness of breath, and of difficulty swallowing. On August 9, she was admitted to the hospital, where a doctor diagnosed her as suffering from a panic attack. But during the first three days, her temperature rose and fell erratically, from 97°F to 106°F. After three days, she developed the classic rabies symptoms—terror of water and air, agitation, alternating between complete incoherence and normalcy. Blood, saliva, and cerebrospinal fluid were collected, along with a skin biopsy from the nape of her neck, and sent to CDC. Her condition worsened, and on August 16, she was transferred to a larger hospital with a CT-scanner. It showed only an old stroke injury in her left cerebellum. Shortly afterward, she stopped breathing and went into cardiac arrest. Although revived, she never regained consciousness and died August 20.

As with the earlier human death, George McKirahan was informed of Barrera's case after returning from Mexico—this time, Tampico—where he had attended a meeting of the same group, the Binational Border Health Association. "She was alive at that point, and hadn't been diagnosed positively that it was rabies, but it was highly suspect." At CDC, the blood, cerebrospinal fluid, and skin biopsy at first tested negative for rabies. However, five days later, rabies virus was detected in saliva. A monoclonal antibody assay found the strain to be Mexican urban dog. A second skin biopsy was taken, and confirmed rabies. McKirahan interviewed family members, who swore there had been no exposure to a suspicious animal. Indeed, they said, she hadn't been bitten by a dog since she was nine years old. She was a lifelong resident of Starr, although she had visited relatives in northern Mexico from time to time. Her last visit was more than a year earlier. Instead, family members suspected she had been poisoned by neighbors, a suspicion lab results quickly ruled out. On further questioning, they acknowledged several animals on the family's ranch had died suspiciously in recent months. McKirahan filed the following preliminary report to Austin:

Texas Department of Health
Austin Texas
Inter-Office
FROM: George McKirahan, D.V.M.
Program Manager, V.P.H.
THRU: Dr. Foy V. McCasland
Bureau Chief Veterinary Public Health

THRU: Dr. Keith Clark
    Director Zoonosis Control Division
TO: Vic Whadford
    Public Health Technician
SUBJECT: Human rabies case - El Sauz - Starr County, Texas

Name: San Juanita Barrera (deceased)
Location of Residence: 20 miles N. of Rio Grande City
    on FM 349
Community of El Sauz
Longitude: 98° 50' (3 miles west)
Latitude: 26° 35' (1 mile south)

Extensive investigations into this case have revealed no conclusive evidence as to the point source for exposure to the rabies virus. However, speculation can be made as to several possible animals that might have exposed the person to the virus. One must keep in mind that none of the animals in question were vaccinated against rabies. In addition, the accuracy of some of the information is questionable because of the circumstances surrounding the case.

Dog No. 1 - 11 year old male crossbreed - As a coyote approached the owner's daughter in broad daylight, the dog attacked the coyote and was bitten by the coyote. The coyote was killed by Mr. Barrera. Subsequent to the coyote attack, the dog became "nervous" - pacing back and forth constantly. The dog killed 3 cats (it had never "messed" with the cats before). The dog appeared to have some stomach discomfort on the last day of its life. The dog died approximately one week after fighting with the coyote and about 3 months prior to Mrs. Barrera's symptoms beginning.

Dog No. 2 - A puppy, approximately 3 months old died choking on a chicken bone. This occurred approximately two weeks before Mrs. Barrera's symptoms began. Mrs. Barrera had no contact with this dog at that time, but the pup had previously scratched her on the leg.

Cat - One of Mrs. Barrera's cats scratched her on the leg about 2 ½ months before her symptoms began. The cat was not noted to be ill, but it disappeared within one week of the incident.

Cow - A cow died one week before Mrs. Barrera's symptoms

began. The cow was not known to be ill until it fell, was unable to get up, had clonic movements, and then died.

Signed George McKirahan D.V.M

"Maybe all four of these animals had rabies—I don't know," McKirahan said later. "We could never determine for sure where she contracted rabies. If the cow had been sick and gone down—but she still had the dog and the puppy and the cat—we could point to the cow. But all were dead, so the process of elimination didn't work. And her husband said, no, the neighbors poisoned her."

After rabies was confirmed, a total of forty-three people received post-exposure shots. Thirty were workers at the first hospital where Barrera was admitted for panic attacks. And although isolation precautions had been in place at the second hospital, an additional seven underwent treatment. They had helped revive Barrera after her respiratory arrest, and were apparently uninformed of her status. Six members of her family also received post-exposure treatment.

From Austin, Michael Kelly with the Texas Department of Health told Laura Martinez, a reporter with the *Valley Morning Star* newspaper, that if Barrera had in fact contracted the disease from the dog who fought with the coyote, then Barrera was the first Texan to have contracted rabies from a pet animal in two decades. "We probably won't ever have a complete story of what exactly happened, because the family is unaware of any bite or exposure from an animal," Kelly says. "It may have been something she didn't think was significant and never mentioned it to anybody." That ignorance of an exposure, he added, is common to human rabies deaths, since people who suspect an exposure typically receive preventive treatment.

Media Coverage is Bare

Perhaps it was the remoteness of the El Sauz ranch, or maybe it was simple disinterest. But the rabies outbreak along the border had so far failed to register much of a blip on the radar screens of newspapers and TV stations throughout the rest of Texas—much less the rest of the country—and Barrera's death was barely noticed outside the Valley. The *San Antonio Express-News,* the closest big-city paper to the Rio Grande Valley, ran a short AP story in the back of the paper Wednesday, August 21, saying that Barrera was in critical condition with rabies. No follow-up story appeared that she had died, although the paper had published occasional stories about the outbreak. A DataTimes search finds no rabies stories in either the *Dallas Morning News* or the *Houston Chronicle* around that time. The scope of the South Texas rabies epizootic, now moving northward at the speed and distance of free-ranging coyotes, did not yet register with the media or the citizens of most of the state as a major health risk. That would come later, with another death, a declaration by the governor, and an announcement of plans for a massive and daring air campaign against the disease.

CHAPTER FOUR

The Little Bandits

As with Sue and Monte Smith's coyote, a rabies outbreak typically begins with an index case. The rabies epizootic in raccoons that spilled across the United States from Florida to New York began back in 1947 with "a seemingly unimportant report of a single rabid raccoon" in Brevard County, Florida, according to a history of the outbreak written by Charles Rupprecht and Jean Smith. Prior to that incident, Florida had seen its share of dog rabies, particularly in cities. A rabid raccoon caused little stir. In the previous decade, ten people had died of rabies in the state. Although the Florida Legislature had failed to enact statewide rabies control measures, many local communities passed their own ordinances, and rabies cases in dogs and other domestic animals dropped dramatically. People began taking note of rabies in wildlife.

The first known case of human rabies transmitted by an insect-eating bat anywhere in the world occurred in Hillsborough County, Florida, in 1953—the victim, a small boy. A pocket of fox rabies was discovered in the Western Panhandle of Florida, and sporadic cases of raccoon rabies further south. Over time, the fox outbreak died out on its own, but raccoon rabies expanded along the vast network of lakes and rivers throughout Central Florida. By 1977, the epizootic had spread into Georgia, Alabama, and South Carolina, and was moving north at roughly forty kilometers per year.

Raccoon rabies might have continued creeping at that pace. But in the 1970s, the disease made a major leap hundreds of miles near the border between Virginia and West Virginia. The reason? Hunters, seeking to restock preserves, brought more than 3,500 raccoons from Florida, according to documents reviewed by CDC from the Virginia Game Commission. And those were the legal shipments, brought by permit. At least one shipment was known to contain a rabid raccoon. That first rabid raccoon in Hardy County, West Virginia, was quickly followed by three more rabid raccoons in adjacent counties. What followed is what Rupprecht and Smith described as "the most intense outbreak of wildlife rabies ever to occur in the United States."

How did the disease begin in raccoons? Researchers believed raccoon rabies had existed in Florida long before it was discovered. It was only the gradual control of dog rabies, and the increase of human populations encroaching on traditional raccoon habitat, that brought the problem to the surface. Genetic analysis of raccoon rabies in Smiths' lab suggested it was unlikely the raccoon rabies epizootic had spilled over from rabies in bats or dogs. The strain was too different, and such spillover rarely takes hold in a different species beyond the infection of one or two unlucky animals. The structure and stability of the raccoon rabies virus suggested it had been around a long time, specifically in raccoons.

From Virginia and West Virginia, the epizootic spread both north and south at about forty kilometers a year. That spread wasn't uniform, however. If it had been, raccoon rabies would have reached both Canada and Texas by now. Both natural and man-made barriers, such as rivers, mountains, and highways, interfered to some extent with the movement of the disease. In the disease's favor, on the other hand, were people. "The rapidity of spread throughout the mid-Atlantic region may be partially explained by the relatively dense raccoon populations associated with an abundance of food and shelter in urban-suburban areas adjacent to parkland, in one of the densest corridors of human population in the United States," Rupprecht and Smith wrote.

The epizootic reached New York in May 1990; Connecticut in March 1991; New Hampshire in April 1992; and Massachusetts in September 1992— in Ashby, near the New Hampshire border, and more than sixty miles north of the nearest reported raccoon rabies cases in Connecticut, according to the CDC. North Carolina was hit from north and south; the outbreak moved from Virginia into northeastern North Carolina in 1991, and from South Carolina into two regions of south-central and southeastern North Carolina in 1992. In the two decades from the index case in Virginia, raccoon rabies virtually blanketed the East Coast, with more than 20,000 rabid raccoons reported; spillover of the disease into several thousand dogs, cats, and other animals; and millions of dollars spent on postexposure treatments. In New York, which in 1993 reported the largest number of rabid wild animals ever in one state, the number of people receiving postexposure treatment increased from eighty-four in 1989, to 2,905 in 1993.

Still, despite the scope of the outbreak, no humans are known to have died from raccoon rabies. Health officials had a few ideas as to why. For one thing, the epizootic occurred as states and cities already had in place sophisticated rabies control programs, as well as improvements in postexposure treatments. But that didn't completely explain it. People had died of both skunk and fox rabies. And raccoons could certainly be aggressive—people had been attacked, and horror stories were plentiful as the epizootic front moved through populated areas. Raccoons shed lots of virus through saliva; that had been well-documented through laboratory studies.

The paradox of these adorable creatures transformed into a deadly menace instilled a specific kind of fear, particularly given their closeness to people. Raccoons are found in greatest numbers in cities, where food is plentiful from garbage cans, backyard gardens, and even the cat dish on the back porch. For many people, the "little bandits," knocking over trash cans or nesting in the attic, weren't a major problem. "People don't seem to mind," says Faye Sorhage, who heads rabies programs for the New Jersey Department of Health. "It's like, 'Oh, the raccoon's in the garbage; How cute.' It's not like a skunk." That sentiment gradually began to change as the outbreak pushed through, and the scary stories became more frequent, accompanied by newspaper headlines such as: "Rabid raccoon bites youth," "Rabid raccoon attacks man near Bucks County," and "Officer shoots self trying to snare rabid fox." The clippings spill from a fat file folder in Sorhage's office in Trenton.

"People were starting to kill raccoons," she recalls. "They were so scared of them they were shooting them. In some towns, we'd estimate half the raccoons were becoming rabid."

New Jersey

New Jersey's first rabid raccoon was discovered along the northwest corner of the state in November 1989. As the disease quickly moved south, a number of voices, particularly from wildlife and animal welfare groups, began demanding action. Some were familiar with Canada's wildlife vaccination program; others had heard of pilot safety studies of a new, genetically engineered vaccine in the United States. "The problem was, we'd have to say to them it's not approved for use," Sorhage says.

Charles Rupprecht, Sorhage, and Douglas Roscoe, a scientist with the state's Division of Fish, Game and Wildlife, had become acquainted at various conferences. Roscoe had offered to find Rupprecht some New Jersey sites for testing V-RG. At the meeting in Berlin, where Rupprecht learned the USDA had approved his plan for Parramore, he had gotten into a shouting match with Roscoe on a bus. "We got into a rather heated exchange because on multiple times he had promised finding us sites in New Jersey and they never came up." Roscoe did come through, and found a location for placebo baiting studies that coincided with the Parramore project. Among Rupprecht's international group of researchers was a Chilean who commuted back and forth between Parramore and the New Jersey placebo trials. He became infected with Lyme disease and had to return to Chile.

For Sorhage, who met Rupprecht at a meeting in Washington, the timing was perfect. Although she had been working with rabies programs for several years—first with the Maryland health department and later with the CDC, assigned to Florida—that Washington meeting had been her first opportunity to hear of wildlife vaccination programs in Switzerland and Germany. With pressure mounting from New Jersey residents to do *something* about the crisis—and with the costs associated with postexposure treatment starting to soar as the outbreak plowed through—Sorhage was prepared to offer up New Jersey as a site for the first U.S. field trial to determine if V-RG, would actually protect wild animals against rabies. The trials at Parramore Island and on Pennsylvania state gamelands had been designed merely to demonstrate the vaccine could be distributed without harm to animals or people. New Jersey's peninsular shape would be ideal to create a vaccine barrier to keep the outbreak from reaching Cape May County, at the southern tip. Some $300,000 in state funds were scrounged from health and wildlife budgets to purchase the baits. For budgetary reasons, they decided to scatter baits along roads, rivers, and the edges of fields where raccoons were likely to travel, rather than dropping them uniformly, as the Canadians did for foxes, and as Texas later would attempt to do to control canine rabies. "Initially we were planning to do a random distribution, which is nice if you can come up with the resources to buy all the bait and the vaccine," Roscoe says.

Another reason for the switch from uniform distribution was the problem of airplanes. Rupprecht and the New Jersey officials had made arrangements with the Ontario Ministry of Natural Resources in Canada to use its fleet of Twin-Otter planes, which were specially outfitted to drop the baits in a grid pattern. But lawyers were unable to come to an agreement over liability issues—who would shoulder the blame if a rock-hard fishmeal bait was dropped from a plane owned by the Canadian government and somehow landed on the head of an unsuspecting New Jersey homeowner? Legal minds could come up with no quick answer to the question, and Canada's offer was declined. In April 1992, the first thirty thousand baits were dropped by hand using a helicopter borrowed from a local mosquito control program, over about a 120,000-acre zone.

Before that could happen, however, the health department tried to win support from those living within the drop zone. Although the area included a large expanse of state park lands, it still contained about forty thousand residents. Kerry Pflugh, a scientist with the state's environmental protection department, was brought in to oversee public relations for the effort. "My concern was that because it was a bioengineered vaccine that people would be afraid of it," Pflugh says. "This was around the same time that the book *Jurassic Park* was released. But it was not even raised as an issue." Pflugh surveyed residents by telephone, briefed local government officials, and held public meetings. "They all wanted to see this trial take place. They were more concerned about rabies as a threat than they were about the vaccine."

Some state officials talked hopefully about creating a vaccine barrier, then moving it further north each year until rabies was pushed entirely from the state. It was clear, however, that initial funds for the project would be inadequate for that, and the protocols for the experiment called only for the creation and maintenance of a barrier for two years. Afterward, the group would analyze data from the study and develop recommendations for New Jersey lawmakers.

The fishmeal baits were dropped in spring and fall, each year for two years, along the northern part of Cape May County, the southern tip of Atlantic County, and east into Cumberland County along the Maurice River. Throughout the study, wildlife officials trapped raccoons within and on either side of the barrier zone. They calculated that the rabies outbreak was moving south through New Jersey at about thirty miles per year. As the front of the epizootic approached the barrier, raccoon populations in its path were becoming rabid at rates as high as 80 percent.

The team held its collective breath as the outbreak reached the barrier and appeared to hold. A couple of rabid raccoons were trapped at the northern edge of the barrier; they were dismissed as having wandered across from untreated areas. A few months later, however, a rabid raccoon was found well into the baiting area. Then another. Spot treatment of baits was made around the site. Wildlife officials discovered a man living above the area, unaware the experiment was under way, had been trapping raccoons as pests on his property and moving them into state wildlife areas within the zone.

But money was running out, and the team members resigned themselves to dropping the remaining 18,000 of 180,000 baits they had purchased, to hold the barrier as long as they could. In November, thirteen days after the final distribution, a rabid raccoon was found two miles below the barrier. Within two weeks, two more were found miles further south. The barrier had been breached.

"The barrier didn't work," Roscoe admits. "But it was effective in the area where the vaccine was put, in terms of both reducing the incidence of disease to a point where it's really rather trivial, and also slowing the ad-

*Examples of fishmeal polymer baits used in the United States. The cylindrical bait
saw only limited use in baiting trials in the Northeast.
Courtesy New York State Department of Health*

vancement of the disease." While positivity rates above the barrier were close to 70 percent, within the barrier they were only 4 percent, Roscoe noted. And the speed of the epizootic was slowed from thirty miles per year outside the barrier, to about ten miles within. Increasing the density of the baits might have made a difference, as would have widening the barrier. The eleven-mile width was selected because healthy raccoons rarely travel more than a mile or two. But in one experiment, Roscoe tagged raccoons, which later became rabid. In their madness, those animals were found to travel as far as seven or eight miles. "It seems reasonable the entire area of 11 miles might have been breached by an animal that was rabid."

As money was running out, Pflugh surveyed residents within the zone to determine if they would be willing to pay a minimal tax—perhaps a dollar per year—to maintain the baiting. "About 60 percent of the people in both those surveys said they would be supportive of that sort of thing. But in this fiscal environment, there is no way a politician will carry this banner. And those (40 percent) who were not supportive, were *very* not supportive."

Pflugh notified residents within the drop zone that the experiment was over, that the barrier they had hoped to create was breached. None of the residents, she says, voiced any criticism of the project or its failure. News coverage was almost nonexistent, despite the heavy coverage that preceded it.

Organizers refused to call the breach a failure.

"Scientific experiments are not failures if the hypothesis didn't occur," Roscoe said in an interview at his laboratory at the Clinton Wildlife Management Area, north of Trenton. "We believe it is only a matter of degree, a matter of planning, to make it effective. It was effective in the area where the vaccine was put, in terms of reducing the incidence of disease to a point where it was really rather trivial, and also slowing the advancement of the disease. The objective of preventing it from getting through the barrier I think may be more a function of the width of the barrier, as well as the number of baits."

The Economic Debate over the New Jersey Experiment

Among the project's main critics was Edward Bruggeman, a staff scientist with the National Audubon Society. After testifying against the idea at public hearings, he published an article in the October 1992 issue of the journal *BioScience* arguing the plan was unnecessary and possibly dangerous. "Public money could be better spent on education" regarding pet vaccination, which is proven effective. Such field vaccination schemes detract from campaigns to increase the percentage of domestic dog vaccination.

Bruggeman, who declined to be interviewed since taking a new job with the National Institutes of Health, also expressed concern in the article with the vaccine itself. Bruggeman noted the vaccinia virus was unknown in raccoons, and introducing it could have unintended consequences.

Although Bruggeman acknowledged that field vaccination efforts had been successful in Europe against foxes, "it is not clear to what extent these results are relevant to raccoon rabies in North America," he wrote. "Similar theoretical models predict that lower vaccination rates are sufficient to control fox rabies." He pointed to one mathematical model that suggested that because vaccination would interfere with the natural population attrition that occurs with rabies outbreaks, it would take an extremely high percentage of vaccinated raccoons to control the epizootic, as many as 99 percent. The most effective control method would be to combine vaccination with culling raccoon populations through trapping and poison. However those methods impact other species, and generally are unacceptable to the public. Bruggeman said, "Because it is apparently so difficult to control raccoon rabies, it may be useful to ask whether raccoon rabies really needs to be controlled." Pointing to the small number of people in the United States who develop rabies—only sixteen between 1980 and 1991, with nine of those acquired in foreign countries—he concluded that the disease is an insignificant risk to human health.

Finally, he wrote, the central argument for field vaccination efforts— that it would reduce the astronomical costs of postexposure treatments— was faulty. Because it would fail to protect 100 percent of raccoons against rabies, any exposure would be treated as a precaution. "It appears that in an affluent society, fear of rabies, rather than actual risk, has created the necessary market for new rabies control technologies."

But Faye Sorhage, whose figures are the most frequently cited by proponents of vaccinating wild animals, disagreed. New Jersey's costs associated with rabies postexposure treatment within the baited area were a fraction of those above the front line of the epizootic. In just two northern New Jersey counties, both public and private rabies costs more than doubled as the epizootic moved through, from $405,565 per one hundred thousand residents, to $979,027. In New York, the number of people who required postexposure treatments rose from 84 in 1989, before the outbreak arrived, to 2,905 in 1993. Although many of those who underwent the treatments were undoubtedly the "worried well," whose exposure did not clearly meet the guidelines for treatment, health officials who have weathered a major rabies outbreak say it is difficult to convince a mother that her child's contact with an aggressive animal is insufficient to require potentially lifesaving protective therapy.

Greener Pastures

In the middle of the New Jersey trial, Hilary Koprowski resigned as director of the Wistar Institute and moved to Thomas Jefferson University in Philadelphia. He arranged to bring the rabies group over with him. "It was clear that the infrastructure at Wistar had changed, and Dr. Koprowski was no longer director," Rupprecht said. "The next administration was not interested in oral vaccination, and we decided to make the move to Thomas Jefferson University, with all the baggage of, 'Do you guys mind being the sponsors of the New Jersey trial?' And to Jefferson's credit, they came into it cold, and were accepting of this new crazy group."

"Thomas Jefferson, I think, really didn't have a clue what they were getting into," Hanlon recalled. "It was done capably, so they were relatively easily sold. But I think initially it was a shock to them." On April 3, 1992, Joseph Sherwin, the associate dean of scientific affairs, notified Robert Miller at USDA that Rupprecht and his group had joined the faculty, "and fully intend, with Thomas Jefferson University's cooperation to continue the field testing of their rabies vaccine product." The change in the trial's sponsor was published in the *Federal Register,* and USDA notified New Jersey health and environmental officials that the transfer would be viewed "in a manner similar to the purchase of a licensed biological manufacturing facility company by another company. This means that all product licenses, manufacturing practices, and authorization previously approved are transferred to the second owner."

But as the trial progressed, "it was clear the project had gotten too big," Rupprecht says. "Rhone was finally taking some responsibility and asking for all the things needed for licensure of a product produced here, instead of imported from France." Hanlon suspected Rupprecht might have lost some interest in the project. "Before we went into the field on Parramore Island, he told me, 'This is no longer science.' He had already moved on to more intellectually entertaining pursuits. Yes, his heart is in this, but he's basically raised a teenager, given it the best he can, and kissed it good-bye. It's on its own. He wishes it well and has been supportive of it, and has really bent over backwards I think to provide as much support as he can." To Hanlon, that was the answer to Rupprecht's critics, some of whom charged his later disputes with the Texans and others were a result of his having lost control of his idea.

In 1993, Rupprecht handed control of the New Jersey project over to Roscoe, Sorhage, and the others. "We were changing over from where we were no longer the principal investigators, as we had been for a ten-year period from the beginning of the '80s," Rupprecht says.

At the same time, George Baer was retiring as head of rabies programs at the CDC. Baer, considered by all to the be the father of the oral rabies vaccination concept, who had edited the seminal text on the disease, *The Natural History of Rabies*, would move to Mexico City to do laboratory work. Rupprecht applied for the job. "I [availed] myself of the opportunity of applying for this position in the hopes there would be greater oversight than what was possible in academia," Rupprecht said. He would continue his involvement with V-RG, but no longer in an immediate way. "It was still clearly in the realm of our mission statement to evaluate this as a public health tool. Certainly it has great potential as an adjunct to traditional vaccination. What I did not have to be concerned about, as I did in both prior positions, was direct salaries for everybody. One of the saddest things I had to do over that ten-year period after building it from nothing was then to start dismantling it and letting people go."

Hanlon moved to the New York State Department of Health to head their rabies program, later launching the first U.S. trial of V-RG to control an enzootic (the term for a firmly entrenched disease—in this case, rabies). "I think the opportunity for Dr. Rupprecht at Centers for Disease Control was a very clear need there, and he was best suited for that position," she says. "The group broke up as a kind of a gradual thing. Only his people left. The remainder of the group is intact and viable, and major players in the rabies research arena. It moved oral vaccination into other logical avenues. It wasn't a bad thing, it was a timely thing. It's no longer basic research, it's implementation."

Mixed Results in New Jersey

Although the epidemiological results of the New Jersey barrier trial seemed to bolster the argument that V-RG might be effective given adequate funding, once again the weakest link in that argument was the measurement of blood titer levels of rabies neutralizing antibodies. In New Jersey, the researchers could only point to about 36 percent of raccoons with rabies titer levels after the first bait drop. On Parramore, that percentage was 45 percent; in Pennsylvania 20 percent.

Jane Rissler's *Gene Exchange,* which had been following the progress of the V-RG trials with a critical eye, cited those antibody results in its February 1994 issue:

> *Scientists doubt that vaccination rates this low can control the disease in wild raccoons. A University of Pennsylvania model of rabies spread in raccoon populations suggests that a 99-percent immunization rate must be achieved to eradicate the disease. The 20-percent to 40-percent rates obtained in the tests may not even be high enough to prevent the spread of rabies to a geographically isolated area like a peninsula. According to government records, a USDA staff scientist, after reviewing the 40-percent antibody-production rate in the New Jersey test, questioned the effectiveness of the vaccine as a barrier against the spread of rabies on the Cape May peninsula.*

The Legacy of the New Jersey Experiment

On one cool winter's evening, Ray Buchanan was vaccinating pets well past dark. The former member of Charles Rupprecht's research team was now animal control officer for Upper Township, a subdivision of Cape May County, New Jersey. The small, cinderblock animal shelter under his supervision, a half-hour drive from Atlantic City, was lit up like a beacon amid the mostly rural landscape of marsh and woods. Lined up outside were dogs of all shapes and sizes, connected by leashes to their owners, interspaced with a few cats transported in cardboard cartons or fancy carriers. Many of their owners had come from miles away to immunize their pets against rabies. They had new motivation to brave the pitch-black backroads to reach this after-hours clinic. Two years earlier, they had agreed to let state and federal health officials scatter vaccine-laden bait on their property in an ambitious rabies control experiment, the first of its kind in the United States.

Now the experiment was over. The barrier officials had hoped to create to stop raccoon rabies from reaching the Cape May peninsula at the southern tip of New Jersey had been breached. Still, inside the eleven-mile-wide barrier, Upper Township was still almost rabies free.

"I don't expect we'll see a rabies outbreak here until summer, when the vaccine starts wearing off," Buchanan said. When the project ended, Buchanan took a job as animal control officer here. "We were running out of money and I was about to starve," he jokes.

Money, of course, is what plagued the Cape May project. For Ray Buchanan, soothing still another skittish dog while a volunteer veterinarian injected it with vaccine, as the line of excited dogs and nervous owners seemed to stretch on forever into the darkness outside, the blame lies squarely with those holding the purse strings. "Yeah, it's hard for me to say the project is over. From a financial point of view, I sort of understand it. There's never a prevention budget; it's always a fix-the-disaster budget.

"People on the outside looking in say it wasn't effective. But it was, because Upper Township, where most of the baits were dropped, only had six cases." He shakes his head. "If I had a thousand doses of the vaccine, I could sell it in three days."

CHAPTER FIVE

The Foxes

With approval from Texas Department of Health leadership to move ahead with developing an oral vaccination strategy, Keith Clark telephoned his former competitor for the CDC job, Charles Rupprecht. It was 1993, and the two men had last spoken at a meeting in Mexico, when Clark congratulated Rupprecht for getting the CDC job; he pledged to work with him and offered assurances there were no hard feelings. On the phone, Clark briefly outlined the state's interest in V-RG, and Rupprecht agreed to discuss the matter further. A short time later, they met at an international rabies meeting in Philadelphia and talked about what would be required to test V-RG in coyotes. Actually, coyotes had been part of the Noah's ark of creatures included in Wistar's initial laboratory tests of V-RG. When the vaccine was squirted into the coyote's mouths, the animals achieved good antibody protection against rabies. However, the coyotes seemed to require a stronger dose than raccoons.

The meeting in Philadelphia in 1993 included Don Hildebrand, president of Rhone Merieux; Gayne Fearneyhough, who had been hired to oversee the Texas Oral Rabies Vaccination Project, as it would soon officially be named; Robert Miller with the USDA; and Rupprecht. The group met again in San Francisco a few months later. The scope of any vaccine barrier in Texas, of course, would be far greater than anything that had been attempted before in the United States. Rupprecht was in favor of the project, but told Clark privately that he doubted Rhone could gear up to produce the amount of V-RG they would require to distribute baits from one end of the Texas to another.

By this time, the Texans had managed to secure a commitment for some start-up funds for research. Gary Nunley, who headed Animal Damage Control in Texas, had informed Clark about a contingency fund within USDA's Animal and Plant Health Inspection Service (APHIS). Animal Damage Control, which was part of APHIS, had as part of its mission the control of animal diseases that threaten humans. Rabies clearly fell into that category. Clark and Nunley submitted a proposal and were awarded $350,000 for development costs. It hadn't hurt, of course, that U.S. Representative Kika de la Garza of Mission, in rabies-plagued Hidalgo County, was chair of the House Agriculture Committee.

As for the research, Miller made it clear the Texans would have to prove V-RG had a reasonable expectation of vaccinating coyotes against rabies. That would require a challenge study. For that, they would need an animal holding facility with specific biohazard capabilities, like those at CDC. Rupprecht volunteered to perform the challenge studies for the Texans. However, he said, the animal facilities at CDC were inadequate for coyotes, and it would cost about $50,000 to upgrade them. Could some of the USDA start-up money be used for those improvements? Clark agreed Texas could provide the $50,000 to CDC from the USDA grant. The overall mood among the group was friendly. Clark, Rupprecht, and Fearneyhough had a pleasant dinner in one of San Francisco's better Chinese restaurants. The conversation centered around Rupprecht's new baby.

Short History of Coyote Control

In one sense, the Texans were lucky that their target was the coyote. Despite the limited time they had to design a baiting strategy and prove it worked, they had a lot of earlier research to build upon. Humans had been developing coyote baits for use with poisons or traps for more than a century. The federal government had launched its campaign against the prairie wolves in 1914, and it could be argued the war had been spectacularly unsuccessful, despite the massive numbers of coyotes killed. Former Fish and Wildlife official Charles L. Cadieux had compared it to the Vietnam War in his book, *Coyotes: Predators and Survivors.* "Many people feel that the Vietnamese mistake was the first war that the United States didn't win. That isn't true. For 45 years, Uncle Sam has fought a war against coyotes—and lost! In the years between 1937 and 1981, minions of the Fish and Wildlife Service scalped 3,612,220 coyotes [scalps were taken as proof the animals were killed]. . . . In 1982 there were probably more coyotes in the United States than ever before."

Still, the war had produced plenty of research into coyote baits and attractants at places like Texas A&M at Kingsville and at USDA facilities like the National Wildlife Research Center in Denver. Much of what is known about coyotes, their social organization and mating habits, food preferences and population distribution, was learned by wildlife biologists with an eye toward reducing their numbers. Of course, trappers had been pursuing coyotes long before the scientists stepped in, and their understanding of coyotes was the stuff of lore. "All old-time trappers had their special scent-lures—secrets to be guarded as carefully as 'an old Spanish waybill' to a lost mine," J. Frank Dobie wrote in his classic *The Voice of the Coyote.*

Many of the scent-lures were based on urine, either alone or in combination with other ingredients. Dobie described one trapper's methods:

> *He selected every trap site with respect to the whole surrounding terrain. But what he mainly depended upon was the few drops of lure sprinkled at the trap site. It was pure urine, undiluted and untinctured with anything else, taken from a bitch that had been shot dead instantly, before she was trapped, wounded, or even scared. He cut out the bladder while the body was still warm and poured the contents into a dark bottle. He claimed that if the bitch had been scared or injured before death, she injected a 'sign,' some sort of indication of her experience with man, into her urine and that the 'sign' would be detected and understood by any coyote who came along and smelled even one drop of the urine.*

The lures were used for generations to bait steel leg traps and snares, or even to draw a curious coyote into the range of a sharp-eyed trapper with a rifle. When the federal government got involved, methods became a bit more sophisticated—particularly with the development of the patented Humane Coyote-getter, which was approved for government use in 1939. The device was a hollow metal tube, sharpened to a stake at the bottom, to be stuck into the ground. At the other end was spring-loaded mechanism that contained a special .38-caliber shell casing filled with a little gunpowder and some powdered cyanide. A piece of wool or a rag was placed over the top and covered by a fetid-smelling lure that supposedly would attract only canines and cause other non-target animals to turn up their noses in disgust. The device was fired by upward pressure, so that people or livestock wouldn't set it off by stepping on it. It worked spectacularly well from the start, although many coyotes soon learned to avoid them. Cadieux quotes the first head of the anticoyote campaign, a Canadian named C. R. Landon, as saying that during the first year of the effort, the coyote-getter accounted for 76 percent of all coyotes killed in Texas, while traps accounted for another 24 percent. Six years later, that percentage of coyotes taken with the devices dropped to 60 percent, as some animals became "getter-shy."

The Coyote-getter was later improved to eliminate the explosive charge, making the entire device spring-loaded. It was redubbed the M-44 and is still in wide use. Anyone who attends a government-sponsored class can use them. Scent-lures topping the devices (among them: beaver castor, mink musk, oil of anise, rotted fish, essence of dead frogs) also became more sophisticated, although no less unpalatable, as the feds became involved. But the M-44s were not without problems. Some counties began banning the devices after pet dogs wandered into areas mined with M-44s and were killed.

But the biggest breakthrough in mass coyote elimination was Compound 1080, or sodium monofloroacetate. The poison was developed by Polish scientists early in World War II, and tested by the Denver Wildlife Research Center. The substance, often injected into raw meat, was inexpensive, stable in the field, highly deadly and, proponents said, more deadly to canines. Conservationists like Faith McNulty disagreed: "It does not break down in the body of its victim, and this means that any animal or bird that feeds on the carcass of a 1080 victim may be poisoned, and its body may become another lethal bait," she wrote. "Furthermore, the dying animals vomit deadly doses of undigested meat, attractive to many animals and birds, wherever they go. Almost all carnivorous birds and small carnivorous mammals will eat carrion, so the possibilities of this chain reaction are extensive."

But 1080 was used widely in western states, with great effectiveness. Cadieux describes it as the only weapon "truly effective against coyotes. . . . When President Nixon banned its use on public lands, coyote population immediately grew." But concerns about its specificity—and public reports of the apparent agony dying coyotes suffered after eating 1080—turned the tide of opinion against the poison. Cadieux acknowledged the poison's effects: "Compound 1080 does not produce a 'pretty' death. It works on the nervous system so that the vital processes are speeded up—as if the motor had lost its governor, and unregulated, ran itself to destruction. Typically, a 1080-killed coyote will end up lying on its back, all four feet going through very rapid running motions as it finally dies. Compound 1080 does not kill quickly, either. Unlike strychnine, which causes a very few sharp convulsions and then quick death, 1080 dooms the animal to several hours of agony before it finally dies."

A scientific advisory panel appointed in the mid-1960s found 1080 effective in coyote control, but said it had been at times used unsafely. They added that they saw little justification for general coyote control on rangelands occupied only by cattle, according to an account in Francois Leydet's *The Coyote: Defiant Songdog of the West.* The panel also noted they saw little evidence that 1080 could be used to control rabies outbreak in coyotes, wolves, foxes, raccoons, or skunks. On February 8, 1972, the Nixon administration banned the use and interstate transportation of 1080. A decade later, President Reagan, responding to appeals from western senators, overturned the ban allowing the compound to be used in toxic collars on livestock (a method thought to be highly specific, in that only those animals that attack livestock would be poisoned), and in experimental use in single-dose baits.

While the ruling allowing the limited use of 1080 outraged conservationists, it didn't particularly thrill the ranchers either, who wanted unlimited use of the only effective tool they had seen to kill off coyotes. So when the South Texas rabies outbreak began its northward spread, they once again sounded the call for widespread 1080 use to control the coyote population. It was, they insisted, a matter of public health.

Family Pets: The Fear of Geometric Progression

But coyotes were only the reservoir, the vector. If the disease had confined itself to coyote populations, health officials would have been far less concerned. There would have been occasional contacts between rabid coyotes and humans, but those would be limited, much the way they were with raccoons, or foxes, or skunks.

No, the real fear concerned dogs—family pets, trusted and beloved, living in close proximity with people. This was their strain, a virus designed to connect with canine nerve cells like matching puzzle pieces. If a beagle or a German shepherd caught rabies from a bat or a skunk, it could become rabid and perhaps infect another animal. But the disease was unlikely to spread beyond one or two cases in a non-host species. Dog rabies could sweep through a neighborhood or a town, particularly in places where enforcement of licensing and vaccination ordinances was weak and where vaccination rates of owned animals were largely a mystery.

Eagle Pass and its sister city, Piedras Negras, Mexico, saw an outbreak in dogs in 1979. Four children had died. The United States was not prepared for such outbreaks on a vastly larger scale, as vast as the considerable range of a sick coyote. Throughout the world where rabies kills tens of thousands of people each year, in India and China and in parts of Africa, it is the canine strain, transmitted by domestic dogs. "Coyotes aren't likely to come into contact with humans," said John Herbold with the San Antonio branch of the University of Texas School of Public Health, and chair of the Texas Veterinary Medical Association's Public Health Committee. "But when it spills over into the dogs, it has a higher potential to go from dog to dog." That was why this outbreak was a national problem, Herbold said. If it swept through Texas and pushed into the rest of the country, the consequences could be enormous. "This is Third-World stuff. You're talking about being in India."

The Canadians Sign On

In the summer of 1993, Keith Clark asked the Canadians for help with the Texas Oral Rabies Vaccination Project. The decision was obvious. The Ontario Ministry of Natural Resources had a fleet of airplanes equipped to drop hundreds of thousands of baits and an experienced crew to fly them. Earlier, the Canadians had offered to help Rupprecht and New Jersey health officials with the first V-RG efficacy trial in Cape May County. The lawyers had been unable to agree on liability issues. But Clark, who had overcome greater problems than lawyers to get the Oral Rabies Vaccination Project as far as he had, wasn't dissuaded. At a gathering of the Wildlife Diseases Association in Guelph, Ontario, Clark asked for a meeting with Charles MacInnes, who headed the Canadian program. They talked for more than four hours in MacInnes's office. "He volunteered at that point to come down and do it for cost," Clark recalled. "That gave us a big boost right there."

Texas Commissioner of Health David Smith had been aware of the Canadians' rabies program for many years. "I have relatives who have a dairy farm up there. So I knew personally about the work that had gone on." But the intergovernmental contract between two nations was a cumbersome thing, liability issues aside. "It was sort of a weird deal," Smith says. "There were signature spots that even included some representative of the Queen. Here we are dealing with rabies, and we're signing something with Her Majesty's Court."

Not everyone was pleased with the arrangement. Smith got one complaint forwarded from a state legislator, who had fielded the call from a constituent and passed it on to Smith. "This one ol' boy complained that we should have just contracted with him. Because he had a Cessna, a grandson, a bucket, and a dog. His grandson could kick those baits out of the back of the plane." Never one to take lightly a request from a Texas lawmaker, Smith patiently explained global positioning satellite technology and the complexities of bait density to the man.

Others, like Rupprecht, felt the Canadians' motivation in assisting the Texans was not entirely charitable. By that time, the Ontario provincial government was cutting back on spending, and the oral vaccination project, which was succeeding beyond all expectations in eliminating rabies in foxes, was also under fire. Outside funding through contracts with the United States would be extra money to keep the Canadian program alive. And although the Canadians would provide the service at cost to the Texans, if it somehow helped get the concept of oral vaccination moving forward in the United States, there might be other opportunities for revenues later on.

Baiting: The Canadian Experience

Each fall since 1989, residents of eastern Ontario have become accustomed to the sight of distinctive yellow Twin Otter airplanes in the sky, flying back and forth over just-harvested fields, dropping small cubes to the ground below. The planes are part of a fleet operated by the Ontario Ministry of Natural Resources for a variety of uses, including firefighting, wildlife surveys, transplanting fish, and transporting bureaucrats. The planes are converted to a bombing mission for a few days each fall, with bombing runs timed to follow the autumn harvest and precede the first hard winter's snowfall.

Canada's oral rabies vaccine program has had remarkable success, and, until fairly recently, unflinching support from the public and politicians alike. Rabies in red and Arctic foxes has been almost eliminated in southern Ontario in a remarkably short timespan. Despite that success, the program has been threatened by budget cuts even as its final objective appears in view.

Fox rabies swept down from the Arctic into Ontario in the 1950s. A second rabies front appeared more or less concurrently, pushing south into Canada's prairie provinces and westward into British Columbia. But that portion of the epizootic fizzled out on its own in 1957—a disappearance some credited to a major fox killing campaign. But the Ontario portion of the outbreak reached Fort Albany in 1954, and southern Ontario near Parry Sound in 1956. By 1959, the disease was firmly rooted across the southern portion of the province.

Dave Johnston, a biologist and one of the pioneers of oral rabies research, was hired by the province in the early 1960s mainly to monitor the outbreak. While trappers and hunters were employed to reduce fox populations in order to control rabies, a fledgling program was begun to feed them birth control hormones in baits. The idea was the same as killing; if you could reduce the population of foxes sufficiently, it might break the cycle of the rabies outbreak.

In 1966, the World Health Organization launched an effort to study rabies worldwide. Although wildlife vaccination research was in its infancy and fraught with problems, the organization recommended vaccination over the alternatives: waiting for outbreaks to die out after what could be fifty- to eighty-year cycles, or killing enough animals to break the cycle.

In 1967, Canada's small program was thrust forward by the tragic death of Donna Featherstone, a six-year-old girl in Richmond, Ontario. The child died after a bite on the face by a stray cat. Although she underwent post-exposure treatment, it proved too late. Suddenly there was a public outcry to do *something*. "We did have a monitoring program—which I was involved with from the early '60s—but really there wasn't the budget to do anything," Johnston recalls. "This little girl died, and within one day I had $18,000 on my desk—which in 1967 was a lot of money." Johnston began working on a vaccine strategy with Ken Lawson at Connaught Laboratories. Connaught, founded by the University of Toronto, had already developed a live-modified rabies vaccine, called ERA, in commercial use for domestic animals. The vaccine was fragile, however, and needed to be modified for stability in the field and inserted into a bait.

Like the Texans, the Canadians did not have to start from scratch with bait development. Trappers had been using poison baits to kill wildlife for years by injecting strychnine into meat and tallow. Johnston worked with a wildlife group in New York State that had used poison baits on foxes decades earlier to reduce pheasant losses. "We did a lot of work on the whole concept of baiting in a wild population. You can go out and take a strychnine tallow bait and you can poison one fox or one coyote, but the question was, could we do this on a very large scale? Could we reach 50 percent of a wild population? Could we reach 100 percent?"

Johnston developed a technique—now widely adapted—to lace the baits with tetracycline as a marker to determine whether it had been eaten. When the baits were chewed, tetracycline was absorbed in teeth and bone. Johnston could even tell how many baits an animal had eaten, since the tetracycline would appear in layers, like the rings on a tree.

The first baits were designed to be simple and cheap: thirty-gram hamburger balls. The best method involved dropping a single hamburger ball inside a plastic baggie, on which a warning notice had been stamped (although those early baits contained no vaccine, they were laced with the tetracycline—hence, the need for a warning). The earliest trials were along Lake Huron in southwest Ontario, just north of Detroit. "We started putting these out by hand, with a truck or just walking through fields. As you can imagine, this is very time consuming and expensive." When trappers

Tallow bait used by Canadians in fox rabies oral vaccination program.
Courtesy Ontario Ministry of Natural Resources

went in and collected animals from the baiting area, Johnston was disappointed that fewer than 15 percent had eaten the baits. "We decided we weren't putting out enough baits, and we weren't putting them out in a broad enough sense to encompass the home range of the animals the trappers were picking up."

They expanded the baited area to include the foxes' maximum home range, dropping the baits from a small airplane. The acceptance rate rose quickly to more than 40 percent, and ultimately more than 60 percent. "That's where the technique of the aerial dropping came from. We'd refine the question of the kind of aircraft, the speed and distance of the line, and the number of baits per square mile. The goal was to try to bring the technique to the point where you vaccinate a significant percentage of the population, but you don't waste a lot of vaccine by putting too much out there. Vaccine is a very costly thing."

The baits evolved into sponge cubes, soaked in vaccine and covered with tallow and flavorings. "It was the old pill-in-the-meatball-for-your-dog thing," Johnston said. "If the pill is too large, the dog spits it out. If you could make the pill so large that it was in fact the bait, as with the sponge that was just simply coated with tallow, then the animal would chew on it." That was necessary because the vaccine had to bathe the back of the throat to be absorbed. "That was the approach we took with the initial work with the ERA vaccine. At that time the vaccine had a fairly low potency and we had to use a large volume, over ten mils of vaccine." Johnston took the sponge baits down to Wistar, where Charles Rupprecht used them in his earliest baiting studies on raccoons. Later, the vaccine baits were sealed in wax ampoules or blister packs and inserted into yellow tallow cubes.

Charles MacInnes was hired in 1973 as supervisor of wildlife research, which included the rabies program. MacInnes took it upon himself to secure a steady source of funds for Johnston's work. "I looked at what he wanted to do and said, 'You're never going to do all that on this small amount of money,'" MacInnes recalls. "I set about to get more money." The Canadians had established an Interministerial Committee on Rabies to oversee the program. The members from several provincial and national departments agreed a steady source of money was necessary if the program were to succeed. Three provincial departments came together and applied for funds from the state lottery. To their surprise, they got it—$1.25 million a year, beginning in 1979.

The bait finally settled upon was a yellow cube of flavored wax containing the vaccine. And in 1986, small-scale baiting trials for foxes were launched. At the same time, wildlife workers were engaged in the smelly job of live-trapping and hand-vaccinating skunks against rabies in Toronto and other cities. The oral vaccine, it turned out, did not work well in skunks.

In 1989, the Ministry of Natural Resources launched a five-year experiment to immunize foxes in eastern Ontario. That year, two Twin Otter planes in the ministry fleet dropped 285,000 baits over fifteen thousand square kilometers during an eight-day period. That region had reported an average of 385 rabid animals each year since 1970. At the same time, baits were hand-distributed around metropolitan Toronto ravines and parklands. The following year, in 1990, the researchers doubled the size of the program, dropping 568,000 vaccine-laden baits over 30,350 square kilometers. The number of rabies cases reported in the area dropped to 293. The scientists continued to tinker with the density and flavor of the baits.

The program was beginning to show results, and in 1991, its third year, the number of reported rabies cases dropped to 116. The following year only thirty-four cases were reported, four of those in bats. Still, the central question for lawmakers funding the project was value, rather than statistics on rabies cases in wild animals. "In North America, rabies is pretty small potatoes as a cause of [human] death," MacInnes says. "We could say in Ontario this program is actually going to save our government money. We have a pretty good estimate of what is being put out to investigate animal-bite cases and give postexposure treatment. In the decade ending in 1994, we were averaging four million dollars a year. Our second premise is that we can completely eliminate fox rabies and then stop baiting. Now our program is costing about $2.5 million a year. So it will probably save money and reduce total expenditures either next year or the year after."

The lottery funds had lasted only three years. The government returned those funds to the general revenue, but gave the rabies program its own budgetary allocation. It continued unmolested until 1991, when Ontario lawmakers found themselves in a budget squeeze. "Since then we've had a hell of a fight," MacInnes says. "Four years ago [in 1992] we were cut without any consultation from $2.1 million to $700,000. Our minimum bait order is about $800,000, so we didn't have enough to go on. We've gotten a little money back." The program was rescued with accounting sleight-of-hand. "Basically we've had our baits paid for out of year-end funds, which is not supposed to be done, and therefore nobody ever admits to. I have no idea where that money comes from. But it means each year I don't know if we're going to go on next year."

Still, in 1993, the program was expanded to cover the entire rabies outbreak in southern Ontario. The planes dropped 554,000 over the original test site during an eight-day period, while another 120,000 were distributed over an adjacent fifty-seven hundred square kilometers to create a barrier and push the rabies control thrust southwest toward the great lake. The number of rabies cases dropped to sixteen, and seven of those were bats.

In 1994, three Twin Otters dropped 1.45 million baits over sixty-two thousand square kilometers. Only five rabid animals were reported in the original zone, three of them bats. The following year, the number of baits increased to 1.8 million. "The traditional rabies outbreak cycle in this area has effectively been disturbed as predicted," a press release stated. "Rabies is under control in this area."

The Business of Bait

Along with their expertise, the Canadians would like to market their baits in the United States. It is a difficult sell. With their own rocky experience with oral rabies vaccine, the Americans have moved toward baits like fishmeal—unappetizing to people—to minimize potential human exposure. The yellow waxy baits used by the Canadians "are very attractive to raccoons, but they'll also be attractive to children," Cathy Hanlon says. "And we've tried very hard to make this bait as unattractive to people as we can." The Americans, who are critical that Canada continues to use a live, attenuated vaccine instead the safer recombinant V-RG, also point to the sweet attractants the Canadians have incorporated into the baits to appeal to raccoons as potentially dangerous, in that they could appeal to children. MacInnes says that's a mistaken idea.

> *The attractants in our original fox bait are unrefined fish liver oil and a chicken soup essence that comes from a company called International Flavor and Fragrances. When we wanted to start working on a bait for raccoons, Ken Lawson did a lot of the work with raccoons who visit his back patio. He came up with the best of attractants being icing sugar, which is necessary to change the consistency of the bait—raccoons don't like the microbond wax. And the marshmallow is not a flavor, its a scent. But Rupprecht and*

Hanlon have heard this described as the icing sugar marshmallow bait, and they are convinced it's attractive to children. We had two kids put our fox baits in their mouths this year. One was a year old, one was two. They didn't get anywhere near the vaccine compartment, because they went 'Yuck!' Rupprecht is very very cautious. His worry is that one bad incident will kill the whole idea of wildlife vaccination in the U.S.

I can't disagree with him. But we're now to the point that we've dropped eight million baits and we haven't had that bad incident. Since ours is rabies virus, we tell people that if they are exposed to the vaccine from the baits, they should take postexposure treatment. We have given postexposure treatment to one person in that way. This was a farmer who was out plowing in a tractor. He leapt out of the cab and saw a bait stuck in the mud between the tires. It had already been squashed by the tractor rolling over it, so he got vaccine all over his hands. He wasn't worried, but his wife had heard all our publicity about it.

MacInnes said the vaccine manufacturer, Connaught, has the only data on human exposures—about a hundred instances of people who were accidentally injected with the vaccine intended for domestic animals. "A typical scenario is a cat who didn't want to be vaccinated and the vet got the owner to help hold it. The vet jabbed the needle through the cat's leg into the owner's hand. A couple of people got flu-like symptoms and spectacularly high antibody titers. Most people got nothing at all."

Rupprecht says the Canadians are foolish to continue using what he considers unsafe and outdated technology when V-RG is available. "Obviously we're at odds with some international collaborators when they point the finger at us with our third-generation recombinant. And we in essence suggest it's outdated technology to keep using the first generation. There's absolutely no scientific reason to keep doing it, aside from you get locked into a technology. Then you've got costs associated with it, as well as biopolitics. Anybody who suggests there's not nationalism involved behind a lot of this is clearly operating behind naiveté."

MacInnes admits he would like to see the Canadian baits sold in the United States. "First of all, we might stabilize our bait manufacturer. We might even bring the price down for our own baits. And secondly, with the business of raccoon rabies, the logical place to fight it is before it gets to

Ontario. And the logical way to do that is to help the people down there get their own program going." To that end, the Canadians have linked up with Laura Bigler, a wildlife biologist at Cornell University. Together, they have distributed 104,000 doses of V-RG in Canadian baits in upper New York state. The Canadians participation with Bigler in New York, and with state health officials in Texas, has drawn criticism from Rupprecht that they are trying to save their financially strapped rabies program by exporting it here. "Nobody's to say it's not a good deal, but it's not free. The Canadians are being paid for their services."

In addition to the orders from Cornell, the company has sold baits to Minnesota, which had experienced an outbreak of mange in its endangered timberwolf population. Those baits contained a treatment for mange. And in early 1996, the company had an inquiry from South Korea about oral rabies vaccine. "That's out of the clear blue sky," MacInnes said. And the Texans have shown some interest. Scott Henke at Texas A&M at Kingsville has tested some of the tallow baits in the field, but they have their limitation in the hot Texas climate. "Our baits have a relatively low melting temperature for sitting out in the Texas sun."

Canada Gets Results

Dave Johnston retired from the Ontario Ministry of Natural Resources in 1994 after thirty-three years of rabies fighting. He left during a wave of government belt-tightening, and now operates a private consulting firm. One of his larger contracts has been to analyze teeth and bones from South Texas coyotes and Central Texas foxes to determine the effectiveness of the bait. He is concerned about the possible demise of oral rabies vaccination technology in Canada just as it appears to be moving forward in the United States. "I think what I'm a little afraid of is the old government story—that once the problem disappears, so does your funding."

"We've had a hell of a fight" keeping the program alive, MacInnes agrees. "Now it's getting really brutal. Now we're looking at actually laying off existing staff. For a while, anyone who has retired is simply not replaced." At this point, he said, the program is "far enough along that we've been able to say: 'Fine. If you wish to be responsible for a government-induced rabies outbreak, you can cut the program.' Because if we stop control, there would have been a really big rabies outbreak within two or three years."

But what exactly had the Canadians actually done to wipe out fox rabies? MacInnes estimates about half the foxes sampled within the baiting zones show evidence of rabies neutralizing antibodies in their blood. And foxes, he adds, "are probably easier to measure than other species." Most of those involved in oral vaccine research agree antibody blood levels are an imprecise measure. An animal dead for two days in a trap will not yield an ideal blood sample.

The Canadians developed a computer model that showed: "if you vaccinated 70 percent of foxes, rabies became extinct quite promptly every time you vaccinated. If you could only vaccinate 60 percent, rabies became extinct seven runs out of ten. If it was 50 percent, then five runs out of ten.

"We have one trial, and rabies is gone. Were we lucky? Or is it that, as is typical with simulation modeling, you're trying to mimic the real world, but you can't have your system as complicated as the real world? And as is typical, for some of the critical numbers there are no measurements for in the wild, so you put in guesses. One of the characteristics of rabies in wildlife is it spreads and it dies back. Some places always have it. But most of the major outbreaks have died out eventually. So my feeling is that rabies in the wild is relatively fragile, and it may not take much of a push with vaccination to knock it out. But that's just a biologist's gut feeling."

And no one is certain how much natural immunity exists in wildlife populations. Some wild animals do survive rabies, which confers some natural immunity. Detecting that immunity, Johnston said, is as difficult as with vaccinated animals. The entire question may be as mysterious as individual immunity in humans, he added. "Say there's twenty people in your office. Sally comes in with a cold on Tuesday, and by next Monday 50 percent of the people have colds. The others don't. Why didn't they get it? There's contact, but there's individual immunity too. There's a lot we don't know."

Another factor, MacInnes concedes, is luck. "We are blessing our lucky stars. We have some evidence and some speculation that hard winters are really hard on fox populations. We are finally having a hard winter—the first we've had since the 1970s. Right in the middle of trying to control rabies, God is on our side."

As for Johnston, thirty-five years of oral rabies vaccination research has given him a better feel for its complexity than most. Like a professional baseball player who knows how difficult it is to throw a fast ball, Johnston is humble about how far they have progressed. "I for one am more amazed than most people that this whole thing even works."

The U.S. Army Lends a Hand

In May 1993, Starr County, Texas, was invaded by the U.S. military. The 1993 federal appropriations act for the first time allowed the military to engage in the kind of nation-building exercises they had long practiced in developing countries for training purposes. The first U.S. site selected was Starr, whose forty thousand residents suffered a jobless rate of 36 percent.

Medical staff from San Antonio's Brooke Army Medical Center, the 41st Combat Support Hospital, and the Texas Army National Guard 217th Evacuation Hospital assembled at the Starr County Fairgrounds in Rio Grande City. For three days they provided check-ups, immunizations, vitamin supplements, and health education materials.

Brig. Gen. Russ Zajtchuk, commander of Brooke Army Medical Center, who led the effort, was visibly moved by the parade of local residents through the tent hospital that had been erected. A native of the Ukraine, Zajtchuk was orphaned during World War II at age six. The army's kindness to refugees like him, he explains, is known worldwide. "After the war, I was living in a displaced persons camp in Germany. I had bad teeth and needed immunization. The American soldiers came by and took care of me. I was immunized, had my dental work done, and they gave me food. Let me tell you, it always makes a big impression." One smiling medic had a different opinion, gesturing at a line of screaming toddlers being vaccinated by soldiers against everything from hepatitis B to measles, mumps, and rubella. "These kids are going to hate the army," he said.

State health officials, who were partners in the effort, were not going to let this opportunity go by without doing a little rabies prevention as well. The Texas National Guard came down at the same time to assist Dr. Roberto Margot, the county's only veterinarian, provide rabies vaccination clinics throughout Starr County. In the first half of 1993, Starr had already reported rabies in eight dogs and five coyotes. Since the epizootic was born, sixty-six dogs and thirty-two coyotes had been confirmed with rabies in Starr. At the same time, the outbreak had spread to twelve South Texas counties, infecting 338 dogs and coyotes.

Enlightening the Outside World

Despite the enormity of the canine rabies problem in Texas, it was clear to Clark that not everyone was impressed. Clark and his staff drafted a paper on the epizootic—certainly the worst rabies outbreak in canines in the United States in decades—and submitted it to the *Journal of the American*

Veterinary Medical Association, the leading veterinary journal in the country. The manuscript was rejected. "We submitted it initially, and apparently some junior editor said: 'Oh, this is only of regional interest.' He actually rejected it," Clark recalled three years later, an equal measure of humor and amazement in his voice. At the time, Clark was chair of the national Rabies Compendium Committee, and the journal each year published the proceedings of the committee. Clark was speaking by telephone to the journal's senior editor about the committee's work, and curiosity overtook him. He inquired about the earlier paper, of which the senior editor was unaware. "You send that back to my attention," the editor told Clark. The paper, which described the epizootic from its index case through 1993, appeared in the journal's February 15, 1994, issue.

CHAPTER SIX

The Vac-Trap and Other Inspirations

The first spark of an idea for vaccinating wild animals against rabies was born in an epidemiology class at the University of Michigan in the late 1950s. George Baer, a young veterinarian whose practice heretofore had been limited to racehorses, had decided to return to school to earn a degree in public health. The professor, a Dr. Horton, was describing an outbreak of fox rabies in New York state. Baer suggested vaccinating them. "It occurred to me there that the only way to control fox rabies would be to vaccinate the animals," Baer said. "The immediate reaction was, that's ridiculous. How could you vaccinate wild animals? But from the beginning, I had in mind it had to be an automatic device, so that the animals would immunize themselves."

After he graduated, Baer was hired by the CDC and assigned to the New York State Department of Health. There he began work in earnest on his idea. In the laboratory, he administered vaccine to mice and foxes, both orally and through stomach tubes, without success. He began looking for some sort of mechanical device, finally coming upon the Coyote-getter—a metal device with a small explosive charge used by trappers and ranchers throughout the West and Southwest to kill coyotes. When the animals bit onto a scented cap, the device blew a charge of cyanide into their mouths. Baer replaced the cyanide with rabies vaccine. He reported that six of fourteen animals vaccinated with that method had immune response to the vaccine. Unfortunately, it also injured the coyotes in the process, and there were concerns the damage to their mouths would cause them to starve. "It was an explosion," Baer acknowledged. "It was not simply laying the inactivated vaccine on the mucosa. If that had been the case, we would have been able to do it by just feeding them the inactivated vaccine. We tried that both orally and enterically, through the intestine, and it just didn't work."

Baer abandoned the idea for a while, moving on to other assignments, including a stint with the Pan American Health Organization in Mexico. But a CDC colleague, William Winkler, picked up the project. He invented a device called the Vac-Trap, which housed a syringe on a rotating arm that actually injected animals with vaccine when they triggered it. Winkler, now retired from the CDC, recalled in an interview the two months he spent testing the device on San Clemente Island, off the California coast, in the mid-1960s. As Rube Goldberg-like as the device was, it successfully immunized 25 percent of the wild foxes and 16 percent of feral cats on the island. Still, said Winkler, "the logistics of carrying these bulky, cumbersome traps around and planting them, and getting only one animal immunized per load, was really impractical."

The impracticality of the device was underscored at one point during the trial, after Winkler had returned to the naval station on the island where he was headquartered. "I had put out a bunch of traps one night and was relaxing, when the base commander said: 'By the way, we're being invaded tonight.' It turned out they practiced war games there, and a bunch of marines were coming in to attack the island. If they crawled up the beach where these traps were and got hit in the head, it would have killed a man."

The ERA Vaccine

Baer returned to CDC in 1969, and immediately began working with Winkler on an oral, rather than mechanical, route for vaccinating foxes. Several developments had come together at once to make the idea suddenly feasible. The first was a new, highly potent attenuated vaccine developed by Connaught Laboratories in Canada, called ERA. The vaccine could be diluted and still produce an immune response when injected. Just as importantly, it didn't kill foxes, as two other recently produced attenuated vaccines appeared to do. Another development was a laboratory method from the Wistar group in which ERA could be grown in baby hamster kidney cells to increase the vaccine's potency a thousand-fold. "We had then the combination of the susceptible species that was involved in rabies outbreaks, and the vaccines that had been shown by injection to be effective," Baer said.

What they didn't have was permission to do research on foxes at CDC.

A short time earlier, a three-legged fox that had been challenged with rabies virus in an experiment had escaped. "It had jumped about ten feet in the air, climbed up a chain fence, and got out of an opening just about as big as a fox's head," Baer recalled. As a result, a CDC chief had banned all research on foxes there. But the work had progressed too far, and Baer was not about to be stopped by some bureaucrat. "I sent someone out to capture a gray fox, which was the fox most common in the southeastern United States. We dropped vaccine on that fox's tongue and cheek mucosa, and bled it two weeks later. Lo and behold, there were antibodies."

He telephoned his friend, Jack Debbie, with whom he had worked at the New York State Department of Health. "I was very excited. No one all these years had believed in it. It was a pie in the sky." When Debbie answered the phone, Baer yelled: "Oh, Jack, I've been looking for this! We were able to drop ERA-BHK on a fox's tongue and get high levels of antibody!"

Debbie asked how many foxes Baer had tested.

"One," Baer replied.

"Jesus Christ, George," Debbie said. "You've got 100 percent of one fox."

Baer's supervisor chewed him out, telling him to stop the work. "I went over his head, to the head of epidemiology, who liked the story very much and gave me the green light to go ahead and work with foxes."

With permission granted, Baer wanted to move the research quickly to New York, where Jack Debbie had agreed to collaborate with him. He feared another researcher, whom he declines to name, would steal the work and publish ahead of him. "In fact, we just were able to beat him out. From the time I got a green light to the time I was in New York was less than a week." They took twelve caged foxes, and gave half of them ERA—sedating them first and then dropping ERA on their throats. Of the six vaccinated foxes, five were protected. The sixth died from effects of the anesthetic. The results were published in the *Journal of Epidemiology* in 1971.

But there was a problem. Cotton rats actually contracted rabies after eating the vaccine. In one experiment by Winkler, as many as half of the rats fed ERA could be infected orally—although it appeared to be a milder form of the disease, since only 17 percent died. The researchers were left with a frightening question: if they distributed vaccine baits for foxes, and the baits were eaten by rats that went onto develop rabies, could the rats sustain or even worsen a rabies outbreak? Particularly as they in turn became food for foxes and other carnivores?

In addition, there were concerns that even the weakened or attenuated live viruses might in some rare cases revert to active rabies and kill the animals they were designed to protect. Baer injected large quantities of ERA vaccine into several foxes—the species most susceptible to developing rabies—and no such reversion occurred. "When you take a susceptible species and inject a massive amount of virus, and nothing happens in many, many animals, then there has to be something to the safety of this vaccine," Baer said. In other experiments, they induced rabies in mice with the vaccine, and then fed those mice to other rodents, which did not get sick. That eased their minds somewhat. But the real answers to those troubling questions would come during field studies in Europe and Canada—and later by the ability to distinguish different strains of rabies through monoclonal antibody analysis.

Meanwhile, Winkler and others continued searching for a bait that would appeal to foxes, as well as allow the vaccine to reach the animal's throat without interfering somehow with its potency. Of course, the logical bait for canids would be meat. A visit to a McDonald's restaurant in the early 1970s inspired a better method. Staring at his soft drink, Winkler envisioned a plastic drinking straw filled with vaccine and plugged on the ends, encased in a hollow sausage. Baer had suggested earlier the Slim Jim sausages available in convenience stores as a possible fox bait. In the laboratory, the baits successfully protected caged foxes against challenge with rabies, and in subsequent placebo field trials in Alaska in 1974, red foxes gobbled up the vaccine-free sausage baits.

But the researchers were already facing bureaucratic barriers to the whole idea of wildlife vaccination. "We have a more conservative, less adventuresome government licensing policy than Europe," Winkler said. "We had a devil of a time, first getting our own agency to even consider approving it—which at that time they hadn't—then to see who would be responsible. Would it be the Department of Health? The Department of Agriculture? The Department of Interior? We spent a year trying to get these people to decide what they wanted. I retired before they ever did." Another problem was the fact that while ERA worked orally in foxes, it failed to protect almost any other species, including skunks, which were a major carrier of rabies in much of the United States, and dogs.

But two other events effectively nailed the lid on oral rabies vaccine research in the United States for the next decade. The first was an act of nature: the red fox rabies epizootic began to die out on its own, eliminating the government's motivation to continue paying for the research. But the second event was more dramatic, and more damaging to the project. On March 29, 1977, a bacteriologist named Jerome Andrulonis was working in Debbie's lab in Albany when he accidentally inhaled aerosolized ERA vaccine. Andrulonis, who had been vaccinated against rabies as a routine precaution, was using a machine to coat sugar tablets with the attenuated virus. The machine suspended the tablets in a stream of air while the vaccine was sprayed onto them. The vaccine, which had been prepared by Baer, was especially potent for oral administration.

The virus traveled the short distance along Andrulonis's olfactory nerve to his brain, before his immune system could mount much of a response. Three weeks later he was hospitalized with rabies symptoms and lapsed into a coma. Although he revived, he suffered severe impairment that left him with emotional and behavioral problems, and the vocabulary of a three-year-old.

After a decade of litigation, in 1989, U.S. District Judge Howard G. Munson awarded $5.98 million to Andrulonis, and criticized both Baer and Debbie. According to a *New York Times* account, Baer, Munson said, had failed to warn either Debbie or Andrulonis of how dangerous the strain he had prepared could be and had allowed the experiment to go forward despite evidence the machine could leak. As for Debbie, the judge added, he could have prevented the accident by using safer laboratory practices.

"It obviously set back the state of oral vaccination research in the United States for a number of years," said Charles Rupprecht, Baer's successor at CDC. "After that, it was extremely doubtful that any traditional modified live vaccine—for instance what the Canadians use—would be licensed in the United States."

"You turn back the clock, it's hard to realize how much resistance there was to oral vaccination, because people thought it would be a dangerous procedure," Baer said. "You were putting live virus into nature, and it could be taken up by other species of animals." Some level of research on oral vaccine continued at CDC, as it has to this day, largely in search of one that would work safely in a large number of species.

The SAD Vaccine

If the United States was not yet ready for an oral vaccination strategy to prevent rabies in wildlife, Europe was eager for one. An epizootic of fox rabies, which began in Poland during World War II, had swept across the continent and now included much of Central and Western Europe, as well as the then-Soviet Union. Like in the United States, the earliest rabies control efforts in Europe focused on reducing the numbers of foxes. But the idea of orally vaccinating wildlife appealed to many.

The World Health Organization organized the project, and after consulting with the CDC, coordinated fifteen research teams in nine countries. Franz Steck and Alexander Wandeler at University of Bern in Switzerland came up with the idea of using chicken heads—gladly provided in bulk by local poultry houses—as baits. Borrowing an idea from the Canadians, they added the antibiotic tetracycline as a marker, which could be detected on teeth to quickly determine whether the foxes had eaten one or more baits. The chicken-head baits were eagerly taken by foxes.

The Europeans faced many of the same questions Baer and Winkler had struggled with: would the live, attenuated vaccine (a new strain, SAD) revert and cause disease? They performed their own laboratory tests and found the risk minimal. In the mid-1970s, the Swiss government approved the first field safety trial on a rabies-free island on the Aare River, in Northeastern Switzerland. The baits were placed, and the researchers waited. Soon, the trial's central question was answered: the vaccine caused no rabies outbreak among the animals on the island.

By 1978, the scientists were ready to conduct the first large-scale campaign. The Swiss, who had demonstrated the most enthusiasm for the idea, selected the Rhone River Valley in which to erect a vaccine barrier against rabies. An outbreak of fox rabies was spreading along the eastern shore of Lake Geneva. Health officials feared it would push deep into the valley and continue east with the river. In October, Steck and Wandeler (Steck later died in a helicopter accident during baiting) dropped 4,050 chicken-head baits by hand over a 335-square-kilometer area, taking advantage of the natural barrier provided by surrounding mountains. Although the rabies outbreak continued its spread up the valley, it was halted at the baited zone, where some 60 percent of foxes had been immunized. Buoyed by the success, they repeated the effort in other Swiss valleys, and the government began funding a full-fledged oral vaccination program. By 1986, Switzerland was largely free of rabies save for a few untreated areas along its borders.

West Germany followed Switzerland, using a slightly different attenuated vaccine. The Germans launched their first field trial in 1983. They also developed the commercially manufactured bait in current use throughout Europe and Canada, an improvement over the successful if somewhat grisly severed chicken heads. The yellow cube-shaped baits contained a vaccine packet surrounded by fish- or marshmallow-flavored wax. They also included the tetracycline marker.

By 1988, 60 percent of West Germany had been treated with oral vaccine baits. By the end of the 1980s, twelve European nations had ongoing oral vaccination programs to control fox rabies. Italy began baiting in 1984, and two years later became rabies free. Austria launched a successful campaign in 1986. Belgium, France, and Luxembourg collaborated on a joint vaccination campaign. Finland, Czechoslovakia, East Germany, the Netherlands, and Yugoslavia followed. Recently, France and Belgium have begun using Raboral V-RG. The stated goal is a Europe free of terrestrial rabies by the year 2000.

"The Europeans fared better than we did, in part because they have a much better handle on their wildlife populations," Winkler said. "The farms tend to be small, the people more evenly distributed in rural areas. I was amazed that when you go out to some farm—wherever you might be—people would say: 'Well, this vixen over here had three kits this year, one of them died, the others are still in the den.' There's not many places you could do that in the United States. We just don't know our wildlife like they do."

Rupprecht agrees. "Europe and Canada have only had to deal with red fox rabies. Here [in the United States] we have this multi-species complex, three of which—raccoons, skunks, and now coyotes—are at outbreak proportions. And the species that everybody, ourselves formerly included, had the most experience with—i.e., red foxes—is certainly not our most important species anymore. So number one, their problem is simpler; and two, their politics are completely different. Their funding is provided [nationally] in almost a socialistic sense—not at the level of a village, a township, a county, a state."

As for Baer, universally considered the father of oral rabies vaccine research, he is philosophical that it was the Europeans and Canadians, rather than the Americans, who saw the technique through its fruition. "We were the initial spark, and even the initial small flame. The people in Europe and Canada did an excellent job putting this in the field and evaluating baits and vaccines. I think that we were—and still are—very happy to have started it all."

In 1991, Baer retired after thirty years with CDC. He returned to Mexico, where his wife was born, and opened a diagnostic laboratory in Mexico

City. He remains active in oral rabies vaccine research, paticularly as a strategy for immunizing dogs in developing countries where abies continues to cause tens of thousands of human deaths each year.

Orally vaccinating dogs "would change the rabies world, Baer said. "I think it's reasonable to assume you can control canine rabies by intramuscular injection, but it's very expensive—particularly getting o areas where you have tremendous number of dogs. In some parts of the developing world you have one dog per person. There are major problems of vaccine quality, costs, organization, administration. Oral vaccination would permit you to reach many more dogs than you're reaching right now."

A Brief History of Rabies

Like a detective piecing together a mystery, Jean Smith has traced the evolution and movement of the rabies virus across the years and continents using the tools of molecular biology and epidemiology. Rabies, along with other diseases, could have migrated with people and animals across the Bering Strait fifty thousand years ago, she and Rupprecht speculate—pointing to legends of a rabies-like illness throughout the Pacific Northwest. The Spanish wrote of vampire bats causing human illness during their conquest of Mexico and Middle America. If bat rabies were present then, the CDC researchers said, then rabies also could have been present in terrestrial animals. However, the first written record of terrestrial rabies in the New World was in 1703, in what is now California.

"Once it became associated with domestic dogs, then it moved all over the world as people moved their domestic dogs," Smith said. The genetic sequence of virus strains from around the world tells the story. "You can trace the dog rabies that's at the Texas-Mexico border all the way back to the European settlers. That particular lineage is part of this grouping of viruses that's found worldwide. It's found in Europe, it's found in Asia, from Canada down to Argentina. What we think happened is, it had as its origin some place in Europe or Africa, and then spread out with the European colonists." Settlers introduced the British sport of fox hunting to the Americas, and imported dogs and red foxes—and, most likely, rabies. A fox rabies epizootic was first reported in New England in the 1800s.

Rabies is among the oldest of diseases, and its terrible symptoms are described in some of civilization's earliest writings. Homer's *Illiad* describes the unhealthy influence of Sirius, the dog star of the Orion. As recently as the nineteenth century, many believed the disease more prevalent in the dog days of summer, associated with the ascendancy of the dog star. Democritus of Abdera, a 5th century B.C. philosopher, was the first to describe rabies, calling it a severe spasmodic disease stemming from an inflammation of the nerves. Aristotle, writing in the fourth century B.C., described the disease in dogs and its transmission to other animals through biting.

The Greek word for rabies, Lyssa—later adapted to include an entire category of viruses including rabies—meant madness. In his essay in Baer's *The Natural History of Rabies*, James H. Steele writes that the Latin word rabies is from the Sanskrit *rabhas*, which means "to do violence." Some have argued its special place in mankind's nightmares is out of proportion to the actual number of human deaths it has caused, largely because it represents such a horrible and certain death. Throughout history it has been associated with its most distinctive and awful symptom, hydrophobia, or the terror of water. Most people infected with rabies will undergo involuntary spasms and choking when water is placed near their lips.

Accounts of rabies epizootics have appeared since the Middle Ages, but more frequently in the nineteenth century. In 1860, an epizootic swept through subfreezing Greenland. Constantinople, long free of the disease, experienced an outbreak in 1839. In the 1860s, so many cattle in Missouri and Ohio were killed by rabies that the owners sought compensation from the government, according to Nathaniel Garland Keirle's *Studies in Rabies,* published in 1909. No cases were noted in London's mortuary statistics between 1603 and 1728, but afterward rabies was diagnosed frequently. The Earl of Richmond was reported to have died of rabies from the bite of a tame fox in the 1880s.

With the disease have come the treatments, some more or less grounded in educated observations of the disease, others leaning toward the bizarre. The Roman scholar Celsus recommended cauterizing the bite wound, and dunking those with the disease in a pond, to forcibly overcome their fear of water. Among the most persistent of treatments was the madstone—gallstones from white cows or other smooth white stones, which were prescribed through this century. If the stone stuck to the wound, then virus was present; some believed it would gradually turn green as virus was extracted. Keirle wrote: "Raw livers of rabid dogs have been fed to patients. The brains of rabid rabbits have been suggested as therapeutic food. In India the entrails of an insect are administered, which causes bloody purgation. The patient is also exposed to the heat of the sun."

Many times treatment was skipped entirely, replaced by more pragmatic solutions. James Thacher, a Philadelphia surgeon, wrote to a colleague around 1812: "Under the unwarrantable pretext of avoiding a bite, the hydrophobous patient, like a demoniac, was abandoned to his awful fate, without the least resource or assistance. But an expedient still more barbarous, or shall I not say, more merciful, was frequently adopted, by consigning the deplorable victim to a premature death, by suffocation with the bed clothes or between mattresses; nor was it till the middle of the 18th century, that such tragical scenes were in some countries prohibited."

In September 1996, a Maryland cardiologist published a paper speculating that the writer Edgar Allan Poe may have died of rabies, rather than of complications from alcoholism as was long believed. "No one can say conclusively that Poe died of rabies, since there was no autopsy after his death," said R. Michael Benitez, an assistant professor of medicine at the University of Maryland School of Medicine. "But the historical accounts of Poe's condition in the hospital a few days before his death point to a strong possibility that he had rabies." Poe was found unconscious on September 28, 1849, outside a Baltimore saloon. According to eyewitnesses, he suffered initially from tremors and hallucinations before slipping into a coma. He awakened and was lucid for a time, but later fell into madness again, requiring restraint. He died four days after hospitalization.

Louis Pasteur, perhaps France's most famous scientist, turned his attention to rabies after his success with developing a vaccine for anthrax. Pasteur took virus from the saliva of rabid animals and injected it into the brain of a rabbit. Then, as that rabbit became ill, he injected material from that animal's brain into another animal, and so on through ninety rabbits. With each transfer, the virus became more virulent to rabbits, but less so to dogs. He had achieved some success developing a vaccine from the dried spinal material from rabbits treated in this way, when a nine-year-old boy, Joseph Meister, was brought to his laboratory in July 1885. The child had been bitten fourteen times on the hand and legs by a rabid dog, and death was considered inevitable. Pasteur reluctantly treated the boy with the vaccine, given in thirteen injections, each containing spinal cords of increasing virulence. The boy never developed rabies. A year later, Pasteur reported he had treated three hundred and fifty people, with only one having developed rabies—a child whose treatment was initiated more than a month after the bite occurred.

At the beginning of the twentieth century, Pasteur Institutes were springing up in Europe and America to offer the Pasteur treatment. In the United States, the death toll from rabies was unknown until 1938, when it became a nationally reported disease. Even then (that year, reported cases totaled 9,412—most of those in domestic animals, forty-seven being human deaths) the cases were vastly underreported, experts believe. Reliable diagnostics tests were not widely available until the 1950s.

World War II marks a turning point for rabies in the United States. Before the war, canine rabies cases numbered four thousand to five thousand a year. After the war, that number dropped to a few hundred. Baer notes: "That was because of the better vaccines, better tests, and the urban programs that were organized by the states and assisted by CDC personnel.

In 1948, Memphis, Tennessee, was in the grip of a major rabies outbreak in dogs, with more than one new case reported each day. This despite a good animal control program and mandatory licensure. About eight thousand dogs were vaccinated against rabies each year. Still, the outbreak called for more aggressive measures, and the Shelby County Health Department organized the nation's first mass vaccination effort in response to a rabies outbreak. Private veterinarians held seventy vaccination clinics throughout the city over a single week, at a cost of one dollar per dog. During the week, some twenty-three thousand dogs were vaccinated, bringing the estimated dog vaccination rate to 80 percent. Reports of new rabies cases plummeted, and the nation had a new model for emergency rabies control. That model was employed again successfully in Houston in 1954, this time using the newly licensed Flury chicken embryo vaccine developed by Hilary Koprowski. Over four days, ninety-four clinics were held and some forty-five thousand dogs vaccinated. Denver, Chicago, Louisville, and Charleston, West Virginia, followed. In each case, the results of vaccinating large numbers of dogs was proven dramatically, leading to stronger state and local ordinances, and improved animal control measures. Soon after, rabies in American cities was a rare and remarkable occurrence.

CHAPTER SEVEN

Coyotes Love Watermelon

Gayne Fearneyhough was thrilled at being handed the reigns of the Texas Oral Rabies Vaccination Program. On the one hand, it was a once-in-a-lifetime opportunity, an enormous undertaking, full of scientific, political, and logistical challenges—one that potentially could head off perhaps the most dangerous threat of rabies the nation had seen in many years. On the other hand, he realized how precarious his new position was. His job had been created by Keith Clark with so-called "soft" money, from the initial $350,000 from APHIS's contingency fund. "I came on board with the under-standing that if this thing didn't begin to show some reasonable assump-tion of success, I could be out on the street in a couple of years. I had some real questions at times about whether I had made the right professional decision."

Fearneyhough, a soft-spoken, prematurely silver-haired veterinarian, had built a successful private practice in Houston for fourteen years before applying for a position with the Texas Department of Health. His main reason for moving to civil service was to spend more free time with his family; in those fourteen years he had taken only five days' vacation. He realized with some amusement that in the first two years of the oral vaccine program, he had taken no vacation at all and only two hours of sick leave. His first job with the state had been as regional zoonosis veterinarian in Tyler. Shortly before the rabies job was created, he had moved to Austin to work in the meat inspection program.

The project faced a severe time line. They had less than ten months to

Gayne Fearneyhough (second from left) discusses the Oral Rabies Vaccination Project with a reporter. Courtesy Texas Department of Health

plan and carry out research that ideally should take five *years*. The research was required to prove the baiting carried some potential for success for the USDA to allow it to take place at all. But the haste was due to the canine epizootic itself. It was necessary to bait in the cool weather months, which in South Texas meant December through February. Research told them that coyotes were more likely to eat meat in the winter; in the summer, their diet became more vegetarian. More importantly, if they missed the winter deadline, they would have to contend with the region's most hated and feared threats, the fire ant. The huge mounds sprouted on farms and ranches in the spring and summer like a pox, and the ants would compete ferociously for any available food. At times, fire ant stings in sufficient numbers had been known to kill livestock. Scott Henke, a wildlife biologist at Texas A&M University in Kingsville whom Clark and Fearneyhough hired to study which bait would work best with coyotes, put it succinctly: "In the wintertime, we had really good, successful pickup of bait. During the summertime, fire ants would jump on the baits within a matter of hours. I don't blame them; no species would pick up a bait after the fire ants got to them."

But the reason most looming over all of them for dropping the baits that winter had to do with Texas' odd shape. The front line of the outbreak—which had caused considerable havoc since 1988, despite the relatively rural area it had traversed—was only forty miles from San Antonio, home to more than a million people. And, if San Antonio animal control director Ned Lammers was correct, fewer than a quarter of its pet dogs were vaccinated against rabies. The problem was, if the epizootic passed San Antonio, it might be impossible to stop. Widening from a southern-most point, Texas would be too wide further north to erect a barricade, as Fearneyhough hoped to do. It would be too expensive. As it was, the drop zone he and Clark envisioned would include some 14,400 square miles, an arc roughly from Laredo to Corpus Christi, with the northern tip resting just below San Antonio, sixty miles wide at its widest point. To do it right would take 850,000 baits, purchased at $1.50 per bait, plus expenses. And that was just the first year.

With Clark concentrating on trying to find money to pay for the whole thing, Fearneyhough began trying to prove it would work to USDA's satis-faction, since the agency would be the one granting permission to drop the experimental baits for coyotes. Robert Miller, the head of USDA biologics, who had overseen the approval process for V-RG over the past decade, was helpful. A former Texan, Miller had spent his early career working in the screwworm eradication program, a hugely successful effort with striking similarities to Oral Rabies Vaccination Program. The program was popu-lar. Miller remembers being introduced to the South Texas ranchers, who shared an inherent distrust of Washington: "They'd take you around to introduce you to people, and they'd say, 'Tell them you work for the screw-worm program. Don't tell them you work for the federal government.'"

The research, which began in May 1994, was divided into two parts: Scott Henke's work to learn which bait coyotes found the tastiest, and the work at Texas A&M's main campus in College Station, to prove the vaccine was effective in coyotes. Miller required thirty coyotes at College Station to be vaccinated under Biohazard Level 3 conditions, which require special isolation and air and water filtering capabilities. Those precautions would last three weeks, since that was how long it was felt the animals might possibly shed some of the V-RG virus through feces or urine. A&M's bio-containment facility couldn't hold all thirty animals at the same time, so they were divided into two groups. Half the animals would be vaccinated first, the other half three weeks later.

At the same time, Clark and Fearneyhough had been negotiating with Rhone Merieux for a particularly potent batch of V-RG. Earlier research had shown coyotes needed a higher dose than raccoons to be protected.

The problem was that the potency the Texans wanted was at the upper limit of what Rhone could produce through normal cell culture procedures in the laboratory. And the USDA had ruled that whatever potency was used to vaccinate the coyotes in the laboratory, the vaccine in the field would have to be even stronger to prevent any potential degradation after the baits were dropped. That ultimately would require Rhone to use more sophisticated methods to concentrate the vaccine, which would drive up their cost per dose considerably. So Rhone had been pushing the Texans to use a less potent vaccine. The debate had become somewhat heated.

Another problem arose from A&M's Animal Care and Use Committee, which prohibited the researchers from withholding food from the coyotes for more than twenty-four hours prior to offering them the vaccine-laden baits. Fearneyhough felt that a slightly hungry coyote would better approximate those in the wild. The coyotes at A&M, which had been captured wild, were still nervous about their surroundings, although they had been given several weeks to calm down. When offered the baits, many of them sniffed them tentatively before eating them. Still, from the dye incorporated into the baits, it appeared they were chewing them enough for the vaccine to bathe their throats—necessary for a proper immune response.

Observers from both Rhone and USDA were on hand when the baits were fed to the first group of coyotes. Everyone then went home, and returned three weeks later for the second group to be vaccinated. Rhone had shipped just enough V-RG for the first group, then sent on a second batch of vaccine to give to the remaining animals. With each shipment, the USDA collected random samples of the vaccine for testing at its National Veterinary Services Laboratory in Ames, Iowa, part of the agency's routine monitoring procedures. After all the coyotes had been fed the baits and had spent three weeks in the biocontainment quarantine, they were moved to outdoor pens until it was time to challenge them with the rabies virus itself. That would be done by Charles Rupprecht at CDC.

The study's design gave the coyotes six months after vaccination to mount an immune response before challenging them with rabies. But barely two months after they were fed the baits, some terrible news came from the USDA's laboratory in Ames. The vaccine they had used was far weaker than what was believed effective for any species, much less coyotes. The correct immunizing dose was supposed to have been $10^{7.4}$ viral particles per milliliter. Instead, half the vaccine they had used was $10^{6.8}$, the other $10^{6.2}$—in immunologic jargon, roughly a whole log weaker in potency.

The Texans' first thought was that Rhone—which had been urging them to use a lower potency—had made the switch deliberately. "We were really upset that Rhone had done this without our knowing it," Clark said. "We got pretty intense with Don Hildebrand (the president of Rhone-Merieux). And at that point, we got sort of to an impasse where we couldn't talk with Don, and it looked like he wasn't going to cooperate with us any more." But it was quickly apparent something inadvertent had occurred, and both the Texans and Rhone began scrambling to learn what had caused the disaster.

Which Bait is Best?

Meanwhile, Henke's work moved a little smoother. First he had to determine which baits and attractants coyotes were most likely to gobble up. In taste tests with caged coyotes, he served up—cafeteria style—two kinds of baits: fishmeal, like those used for raccoons along the East Coast; and dog food. Added to the baits were various scents and flavors designed both to make the bait tastier, and perhaps even help the coyotes sniff out the baits in the field. The attractants included watermelon (born of the observation that hungry coyotes have invaded more than one watermelon patch); raspberry; chicken; a rotten-meat scent long used by trappers; and a plain version consisting of just the bait and the lard-wax plug inside.

This phase of the research involved simply counting how many baits served in a seven-dish tray each coyote ate. The animals could eat as much of any or all of the baits as they wanted. "Basically we found there was no true preference by coyotes," Henke said. "The individual coyotes would have a preference—some would go for the watermelon–dog food, others for the fish meal–watermelon—but for the group as a whole, there was no one preference."

To make sure that being cooped up didn't change the coyotes' taste preferences, the experiment was repeated in the wild. They set up bait stations along the edges of dirt roads. "Every half-mile we would clear a meter circle of vegetation and get the ground good and smooth, and put the baits in the center. We had done ten rows, and each row contained a bait station with various flavors of baits." Again, the coyotes showed no preference between baits.

So it was the plain dog food baits, with the plastic vaccine sachet sealed in the hollow center with plugs of lard and wax, that were selected. State health officials were pleased, since at about $1.50 a piece, the unscented were less expensive; the lower the cost, the more baits they could afford to buy. "The scatological smell and the watermelon were the most expensive types," Henke said. "It would have upped the cost hundreds of thousands of dollars in the large quantities they would need for the big drop." The next step was to see how many baits would *need* to be dropped to be eaten by sufficient numbers of coyotes.

For that, six ranches between Laredo and Frier along the border were selected as a test site. Using a small plane borrowed from the Texas Department of Agriculture's animal damage control program, researchers dropped fifty baits per square mile over half the test area, and 150 baits-per-mile over the rest. More than twenty-two thousand baits were dropped over more than two hundred square miles. Unlike the Canadian Twin Otters they would later borrow, with their elaborate conveyer system that timed the bait drop by air speed, Henke's test flight was a little more primitive. A graduate student with a stopwatch sat in the back and chucked the baits out an open chute.

In fact, graduate students at A&M took the most abuse during the testing. They filled the initial load of baits with Rhodamine B, a bright purple-orange fluorescent dye that would serve as a marker in coyotes, but would remain on the students' hands for weeks as well. Months after the test, as Henke provided a tour of his lab, streaks of the fluorescent dye could be seen in every crevice. The baits also contained tetracycline as a marker.

A week after the drop, Animal Damage Control personnel returned to the area, and from helicopters or on foot shot and killed 148 coyotes. To account for possible migration, they only captured animals within the inner sixteen square miles of each ranch's thirty-six-square-mile drop zone. They found ninety-nine of the coyotes had taken the bait. At 150 baits per mile, 75 percent were taken by coyotes. At fifty baits per mile, 68 percent were taken. Computer models had predicted the disease would die out if 70 percent of the coyotes were vaccinated. Since there was no statistical difference between the two densities, Henke felt safe recommending the lower density, which again meant the state could afford to purchase more.

One of the biggest questions facing the researchers was whether a coyote would chew up a bait or swallow it whole. The vaccine had to bathe the tonsils to be effective. And as Fearneyhough and Henke agonized over the appropriateness of penned versus free-ranging coyotes as test subjects, the question was not so absurd. A hungry coyote in the wild could very easily gulp the matchbox-sized baits whole, making the whole expensive oral vaccination enterprise useless. Years before, Henke had autopsied a coyote and was astonished to find the stomach was the size of a basketball. "I said, jeez, it must have eaten a huge jackrabbit. I was shocked when I opened it up. Three adult ravens, unchewed—beaks, feet, the whole works. How it swallowed them, I have no idea. But if they can swallow something that large, I can see how they could gulp down a bait pretty easily."

When Henke fed the penned animals baits with the fluorescent dye, the baits were chewed and the purple-orange stain was found coating the backs of their throats. But would coyote behavior be different in their natural environment? In the haste to complete the research by deadline, the question was never adequately asked or answered. But in Henke's field taste tests involving the bait stations and wild coyotes, he found some evidence the baits had been chewed. "We did recover some of the [vaccine] sachet packages in coyote scat. It's proof positive when you have purple scat on the road," Henke said.

Pushing Forward

After the disaster at College Station, both Fearneyhough and Rhone tried to figure out what had gone wrong. They ground up baits and poured vaccine over them, to see if perhaps something in the baits was damaging the virus in the vaccine. When that failed to turn up any answers, they began going over the production process step by minute step. That process had changed since Rhone had produced baits for Rupprecht and the various small pilot projects in the Northeast. For one thing, they were no longer using wax ampoules to contain the vaccine. A bubble pack made of a plastic film—similar in appearance to the plastic ketchup packets at a fast-food restaurant—held the V-RG, which was hand-inserted into the hollow baits and sealed with a hot lard-wax plug. As they studied the production methods, the more likely it seemed that the hot plug might have killed off some of the virus.

The new process used hotter temperatures to seal the sachets in the baits than had been required for the older wax ampoules. "The only potential cause they could come up with was that these baits were hand produced, and in the process of putting the vaccine into the plastic sachet in the hollow cavity of the bait, sealing wax was used to hold it in place," Fearneyhough said. "The sealing wax may have been too high a temperature, and inactivated it." A new procedure was put in place, this time using cooler temperatures to seal the vaccine sachet.

It wasn't until many months later that the real problem was identified: the plastic film itself was found to have virus-killing properties. The plastic was replaced with another, solving the problem. But at the time the group was satisfied that heat was their culprit. That still left the question of the coyotes at A&M that had been vaccinated with the weaker V-RG. Only three months had gone by—midway through the original six-month protocol before the coyotes were supposed to be challenged. After lengthy discussions between the Texans, Rhone, USDA, and CDC, it was decided to challenge the coyotes with rabies virus right away, instead of waiting another three months.

"When we got the results from Ames that the titer was so remarkably low, we basically had two alternatives," Fearneyhough said. "We could go ahead and take a chance that coyotes would respond with that low virus titer—and nobody had done any research to indicate any level of success at that potency. That was a very dangerous thing to do. If we had failed, we would have waited six months before we got any results, and it would have been to late to get into the field. So we made the decision that what we would do was challenge those animals at three months."

They selected twenty-two of the thirty coyotes, fifteen that had received the slightly higher potency vaccine, and seven from the lower potency group that had shown some level of immune response. The animals were shipped to CDC, where they were injected with live rabies virus. Within a few days, all but four were dead.

It was a crushing blow. "It looked like the thing was dying," Fearneyhough said. "Sometimes I'd drive home thinking it was all over, and it was never going to happen." Clark and Fearneyhough met in a gloomy post-mortem with Glenn Provost, standing in for Health Commissioner David Smith; and Diane Simpson, their associate commissioner. Time was running out, and the efficacy study had been a spectacular failure. Clark methodically laid out where they had been and what their options were. The big question was left hanging for the end. "I said, 'What do we do?'" Clark recalled later. "The consensus was, we had a public health emergency, we're not where we'd like to be. Still, we've got to give it our best shot."

They returned to the lab. Rhone had a dozen more coyotes, in which vaccine of varying degrees of potency was squirted directly into their mouths. Those animals survived the challenge with rabies, proving again that V-RG would work in coyotes if the method of delivery could be worked out. An additional four coyotes from A&M were fed vaccine-laden baits at a higher vaccine potency. But the issue of the plastic sachets had not yet been resolved, and those animals, too, died of rabies when challenged.

Funding the Program

David Heard understood the project was important to the chairman of the House Agriculture Committee. The rabies epizootic had hit hardest in Eligio "Kika" de la Garza's South Texas district, and he had taken a personal interest in the Oral Rabies Vaccination Program. Heard was one of the few Texans on the Agricultural Committee staff, and was frequently handed projects important to Texas. Fresh out of college, Heard had earned his public administration degree at Texas A&M, and had worked as an aide to the former Texas A&M University System chair, who had helped him land the committee job.

The Texans had managed to get $350,000 from the U.S. Department of Agriculture for their earliest research into V-RG and coyote baits. The money came from a contingency fund, designated for emergency agricultural projects around the country, operated by USDA's Animal and Plant Health Inspection Service, which included Animal Damage Control, the agency responsible for keeping down the numbers of coyotes. Gary Nunley, the director of Animal Damage Control in Texas, had told Keith Clark about the contingency fund when Nunley had been called in to help with reducing coyote populations in the rabies hot spots. Animal Damage Control had never gotten any of the contingency money, Nunley said, but the rabies project might be something that would. The Texans put a proposal together for the Oral Rabies Vaccination Project's development costs, with part of the money going for testing the vaccine at Texas A&M–College Station, and the rest for testing the bait at Texas A&M–Kingsville. Clark had already met with officials at College Station and had found out they had a captive colony of coyotes. No one seemed certain who they belonged to, but the A&M faculty were amenable to participating in the research. Clark asked them to begin on faith, since the funding had not been approved.

USDA had approved the initial $350,000 grant, after some prompting from de la Garza. However, Lonnie King, the acting administrator of APHIS, thought that he had made it clear to Clark that USDA would only pay for the start-up research costs; an ongoing rabies program would have to be paid for by Texas. Now, a year later, the Texans were asking USDA to pay for the full cost of the first-year's bait drop, and King was telling them it was impossible. But it was early 1994, the Texas Legislature wasn't in session, and there was no place else for Clark and Fearneyhough to turn. Clark asked de la Garza's office for help, and David Heard was handed the ball.

First, Heard was briefed by the Texans on the project. The epizootic front was at San Antonio's back door, they said; if it moved beyond the city, it would probably be too big to stop. "They made it clear it was critical they get this money to do their project. They went through the whole list as to why—rabies was becoming such a big problem in South Texas, and what this would mean for the future of Texas and really the entire United States. How this was different than the epizootic going on with the gray fox in West Texas, that this was far more insidious. And not only did they need money, but they needed this exact allotment for the project. If they only had half the money, they couldn't go forward."

Heard could hear a silent groan behind Lonnie King's voice when he called the acting administrator and brought up the Texas project. "Look," Heard recalls King saying. "Chairman de la Garza has been very good to us, and we'll see what we can do—but I have to tell you this may not work." King was familiar with the problems the research had encountered. King suggested: "You ask Dr. Clark how his first tests went. They didn't go very well." Heard later asked Clark about the tests. Clark admitted the poor initial results, but insisted there were other circumstances they were certain they had overcome. The vaccine would work. But King was unhappy with the pressure, and made it clear that no funding could be allotted unless the vaccine could be demonstrated as effective in coyotes. In addition, the deadline for the funds were approaching, leaving the Texans with the dual problem of proving the vaccine would work before the fiscal-year funding cycle ended.

King was skeptical about whether the Texans would succeed. He told Heard such research should not be rushed with a bubble-gum-and-bailing-wire kind of approach. "I realize you have a critical problem, but you're one of many," King told Heard. "When it comes to prioritizing these things, it's very difficult, but we have to do it." But King was diplomatic, realizing that he was, in effect, speaking to de la Garza and that this was important to the chair.

In fact, de la Garza had been extremely good to the USDA as chair. Year after year, there had been pressure to slash farm subsidies and other agriculture programs, yet de la Garza had been firm in his support for the agency. On the other hand, such contingency funds in government agencies are rare and protected jealously. "You don't have a lot of that kind of money up there, where an agency gets a sum of money from Congress that they can dole out as they please. That's why it became very political at the USDA's level. They have so little control over their purse strings, the little they have they're not thrilled about abdicating to the will of the chairman," Heard said. In other words, King hinted, if de la Garza wanted the project funded, he should appropriate the money for it.

King kept referring to the seed money he already had provided the project. "He did not like the fact they had given money the prior year, and then were giving it again. His view was that we in Texas had been a little disingenuous, getting the seed money, saying: 'Yes, yes, give us the money and then we'll go to the legislature,' and then a few months later, here we were again—asking not just for a little more money for the project, but the entire project." Whether this reflected miscommunication is unclear; Keith Clark said later he and Gary Nunley had repeatedly told USDA officials not to approve the start-up funds without agreeing to pay for the first operational year, since the Texas Legislature met only every other year. Nevertheless, the fact the project's survival hinged on the entire funding request, Heard said, was particularly difficult for King. "A lot of times in those situations, you can say, 'Well, I can't give it all to you, but here's 40 percent.' But the state leg was not in session, their budget was set. This was a situation where the project had to be funded fully."

Heard had a few more conversations with King on the matter. In one call, King warned that the agency's legal department had determined the USDA could not pay for the vaccine, since it was charged with approving its safety and efficacy—a clear conflict of interest. "What he really said was, there's ways we can get around It. But he wanted you to know what a pain in the butt this was."

But in the end, de la Garza's clout overcame all obstacles. On October 27, he wrote directly to Agriculture Secretary Mike Espy:

> *Dear Mr. Secretary:*
>
> *The rapid spread of the rabies epizootic in South Texas is currently threatening the health of the residents of the State of Texas as well as individuals living beyond its borders. On July 18, 1994, Governor Ann Richards declared the epizootic a state health emergency.*
>
> *The epizootic is currently moving northward from South Texas at a rate of 40–50 miles per year. As of September 20, 1994, the northern-*

most canine rabies cases were recorded 45 miles southwest of San Antonio. The epizootic will probably enter the highly populated areas surrounding San Antonio (Bexar County) before the end of 1995.

The canine rabies epizootic is not just a problem for South Texas. It is a problem that is potentially national in scope. This situation is analogous to the raccoon rabies epizootic that spread out of Florida in the 1960s. Therefore it is critical that immediate efforts are made to contain and restrict the spread of the epizootic.

The Texas Department of Health, in cooperation with the Texas Animal Damage Control, the U.S. Department of Agriculture, and the Centers for Disease Control and Prevention, has developed the Oral Rabies Vaccination Project as an innovative approach to containing the spread of the epizootic. TDH and TADC are requesting FY 1995 contingency funding from the Animal and Plant Health Inspection Service. These funds would be devoted to the implementation phase of the project (scheduled to begin in January 1995) and are essential for the purchase of a vaccine/bait in sufficient quantities to create a zone of vaccinated animals along the northern front of the epizootic.

I fully support the TDH request for APHIS contingency funding and would appreciate any efforts you could make to ensure that the ORVP receives the proper funding.

I would also add that the project is on a very strict time schedule due to the rapid spread of the epizootic, its proximity to large urban areas, and the efficacy based need to distribute the vaccine baits during the cooler months of January/February. Therefore, it is crucial that the contingency funds be made available to TDH and TADC as soon as possible.

Additionally, it is critical that the ORVP receive a level of funding that will allow for the full implementation of the vaccination phase. Partially vaccinating the animals in the "containment zone" will not ultimately restrict the spread of the epizootic and will only waste any of the federal funds supplied to the project.

Thank you for your prompt attention to this matter.

With best wishes, I am

Sincerely,

E (Kika) de la Garza

Chairman

Heard, who had recently completed political science courses at A&M, marveled at how the episode appeared to be "a textbook example of chairman politics, how they'll form an alliance with the agencies. Sometimes you'll have an adversarial relationship, as you do now with the Republicans scaling down. But between our agency and the USDA at the time, there was a huge spirit of cooperation—a feeling we're all in this together."

Political Impetus

Back in Austin, Keith Clark was trying to herd Texas bureaucrats in line as well. The USDA wanted the state to declare a public health emergency before the agency would approve the emergency request for contingency funds. But even within his own state, politics and side issues remained a distraction. While he could assure state leaders that the South Texas canine rabies epizootic was an urgent threat, those leaders were starting to feel pressure to do *something* about rabies—not so much because of South Texas coyotes, but rather Central Texas foxes. In the more heavily populated Central Texas area, local governments were starting to get loud about the need to head off gray fox rabies in its tracks.

The first rabid fox appeared in Sabine County, on the border between Texas and Louisiana, in 1946, the year after World War II ended. "It probably started in Alabama or Georgia," Keith Clark said. "We know it came in from Louisiana and swept westward." It moved well into Texas, but by the 1960s, fox rabies was beginning to die out in the eastern portion of the state, where it began. The reasons could be many, Clark believes, including a rise in fur prices; fewer small farms providing a reliable food source; drought; the disease itself reducing fox population below that needed to sustain enzootic rabies. In any case, by the late 1970s and early 1980s, fox rabies was confined to a small region in West Texas.

But in 1988, it began to expand again, perhaps triggered by a reversal of many of the same conditions that caused it initially to die off. The new outbreak began in Sutton County, west of the Texas Hill Country, and became centralized in Val Verde County, which contained the border town of Del Rio. That year there were seven counties reporting twenty-three rabies cases, largely in foxes but spilling over into other animals as well. The following year, only twelve cases were reported, eleven foxes and one cat. Health officials hoped it might be dying out again. But in 1990, it ballooned again to thirty-eight cases.

Then, in 1991—the same year the canine epizootic exploded northward from Starr and Hidalgo—fox rabies also erupted southeast, with sixty-nine cases in twelve counties. It continued to grow each year, reaching northern San Antonio in 1994 (San Antonio, squeezed by two rabies epizootics, had canine rabies only forty miles to the south), and threatened other large metropolitan areas like Austin and Waco.

An odd side note to the gray fox epizootic was that almost every year, it seemed to spill into at least one strange species. In 1991, it was a porcupine ("You'd have to be mad to pick a fight with this critter," one state health official noted), and in 1992, a rabid llama was reported. And although there were a few scary incidents involving humans and rabid foxes—and some limited spillover into domestic animals—the danger from fox rabies was clearly less than that posed by canine rabies in South Texas.

Gov. Ann Richards's office convened an interdepartmental task force to deal with the rabies problem in foxes and coyotes. Richards's agriculture policy advisor, Keith Jones, chaired the task force. "We were getting a pretty significant increase in the incidence of canine rabies in South Texas, but really what prompted the concern was that we were getting a major increase in rabies in gray foxes, from about Llano west to San Angelo," Jones said. For the residents of the Texas-Mexico border, who often complained bitterly that the state ignored their problems until they also became problems for Austin and San Antonio, those suspicions appeared to have some merit.

From the first meeting, it was clear to Jones and Clark that the Texas Sheep and Goat Raisers Association had mustered a considerable voice in the discussion through the Texas Department of Agriculture's representative, and a staff member from the office of state Sen. Bill Sims of San Angelo. The ranchers idea of how to stop coyotes from spreading rabies was as old as ranching in Texas—to kill them. For that, they hoped the rabies outbreak would provide the leverage to convince the Environmental Protection Agency to allow them the emergency use of Compound 1080—a poison they had lost two decades earlier. President Nixon had banned 1080 and sharply restricted the use of the M-44 cyanide gun. Those restrictions were eased considerably during the Reagan administration, but the ranchers wanted unlimited use.

It was a political dilemma for both the governor and for Texas Agriculture Commissioner Rick Perry. Rabies, Jones says, "was beginning to be an issue that could be used in campaigns. Commissioner Perry was pushing all the buttons to make sure his constituency group got taken care of."

Clark, who opposed the 1080 idea, instead stressed the health department's idea to drop vaccine-laden baits over South Texas. The problem was, under the regulations governing the contingency fund, the governor would have to declare rabies a state health emergency. That made both Jones and the governor nervous.

"We were thinking about tourism, we were thinking about all kinds of things—what that would say. And so it really did take us about two or three weeks to make the final decision to do it. Also it ratcheted up the pressure. Once you say this is a public health emergency, then everybody can start beating up on you if you're not moving as rapidly as they think you ought to move."

In the end, 1080 and V-RG were the only options at the table, and the group decided to move ahead with both. The Texas Department of Agriculture officially asked the EPA to consider the 1080 issue in Texas, in light of the coyote epizootic. After several months, the answer finally came back: not a chance.

And while Jones thought V-RG was the best of the two options, he couldn't help but think the idea was "kind of screwy. I kept pulling him [Clark] aside and saying: 'Keith, are you sure this stuff's going to work? Because if we spend $1.4 million trying to vaccinate coyotes, we're going to look pretty stupid if it doesn't work.'"

On July 18, 1994, Gov. Ann Richards sent this letter to David Smith, the Commissioner of Health:

> *Dear Dr. Smith.*
>   *I am declaring the serious rabies problem in West-Central and South Texas to be a State Health Emergency.*

Promising to convene still another meeting of state health and wildlife officials and other experts to consider options in the rabies battle, she concluded:

> *We must protect the people and animals of Texas against rabies, and I am committed to taking whatever action is necessary to control the rabies problem.*
>   *Sincerely,*
>   *Ann W. Richards*
>   *Governor*

V-RG is Judged "Safe"

The annual meeting on rabies in the Americas took place in Niagara Falls, Ontario, in 1994. Fearneyhough hoped to take advantage of the expertise there to keep the Texas project alive. He had been granted one bit of luck: in calling around to find more coyotes, he had spoken to Fred Knowlton with the Animal Damage Control's Denver Wildlife Research Center in Logan, Utah. Knowlton, who had done some of the best-cited work on coyote density in South Texas, had forty-seven coyotes at Logan. However, all but seven had already been vaccinated for rabies. But the researchers there had been comparing two different rabies vaccines for effectiveness in coyotes, and only two weeks earlier had measured the level of rabies-neutralizing antibodies in all the animals. In addition, those animals roamed in a large enclosure, more typical of their natural habitat. The A&M coyotes had been penned in cages, and fed a regular diet in addition to the baits. If the Texans could use the Utah coyotes, Knowlton said, they were welcome to them.

Fearneyhough then met with Robert Miller, who also was helpful, repeating his view that the project could proceed if the Texans showed V-RG was safe and had at least a chance of being effective in coyotes. The safety issue had pretty much been addressed in previous studies. It was now a matter of demonstrating they could vaccinate coyotes with the vaccine baits. Fearneyhough met with Miller and Kent Van Kampen, a consultant Rhone had hired to help with licensing V-RG. Van Kampen's biggest value was as peacemaker, soothing ruffled feathers between the Texans, Rhone, and the CDC, organizing weekly conference calls to keep everyone on track. "He got us all talking to each other again," Clark says. The group discussed how they might use the coyotes in Utah. They certainly could test the vaccine in the seven unvaccinated coyotes. This time, however, the animals would be less skittish, more likely to behave in their normal manner. In addition, the researchers could withhold food so that the coyotes would be hungry— again, approximating their condition in the field during winter.

But the forty previously vaccinated coyotes might also be useful. A vaccinated mammal will undergo an amnestic response when vaccinated a second time—a spiking of the immune response to an antigen the body has seen before. With their current rabies immunity already measured, the vaccinated coyotes could then be boosted with the oral vaccine. If the animals achieved a four-fold increase in rabies-neutralizing antibodies after eating three baits, that would demonstrate V-RG would work in coyotes. Miller agreed to the proposal. In fact, because of time constraints, the USDA considered only blood tests in their decision to let the project move forward. The seven unvaccinated coyotes weren't actually challenged with rabies until much later. Under different circumstances, the USDA might not be so generous, Miller allows. But behind their decision was the same thing driving the Texans: the northward spread of the epizootic. If rabies moved into San Antonio and beyond, there might be no way to stop it.

"That was one of the things we considered in approving that initial study," Miller said. "There was a real need to get started now instead of waiting for additional information, and if Texas has got the money to go ahead and do it—let's not stand in the way of that. Let's let the product talk for itself. We felt it wasn't going to do any harm to let them go ahead with that study, and if it's going to do some good—then that's good."

Fearneyhough then sought out Charles Rupprecht for his blessing of the idea. Although Rupprecht was not a member of the USDA's oversight committee for the Texas project, he was a member of the agency's Vaccine Advisory Board, and therefore had a lot of influence. Besides, he was the father of V-RG. The meeting took place at a restaurant adjacent to the Niagara Falls conference hotel. Besides Rupprecht and Fearneyhough, others present were Cathy Hanlon, Guy Moore from the Texas Department of Health, and Van Kampen.

"The lobbying that I was doing with Chuck was just asking him to at least look at this thing with an open mind," Fearneyhough says. "Let us see if we can find a way to measure immune response and to show that we're showing a positive effect. And if we can, will you at least agree that it is a reasonable assumption of success, and give your blessing so that USDA can feel like they can release the money to let us go ahead?"

But the tone of the meeting quickly turned combative. Rupprecht felt he was being painted in a corner by the Texans, who were moving too fast with too little scientific evidence. "I recall a very heated dinner," Rupprecht says. "Certainly there was very strong rationale to proceed with an experimental project. But that was a lot different than asking the public health service to say that this is a bona fide control program, with a very high chance of success. We had no efficacy data on this."

Rupprecht challenged the decision by the Texans to use both fishmeal and dog food baits for the drop. With a Texas firm supplying the dog food, he implied there were commercial reasons for the choice. Fearneyhough denied it. "We knew fishmeal had been used on the East Coast with raccoons, but some of the preliminary work we had with coyotes—they didn't necessarily like fishmeal. Maybe this was the point in the scientific investigation where you have your biases, and we just made the assumption that coyotes out in the middle of brushland in South Texas didn't eat fish. We thought, well, we should look at something else besides fishmeal. Dog food was a natural choice. We looked as something that was a nutritional source, that was readily available and easy to use."

As it turned out later, the Texans would find dog food less effective than fishmeal. But at the time, they stuck to their guns. "Chuck was holding the hammer over us pretty hard," Fearneyhough said later.

The Experiment Begins

Fearneyhough arrived to the cold and snow of the Denver Wildlife Research Center in Logan with guarded hope. The coyotes roamed relatively freely in one of four half-acre fenced enclosures arranged in a cloverleaf around an observation tower. Soon after his arrival, Fearneyhough went straight to one of the enclosures and tossed a bait to a hungry coyote. The coyote promptly urinated on it. Not a good sign, Fearneyhough sighed. He tried a second coyote. It also urinated on the bait, then rolled it in the dirt with its nose. The third coyote actually buried the bait in the frozen ground, digging a hole with its paws, pushing the bait in, covering it with dirt and tamping it smooth with its nose. Fearneyhough watched with equal measures of fascination and despair. Still, "the opportunity here was to learn. With each of these responses, which appeared negative at first, the animals finally did take the baits." Urinating on a food source, it turned out, is natural coyote behavior—marking it with scent. So was storing it for a later meal. "It doesn't matter what process occurs prior to it, so long as the end result is consumption of that bait and rupture of that vaccine packet. And that's what occurred."

Three laboratories performed the blood tests on the coyotes, including those at CDC, Rhone Merieux, and at Fort Sam Houston Army Base in San Antonio. Seventy percent of the forty coyotes that had already been vaccinated against rabies showed a high enough "spike" in rabies neutralizing antibody levels to suggest the V-RG baits would induce an immune response. In addition, five of the seven coyotes that had never been vaccinated also demonstrated an adequate immune response after eating the V-RG baits.

Those seven newly vaccinated coyotes were shipped to CDC for challenge. The five that had shown an immune response survived injection with rabies virus. However, the challenge itself caused additional friction between Rupprecht and the Texans. "When we brought those wild trapped animals in from the field [to A&M], they were left totally alone for two weeks to just acclimate and readjust," Fearneyhough said. "That's just common protocol for dealing with an animal that's been moved or stressed. You allow them to bring their body systems and immunological systems back to normalcy. Chuck didn't do that. He zapped them [with rabies] right away."

Clark is more blunt: "I'm convinced that Rupprecht did his very best to scuttle us right there. Five of the seven had titers. We shipped them over there. All convention dictates that you let them settle down, get over the stress of shipping before challenging them. He did it right away, trying to kill them. They survived anyway."

Rupprecht says the accusation is groundless: "I see the big L-word ludicrous come down the pike. Number one, it was the Texans who were pushing left and right for expediency—and why in God's name would anybody want to sabotage this project? It's completely without any substance. The kinds of treatments that were done were to try and expedite at their own requests, answers ASAP, so they wouldn't look foolish when stuff went

A coyote gazes warily from an enclosure at the USDA Denver Wildlife Research Center in Logan, Utah. Courtesy Texas Department of Health

into the field. It's the only data at all that demonstrates there's any efficacy at all to the vaccine in an animal that consumes a bait against challenge. It would have seemed peculiar to put more than a million doses in the field and never have any efficacy via baits ever described.

"It wouldn't have mattered if they were here for a year," Rupprecht added. "If anything, we would have lost more of them."

In any case, the Logan study had been the success the Texans had prayed for, at least as far as resolving the questions the USDA had asked of them. For their part, USDA officials privately told the state health department the drop would be approved. But the wait for official notification of approval dragged on and on, until the very last minute.

Funding, Again

While Fearneyhough was still in Utah, trying to salvage something from the research, Keith Clark had a dilemma. To produce the volume of baits the Texans needed, Rhone Merieux needed to purchase a $100,000 piece of equipment that would automatically produce and fill the vaccine sachets. But without an order in hand from Texas to actually buy the baits, they were reluctant to obtain the machine. After all, the vaccine baits used in Europe were produced in Europe; only a relatively small number of U.S.-produced baits had been required by Rupprecht and the group in New Jersey. "We were putting pressure on them to buy this piece of equipment they'd need to manufacture it, without being able to guarantee at that time we'd ever be able to buy one dose from them," Clark says. "And finally it came down to, when we had to order the vaccine, we didn't have the money." With everything on the line, and no money to back it up, Clark ordered several hundred thousand baits. "I went out on a limb," he admits, grinning. "I remember sweating bullets. It seemed like a couple of weeks. Maybe it wasn't that long."

On November 4, 1994, the USDA issued a press release stating that $1.3 million had been approved to pay for the Texas bait drop. The release did not say that permission for the field trial itself had not yet been granted by the agency. That permission wouldn't be granted until the last minute. "USDA is taking an innovative approach to prevent further spread of this disease," said Patricia Jensen, acting assistant secretary of Marketing and Regulatory Programs. "USDA's Animal and Plant Health Inspection Service is working closely with Texas officials to develop a comprehensive management plan to control the rabies outbreak, and will continue cooperating with the Texas Department of Health and others in implementing the plan and gauging its effectiveness."

The release included a few carefully phrased remarks from Rupprecht as well: "We feel that this is one of the most progressive uses of oral rabies vaccine to date in the United States. We're hopeful that this will lead to more effective rabies control in South Texas."

A few days after that release, Lonnie King wrote a letter to Keith Clark, congratulating him on the funding, and clarifying their new partnership in the oral vaccine project:

> *Keith, the experimental nature and high visibility of this project*
> *raise a number of issues that require our mutual agreement and*
> *understanding. . . . [A]n epizootic of this magnitude will require*
> *funding and other resources beyond current availability and*
> *timeframes. Funds have not been included in our FY [fiscal year]*
> *1996 budget request to support this project. Contingency funds can-*
> *not be used to fund what has now become an 'ongoing' program.*
> *Therefore, I hope we can agree that the State of Texas will seek*
> *appropriated funds to support this work in future years. Any par-*
> *ticipation of APHIS in the future will be based on congressionally*
> *appropriated funds.*

King also recommended establishment of a scientific oversight group to review progress of the project, including representatives of the CDC, APHIS, and the Environmental Protection Agency. Finally, King said it would be important for the public to recognize the cooperative nature of the project:

> *Thus, it would be helpful to give both the Texas Department*
> *of Health and APHIS recognition in all public information re-*
> *leases. . . .*

CHAPTER EIGHT

Face on a Plague

Rolando Bazan's first complaint was an odd one. In a telephone conversation with his father, a U.S. Bureau of Alcohol, Tobacco, and Firearms agent assigned to Corpus Christi, the fourteen-year-old complained of feeling "sad all over" and described a tingling sensation in his back, neck, and shoulders. Later, relatives would recall he seemed a bit agitated, somehow *different*. But at the time, it wasn't a major concern. After all, Rolando—by all accounts happy and well liked; a good student in his eighth-grade class at South Junior High School in Edinburg, who enjoyed playing tennis and drums in the school band—could be a bit of a hypochondriac.

"My son was the type to let me know," says his mother, Cindy Parras, a clerk in an Edinburg law office. "Every little cut he had, he wanted to go to the doctor. He'd call the doctor on his own." A few weeks later, when a team of investigators from the Texas Department of Health descended on Edinburg, searching for the source of Rolando Bazan's illness in order to turn up any other potential exposures, they were frustrated by the boy's well-documented tendency to complain, given the lack of other clues. No, they were repeatedly told, if Rolando had been bitten or scratched by a dog, particularly by some wild animal, he would have mentioned it. But he had said nothing at all.

Socioeconomic Factors in the Rolando Bazan Case

By the time Rolando first complained of neurological symptoms in November 1994, the canine rabies outbreak in South Texas was six years old,

*Rolando Bazan, the fourteen-year-old Edinburg boy who was
the second Texan to die of the canine rabies strain. Family photo*

by official estimates. More than five hundred animals—including two hundred and sixteen pet dogs—had become rabid, exposing some fifteen hundred people in eighteen contiguous counties. One person, a fifty-five-year-old woman living in a remote part of Starr County, had died of the disease. That summer, Gov. Ann Richards had declared the outbreak a public health emergency. Despite sporadic news coverage of the problem, it was largely ignored by the rest of the state. Another health crisis along the border? It was no big deal.

The border between Texas and Mexico is the poorest region in the state—indeed, among the poorest in the nation—and health conditions there are notoriously poor as well. The year after the first rabid coyote was discovered in Starr County, a mysterious and terrifying cluster of anencephalic births was taking place in nearby Brownsville. Dozens of babies were born with all or part of their brains missing. The Texas Department of Health and CDC responded quickly, but were unable to identify an epidemiological smoking gun, although outraged residents were quick to point a finger at industrial pollution from the *maquiladoras,* or maybe the foul-smelling pesticides sprayed upon the cantaloupes and navel oranges. The parents of sixteen babies born with anencephaly or spina bifida, another neural tube defect, filed a lawsuit against eighty-eight U.S. and Mexican companies, charging that the birth defects were caused by exposure to hazardous substances in the environment. Many of the firms eventually settled with the families.

The EPA launched an expensive probe of pollution along the Rio Grande in response to the birth defects cluster. Almost instantly, they found incredibly high levels of polychlorinated biphenyls, or PCBs—among the highest ever recorded—absorbed in the fatty tissues of a carp caught in an irrigation canal near the Donna Reservoir, about fifteen miles southeast of Edinburg. The Rio Grande, which separates Texas and Mexico along their 889-mile common border, had long been an illegal dumping ground for toxic waste, a situation underscored by the federal convictions of four people associated with Weaver Electric, a Denver company that recycled electrical equipment. Acting on a tip from a woman who wondered why the truck parked in a lot next door to her was leaking, El Paso health inspectors in 1991 discovered one hundred and seventy-five barrels of PCBs abandoned in a residential neighborhood. The shipment was traced to Weaver Electric. Mexican authorities later reported finding empty PCB barrels used by poor residents of *colonias* to store water.

The chemical pollution was in addition to the long-documented problem of raw sewage contamination—billions of gallons of human waste released into the Rio Grande by Mexican cities from Juarez to Matamoros. Nuevo Laredo alone was dumping between twenty million and thirty million gallons of raw sewage a day into the river. Both the American Medical Association and the environmental group American Rivers described the Rio Grande as a "virtual cesspool." "How many rivers in the country have raw sewage going into them as a matter of course in this country?" asked Alan Jones, a scientist with the Texas Water Commission. "We wouldn't think of allowing that in the Colorado River. And of course, the reason is we share that river, that resource, with another nation." The health effects were demonstrated in one study examining the residents of San Elizario, a tiny *colonia* near El Paso. Researchers found that 35 percent of San Elizario children had been infected with hepatitis A by age eight. By age thirty-five, that number was close to 90 percent. The magnitude of the environmental harm to the river, and the communities that rely on it for drinking and irrigation, offered plenty of ammunition to opponents of the North American Free Trade Agreement, which was narrowly approved in 1994 with the last-minute inclusion of funds for border clean-up projects.

Rolando's Case Focuses Attention on the Problem

On Sunday, November 15, the boy who would put a face on what had previously been a vast and anonymous danger knew only that he was ill. He asked to be taken to a hospital emergency room, where he complained of a sore throat, muscle pain, and discomfort when urinating. The emergency room doctor gave him an antibiotic, amoxicillin, for his sore throat, and told him to take Tylenol or ibuprofen for his other symptoms. Rolando was then sent home to recover.

By Monday, his condition was no better. As he was prone to do, Rolando himself called his pediatrician in McAllen, Joseph McDonald, and asked for an appointment. To his mother, "he just told me he had some sort of a problem, but he didn't want anybody to know," she recalled later. By the time they arrived at McDonald's office, Rolando was exhibiting some disturbing neurological symptoms. One minute he seemed jumpy and hyperactive, the next quiet and withdrawn. His jaw and upper body were jerking in involuntary spasms. To his doctor, who knew the boy well and considered him a friend, Rolando admitted being overwhelmed by a feeling of impending doom. McDonald's office was connected to a hospital—different from the one where Rolando had been seen the previous day. The pediatrician was concerned enough by what he saw to put the boy in a wheelchair, and pushed it himself to the hospital next door. After he was admitted, Rolando's condition deteriorated rapidly. A tube was placed down his throat to help him breathe. Doctors puzzled over whether he might be suffering from meningitis, encephalitis, or a brain abscess. They decided to transfer him to Methodist Hospital in San Antonio, 130 miles away. Methodist would be better equipped to diagnose and treat a serious neurological disorder. Eight hours after he had been admitted to the first hospital, he was rushed by air ambulance to San Antonio and admitted to the pediatric intensive care unit at Methodist. William Norberg, Jr., director of the unit, diagnosed him as having probable encephalitis. But, as Norberg said later, doctors go through a long list of suspected diseases as they try to determine the cause of encephalitis; rabies is at the bottom of that list.

A battery of tests identified one possible, if bizarre, culprit: an overdose of the herb *yohimbe,* which is used in folk medicine as an aphrodisiac, but is also contained in a few legitimate pharmaceuticals. Norberg, after talking to McDonald and the boy's family, really didn't suspect drug abuse. Some toxic exposure was a possibility, though, and he questioned relatives about any possible source. They were unable to provide any answers. Meanwhile, Rolando's condition steadily worsened, bouncing between anxiety and hallucinations and unconsciousness. Intubated and unable to speak, he sometimes was able to squeeze his parents' hands when they asked if he could hear them. His heart rhythm became unstable; his kidneys failed, requiring dialysis. His lungs filled with fluid.

"It was one of those absolutely progressive diseases," Norberg said later. "You could see deterioration happening, and you knew you were powerless to interfere. Medical technology could support him, but it couldn't check the illness." On November 23, Norberg began to suspect rabies. A skin biopsy from the nape of Rolando's neck was taken, along with some saliva, and sent to the CDC, which didn't receive them until the day after Rolando finally died November 27, after a massive lung hemorrhage. On December 1, the word came back. Indeed, Rolando Bazan had died of rabies. The strain was later confirmed as Mexican urban dog, the canine strain sweeping through South Texas.

Rolando's death was the third from rabies along the border since the outbreak began in September 1988, the second from the canine strain. The first victim, twenty-two-year-old Manuel Riojas in 1990, had died from a bat bite. But the canine strain of rabies had reached much further. In all, twelve people in the United States had died of rabies during the period. The first was an eighteen-year-old in Oregon, who apparently had contracted canine rabies in Mexico eight months earlier. In 1993, a sixty-nine-year-old California man also died from canine rabies acquired in Mexico. An eleven-year-old child in California died in 1992 of canine rabies acquired in India. The remaining six U.S. deaths were identified as bat strain, mostly silver-haired bat—although only one of the victims had recognized a bat exposure—Riojas, who had been bitten on the hand.

But Rolando's death brought sudden focus to all the earlier warnings that had largely been ignored. Immediately, investigators turned their attention to Edinburg, where Rolando had lived most of his young life. It was an unlikely location for such a tragedy. During the first eleven months of 1994, only two animals—a bat in August and a coyote in October—had been rabies positive for all of Hidalgo County, a relatively small number given the scope of the epizootic.

Edinburg lies at the northern end of a cluster of towns and *colonias* that dot the border, near the center of the agriculturally rich Lower Rio Grande Valley. It is small and pleasant, with about thirty thousand year-round residents, and a few hundred mostly retired "snowbirds" who escape the bitter winters of the northern United States each year, driving Winnebegos or pulling fifth-wheels, enticed by billboards extolling the amenities offered by one community or another, each competing for a piece of the lucrative snowbird trade. Edinburg is home to the University of Texas–Pan American, which provides a comfortable economic base by border standards—although not nearly as comfortable as the booming McAllen, twenty minutes to the south along good expressway, with its *maquiladora* plants, shopping malls, and hospitals. Edinburg is the county seat of Hidalgo County, and the county courthouse and adjacent square is the commercial and social epicenter of the town.

The investigators learned almost immediately that Rolando had been given a puppy, which had died a few days after it was born. They thought they had their answer, until they learned the rest of the litter was fine, and it was unlikely the puppy had been exposed to any other animal after it was taken from its mother. The family also had an adult dog, which also was healthy. Nearly everyone Rolando knew was interviewed to see if he had mentioned a scratch or bite. He hadn't. As the investigation stretched on, no other leads surfaced. The investigators went back over the records of reported animal rabies cases. Although only two rabid animals were reported in Hidalgo County in 1994, there were nineteen the previous year, and thirteen of those were from Edinburg. Since the incubation period for rabies can be years (although the average incubation period is only about a month), it was possible Rolando had been exposed long ago. He might even have told someone about the exposure, a casual remark that by now could have been long forgotten. Like the earlier victim, the fifty-five-year-old Starr County woman, there was no clear incident of exposure. And that absence of known transmission cost both victims their lives, says Dr. Michael Kelly, director of communicable disease control with the Texas Department of Health. "It represents a breakdown in the system, because people shouldn't get rabies. If they recognize an exposure, they should get the shots. And you don't get rabies if you get the shots." For Cindy Parras, the source of her only child's infection with rabies continues to haunt her. "I wish I would have known something had bitten him. I don't think I'll ever know what it was."

The Reaction

Margot Martinez, who heads the Texas Department of Health's new Rabies Center of Excellence in Laredo, was not surprised the state's most infamous rabies death occurred in Edinburg. Although the city later stepped up its prevention efforts following the boy's death, it had not been particularly aggressive before, she says. "Edinburg thought they had a tight rein on things for years, and they wouldn't let (the state health department) in there," Martinez said. "They tell you, 'We've been doing *vacunas* (vaccination clinics) for twenty years; we know what we're doing.' Then you start an evaluation and find out, yeah, they were having *vacunas,* but they had them from like 3:30 in the afternoon to 4:30. They're trying to vaccinate the dogs of working people, who don't get home until six or seven. So when are you going to pick up your old, smelly, tick-loaded, flea-bitten dog, put it in your nice car and drive ten miles down the road to get to the *vacuna?*" And there were a hundred towns, just like Edinburg, all along the border and throughout South Texas.

If Rolando's death shocked his hometown, it served as a wake-up call to the rest of the state. Suddenly the canine rabies outbreak had a human face (if a bit blurry in newspaper reproductions) in the form of a clean-cut, grinning fourteen-year-old, posing for a snapshot in the family dining room. Throughout the state, but particularly in South Texas, communities organized low-cost rabies clinics, and pet owners lined up in droves to vaccinate their animals. That fact alone provided Rolando's mother some small comfort, she said later. But the boy's death was also hard to ignore for the USDA, which was monitoring the South Texas epizootic, as well as the trouble-plagued research required before they would approve the airdrop of hundreds of thousands of vaccine-laden baits to erect a barrier against further spread of the canine strain by rabid coyotes.

The morning that the lead story in the *San Antonio Express-News* heralded Rolando's death from rabies, state and regional health officials arrived at the city's convention center for a conference on the canine outbreak. The conference had been organized months before Rolando's illness, but the timing was ironic. Fernando Guerra, San Antonio's health director, opened the meeting by holding the newspaper over his head and reminding the audience that this canine outbreak carried a risk to human life that health officials hadn't seen in many years.

Although he didn't state it, Guerra's own animal control director, William Lammers, estimated that fewer than one in four owned dogs in San Antonio was vaccinated against rabies, one of the lowest rates of any major city in the country. The reason for the dismal rate was a combination of factors: the city's high poverty rate and the fact that for many families a dog was protection, rather than a pet; poor enforcement of rabies ordinances already on the books; and a general perception that rabies wasn't a threat. Within Guerra's department, there was disagreement over what to do, with the front of the outbreak only forty miles to the south.

The next to rise at the conference was Keith Clark. One of his early slides was a graph showing that over the past several decades, the decline in dog rabies from widespread use of vaccine was almost identical to the drop in human deaths from rabies. Dog and human rabies are inextricably linked, Clark said. "Canine rabies is what kills people, and we've got two dead people to prove that." He later outlined the plan to launch the first large-scale attempt to vaccinate wild animals, in this case coyotes. The seven-year, $11.7 million effort would drop hundreds of thousands of vaccine-laden baits over a forty-mile-wide band stretching from the Texas-Mexico border near Laredo, to the Gulf of Mexico near Corpus Christi, with the northern edge of the drop zone touching South Bexar County, which contains San Antonio. The target date was February 1995. "Canine rabies is on its way to San Antonio, and we feel like there's a very narrow window of time where we can do anything about stopping that," Clark told the group.

CHAPTER NINE

In the Path of a Plague

On a typical day on his rounds, Mike Guerra, a veteran animal control officer with the city of San Antonio, watched expressionlessly as the man who had summoned him struggled to lift an old dog into a small cage on the back of his truck. "He's a good dog," the man explained. "I hate to see him go. He never barks. But *she*"—he nodded in the direction of his wife—"can't stand the smell."

"I keep tripping over him," the wife explained. "I broke my elbow."

Guerra nodded, giving the man a form to sign. Only as he drove away did he reveal a small measure of frustration. "Isn't that a sorry excuse?" Guerra said, shaking his head. "If you keep tripping over him, turn on some lights. The smell? Give him a bath." He sighed. "I can't get shocked any more over these excuses."

As the canine rabies epizootic crept closer to San Antonio, the ninth largest city in the country, local health officials were frustrated over the dismal pet vaccination rate. They pointed to the persistent notion among too many people that dogs and cats are disposable commodities. William Lammers, the city's animal control veterinarian, could only guess, but he estimated fewer than one in four owned dogs were vaccinated—one of the lowest rates of any major American city.

Guerra, who had adopted four dogs from the pound for himself and his parents over the years, seemed resigned to public indifference regarding their own pets. Oddly enough, many were instinctively hostile to the twenty-three city and four county animal control officers patrolling their neighborhoods, picking up strays. Strangers cursed them as they drove by. Owners of unrestrained dogs had been known to physically attack them.

But life without them would be hard to imagine. In 1994, some forty-six thousand animals were impounded by the city, the most of any city in Texas. Of those, forty-two thousand were destroyed. Half were animals voluntarily given up by owners who didn't want them any more.

"Every single dog and cat who came in here was an innocent victim," Lammers said. "It's true some of them may have been socialized improperly. But most of them just did what dogs and cats do. The biggest mistake they made was to pick the wrong owner."

The numbers were almost beyond comprehension. Besides the forty-two thousand animals destroyed, public works officers picked up another fifty thousand dead animals. San Antonio had been trying for years to solve a critical landfill shortage; at the same time, more than sixty-three tons of dead animals were being buried each year at the dump. Some animal groups were calling for mandatory spay-neuter initiatives; Lammers felt that would be too expensive and would barely put a dent in the problem. "I'm very concerned that with forty-two thousand animals euthanized last year, and another fifty thousand dead picked up by public works—that's ninety-two thousand animals last year that were effectively spayed and neutered. And it hasn't changed a thing. We've been doing pretty much the same thing every year."

Now the city was facing a new threat. Two wild animal epizootics were converging. To the north, an epizootic of gray fox rabies had already reached the city. But the greater threat was approaching from the south, where canine rabies had been moving up from the border over the previous six years, carried by the far-ranging coyotes. It had reached Atascosa County, just below Bexar County (which includes San Antonio). That outbreak, all agreed, was capable of raging through the city's vast population of unvaccinated dogs, just as it had done in smaller towns along the border.

That vulnerability was behind much of the state health department's urgency to create a vaccine barrier against canine rabies, dropping nearly a million baits in an arc from near Laredo to the Gulf Coast, with the northern tip touching southern Bexar County. If it worked, they hoped to move the barrier further south each year until rabies was pushed from the state.

Many feared San Antonio would be the first large city in decades to experience an urban outbreak of dog rabies, something that had been virtually unknown since modern vaccine and animal control methods were introduced. "You'll be going back to the '30s and '40s when dog rabies was prevalent throughout the United States, and you had newspaper headlines about mad dogs coming down Main Street—whether it be in Central Texas or Central Ohio or New York," says John Herbold, professor with the San Antonio branch of the University of Texas School of Public Health. Herbold points to the raccoon rabies epizootic in the east, which had traveled thousands of miles without a single human death. The canine strain already had killed two.

But no one knew for certain if this bait drop would work. In the meantime, the city and private veterinarians got together to launch a massive series of low-cost vaccination clinics. At a press conference to announce the clinics, the mascot of the San Antonio Spurs basketball team, the Coyote, was on hand. The city health director, Fernando Guerra, pretended to inject the Coyote with an oversized hypodermic needle. Between February and November 1995, twenty-two public rabies vaccination clinics were held, an effort that immunized more than twelve thousand pets. Additional clinics were held by animal welfare groups, suburbs, and businesses. Many private veterinarians dropped their prices for rabies vaccinations. Lammers, who had based his earlier estimate of less than 25 percent vaccination levels among owned dogs based on conversations with local vets, raised that estimate. Better than half now were immunized. Still, it was just a guess—and still inadequate, according to disease models developed by some experts. "We estimate that 70 percent of the animal population needs to be currently vaccinated to withstand the entrance of the epizootic and protect the community. We're never going to get to 70 percent," Lammers said.

Privately, Lammers was pushing for more enforcement of existing statutes that already required pet vaccination. Already San Antonio issued about 150 citations each month for animal code violations. The minimum fine was one hundred dollars, with an additional forty dollars in court costs. In San Antonio's municipal court, charged with hearing animal code cases, the conviction rate was running about 80 percent. Lammers believed that a combination of low-cost clinics, public education, and much stronger enforcement was needed. His boss, Guerra—whose career had been spent as a pediatrician in San Antonio's *barrios,* who founded one of the earliest inner-city health clinics, whose patients included the children of former mayor and later Secretary of Housing and Urban Development Henry Cisneros—was reluctant to penalize the poor for any reason, favoring an education-only response.

"Of the forty-six thousand animals we impounded last year, approximately 50 percent were owned pets the owners decided they just didn't want anymore, and they called the city to come and get them," Lammers said. "They may have mange, they may have some type of medical problem, and the owner doesn't choose to have them treated. Or maybe they're just tired of them. I know we've got to back education up with enforcement. That's where I don't think Dr. Guerra and I agree. Dr. Guerra is a pediatrician, and he's used to people coming in and getting immunized. They have to show proof of it to go to kindergarten. That doesn't happen with dogs. Like it or not, we have to do some unpopular things."

Lammers said the bulk of the city's problem, not surprisingly, was in low-income neighborhoods, where dogs are often less pet than protection. Under those circumstances, people often had little surplus money for vaccine or fixing fences. Getting a handle on the stray population, of which Lammers estimated 75 percent were owned by *someone*, was essential, since it was unlikely vaccination alone would provide a great enough level of protection in the community. The next best thing was to make sure strays were confined or impounded. But the city's animal control program, with a $1.5 million budget, was among the poorest-funded in the country. The median per capita expense for animal control among all big cities was about $2.50 in 1994. Los Angeles, which ranked nineteenth among cities, spent $2.38 per resident. San Antonio, ranking next at twentieth, spent $1.23. Lammers had been lobbying for years for more money. "Of course, a lot of people who heard me probably think, 'Well, Ned's just trying to get more people.' And they're right, I am. But not because I want to build an empire. We've got to somehow protect the community.

"In the summer months," Lammers added, "animal control officers will get eight hundred calls per day. These guys will leave here with two or three sheets of calls to make, and we know they can't make all these calls."

Guerra's History with Rabies

The specter of rabies held vivid memories for Fernando Guerra. He was among the few physicians in the United States to have treated three American children with rabies early in his career. All three had developed symptoms within a month of each other and were referred to Santa Rosa Children's Hospital in San Antonio.

Gerardo Castano, eight years old, of Eagle Pass—a border town between Laredo and Del Rio—was transferred to Santa Rosa in June 1979 with mysterious neurological problems. His parents initially had taken him to a local doctor for a painful throat, but by the time he arrived in San Antonio he was barely coherent. Guerra had returned from a meeting in Austin on a Saturday afternoon and was asked to see the boy in Santa Rosa's intensive care unit. "He had a very perplexing set of symptoms. He presented with a waxing and waning neurological picture, at times somewhat conscious, sometimes sort of being in a comatose state. Then hyperirritable."

Guerra questioned the parents, who spoke only Spanish, pressing them for details. Rabies was in the back of his mind, although it was fairly low on the list of possible causes for meningal encephalitis. He asked if the boy had had any animal bites or wounds. "It was only on specific questioning, trying to get them to recall over a period of weeks that they remembered that he had gone out one night to separate two dogs that were fighting in the back yard. One was his, a small puppy, which had come upon this dog from the street. They remembered he had gotten bitten on his hand, on the webbing of his right hand between the thumb and the index finger. It broke the skin and he had some scratches, but they didn't think it was anything serious. It was not associated with any particular pain or discomfort, it didn't require suturing." The puppy had run away a short time later.

With the history of the dog bite, Guerra suspected rabies. "I had taken my pediatric boards just a few years before that, so some of that information was still present. So I said, well, why not? It makes sense." A skin biopsy and cerebrospinal fluid was sent for testing. Meanwhile, the child lapsed into a coma and had to be placed on a ventilator. He suffered high, spiking fevers that required cooling blankets.

When the positive test results came back, "then he suddenly became a very interesting case, and all these super-physicians from the medical school were coming, and disagreeing mostly," Guerra smiled. Also arriving were CDC investigators including veterinary epidemiologist Ted Baker, who participated in a press conference at the hospital. "Whenever you have outbreaks of rabies, especially in the dog population, because it's so close to the human population, this is something to be very concerned about," Baker said. By this time, it was found that Eagle Pass and its sister city, Piedras Negras, Mexico, had been reporting an increase in rabid dogs since February. And Mexican officials acknowledged a nine-year-old girl had apparently died of rabies in Piedras Negras about the time Gerardo Castano became ill.

Even though death was inevitable, Guerra labored to treat the boy. "We even were trying to make arrangements to bring from Stanford, from one of the research labs, some interferon—which at the time was about the only high-powered antiviral agent that was available. It was strictly for research purposes, and it was very expensive. It was probably going to cost something like twenty thousand dollars a dose. They were willing to consider its release under the circumstances, but the consensus was that this child was so far gone, and had so much brain damage by then, that we would not have been able to reverse the course."

With that battle ongoing, another Eagle Pass child was admitted. Marianita Garza, eight years old, had suffered a deep bite to the leg by a dog. A decision had been made to await results of the dog's rabies test before beginning postexposure treatment on the girl. "This was one who should not have died," Guerra said, still upset at the memory of the long-ago case. "They were waiting to get a confirmation on the [animal] brain that was submitted before they started prophalaxis, which is totally inexcusable. I discussed it with the family, and it's not to be critical of the management of her case, but there was still that tremendous misperception at the time that once you committed to treatment, you had to undergo that whole series of painful treatments." In fact, human diploid cell vaccine had been introduced making postexposure therapy less of an ordeal.

The girl arrived at the hospital in a coma and never recovered. Four days after her arrival, "she suffered six separate cardiac arrests on Monday night, but was successfully revived by the hospital staff each time," he said. The following day she died.

Before Marianita Garza died, a two-year-old girl from Poteet, only thirty miles south of San Antonio, was admitted directly into the hospital's neurological unit with suspected rabies. Initial tests were negative, but an examination of cells from her cornea detected the virus. Although city officials in Poteet hurriedly began rounding up strays and planning clinics, the mayor told a *San Antonio Express-News* reporter that the girl, whose name was withheld, apparently had become infected on a trip to the border. A hospital spokesperson said the child's condition also was up and down, occasionally improving to the point she could play with toys.

Meanwhile, more CDC and state health officials were in Eagle Pass and Piedras Negras, where some sixty people were undergoing postexposure treatment. A massive campaign was organized to immunize pets, with health workers going door-to-door. More than six hundred strays were destroyed. The mayor told a reporter that city officials were "a little optimistic" they had convinced local residents of the seriousness of the outbreak.

As for Guerra, beset with the remarkable coincidence of having three young patients, "suddenly I became the rabies doctor for South Texas and Mexico. I was getting patients coming from Mexico. Some of these were from fairly affluent families who would spare no expense. They would fly up on a chartered plane just to get the child started on the vaccine." One wealthy family from Mexico listened politely to Guerra's advice regarding their children's exposure and decided to seek a second opinion. "They decided the state of the science for the treatment for rabies was much more advanced in Europe, so they flew to Europe to the Pasteur institute, which had some prototype vaccine."

Most of the exposures were low-risk. One, however, involved a confirmed rabid dog that had exposed a large group of young children on a playground in Saltillo, Mexico. "There were about thirty kids from a nursery school in Saltillo that were in contact with a stray puppy that came in that summer to play in the playground. It licked all of these kids, some got scratched, maybe some got bitten. And talk about panic. So we had to make arrangements to try and get them enough doses of that so they could protect those kids."

Guerra, who had been vaccinated against rabies, underwent a booster. Dozens of hospital workers were also treated. "Once you consider rabies as a compelling diagnosis, then it becomes an almost hysterical level of fear in everybody, and understandably so. We ended up having to prophalax a lot of people who were in contact, even those that were somewhat remotely associated with the individuals. People who thought that when they were suctioning a child there might have been a spread of secretions."

Guerra never treated another rabies patient. But after observing the three children, he wondered if perhaps he had seen rabies before. "When I was in Vietnam doing my obligated tour as a battalion surgeon, we had at times to take on responsibility for caring for civilians brought in who were very sick. I know there were some kids and adults who must have died of rabies that I didn't recognize at the time, but had profound neurological presentations."

Margot Martinez

While Clark and Fearneyhough were figuring out how to apply cutting-edge biotechnology to the canine rabies epizootic, Margot Martinez was approaching the problem from the other end using traditional rabies control methods to fight the disease. The state had hired Martinez and opened a Rabies Center of Excellence in Laredo in May 1994 for the primary task of increasing the domestic animal vaccination rate along the border through clinics and education. Surveillance was another of the center's duties.

Martinez was particularly suited for the new job. A lifelong resident of the border, she was attuned to the culture and sensitivities in the area. Unlike her colleagues, she believed the canine rabies epizootic did not originate in Mexico.

> We've always had rabies outbreaks being reported periodically in cities along the border. But we've never seen the population numbers we're seeing now. Rabies is a disease of human reporting. We know it appears in wildlife, it cycles all the time. The bottom line is, you need to have a human there to say, "Oh yeah, this dog looks sick and he could be rabid, let's submit the head and see." So more people are around to observe this abnormal behavior in animals; it's not just animals dying cyclically in wildlife. They're now being reported.
>
> When they say this started in 1988, that was the first coyote attacking dogs that was reported. My point is that it was a coyote attacking dogs at the right place at the right time. There's been a massive boom, building in all these communities. And as those areas are being developed, animals become displaced. On top of that, you have a deadly virus that is transmitted through the expression of aggressiveness. These animals may be defending their turf because they're being packed into smaller spaces. That's part of their normal behavior. So you increase the human numbers, you displace the wildlife population. The hunters are not as aggressive as they used to be with all this ecologic consciousness. It's a very complex thing to where a whole bunch of factors come into oneness with the stars, and here we are on this big rabies conversion.

Buried in that argument was a political reality well-understood by border residents. If rabies came from Mexico, the officials in Texas would simply shrug: Why, they would ask, should we put any money into controlling it? The border is notoriously porous; stop this outbreak and there will just be another outbreak down the road. On the other hand, if canine rabies has always been on the Texas side of the river, just cycling unobserved over the years, then it was Texas' problem. Martinez was particularly frustrated at hearing the attitude from local officials along the border that Mexico was to blame. "The local and county governments do not want to spend money on animal control and rabies prevention in their communities. Why should they? Everybody knows rabies comes from Mexico. It's only twenty miles away, they think it can cross the river and that's why we're having rabies in Texas. I think that's just an excuse not to meet the responsibility of the community that elected them."

Martinez, who had done graduate studies in rabies cycles, maintained the cycle in Mexico was different that in Texas. The canine strain had been seen in periodic outbreaks for years, including Martinez's hometown of Eagle Pass, which had seen fairly serious rabies outbreaks in 1974, and again in 1986. "The reality is, we've had our own cycles. The viruses may look very similar. But you have to do rabies control in your own backyard, and if you don't, you're going to have continuing cycles."

While Keith Clark understood and sympathized with Martinez's position, he disagreed with her reasoning. The Mexicans, who were often reluctant to share hard information on rabies in Mexico, had told them they had been aware of coyote rabies for some time. "We had a meeting with Mexican veterinarians here in Austin. They were telling us about seeing rabid coyotes as early as 1986."

But Martinez felt the way many border residents did—that their problems were only being addressed when they started being problems for the big cities further north. "The rabies center is addressing needs that have been here for eons. They just never had the political clout or the money to back it up. Now, as these problems start to close in on San Antonio and Austin, all of a sudden it's like: 'Oh, gee. Maybe we should have stopped it on the border.'"

Still, Martinez was finding her job more difficult than she expected. For one thing, there was pressure on the health department not to encroach on the private practices of local veterinarians by holding too many vaccination clinics. "There was never any intention of our putting on clinics in competition with private veterinarians," Clark said. "It has always been my contention that the veterinary community has its responsibility to public health, that we ought to be out there making rabies vaccinations affordable and available to the public. But a whole generation has grown up down there without any terrestrial animal rabies. They were able to get by without vaccinating."

But Martinez heard a different story from pet owners. "The community will tell you it's too expensive to go into the veterinarian's offices. They wind up paying visitor's fees and vaccination costs. You can't walk in and out without a seventy dollar bill. We have no influence on that. It's private enterprise. They can price their vaccine at whatever is fair to them. But with that comes the reality that people will cut back and give up some-where. It's always easier to give up on the dog."

Another problem was local politics. The countless small towns and villages had their own budgets and bureaucracies and associations. "El Seniso and Río Bravo (two suburbs of Laredo) don't have animal control. They can't get services from Laredo because they've been incorporated as private cities. They say, wait a minute, we are Webb County taxpayers, can't Webb County service us? But the city of Laredo holds the contract to Webb County. It's all kind of politics meshed in there. In all of these small cities, animal control is usually the last thing on the list, and it's the first thing that gets cut. And so a lot of times our role is to educate the leadership that it's cheaper to spend two thousand dollars on a *vacuna* (a vaccination clinic) than to wait until thirty people are exposed to rabies and spend $750 per person on postexposure treatment."

But it was clear the efforts were paying off. When the state later did a retrospective study of Starr County pet vaccination levels, they found that only 18.2 percent of dogs who were known to have been exposed to a rabid animal were vaccinated against rabies in 1988, when the outbreak began. By 1994, that percentage had climbed to 50 percent. So intensive rabies educa-tion programs and vaccination clinics did appear to be having an effect.

A Short History of Rabies in the United States

Martinez was correct that the rabies outbreak in coyotes was not the first, either in Texas or the United States. History records a major coyote rabies epizootic that began in central California in 1909 and ultimately pushed north into Oregon and Washington, and east into Idaho, Nevada, and Utah. By 1923, more than two thousand people had been bitten by rabid coyotes and dogs, fifty-six of them fatally. Livestock losses in Nevada totaled half a million dollars. Congress appropriated $125,000 in 1916 to combat the dis-ease through predator control methods. The same year, a rabies conference was held in Salt Lake city by representatives of state health departments, wool growers, cattle raisers, and railroad companies. The conferees recom-mended "as a plan for promptly eradicating rabies, that wild animals should be destroyed by authorities of each state, in cooperation with the federal department of agriculture; and that the control and prevention of rabies in humans and in domestic animals be in charge of state health boards cooperating with the federal public health service, a detail of officers from the service being requested for this work." The coyote outbreak in the West eventually burned itself out, just as the outbreak in Arctic foxes across the northern United States would many years later.

Texas, too, had its rabid coyotes. Dobie recounts in his book, *The Voice of the Coyote,* encountering one as a child: "In my boyhood, a cousin and I walking along a wagon road were followed for a mile by a coyote that took refuge, at the end of our walk, in a cow shed, where a man shot it before dogs attacked. It manifestly had hydrophobia, and like many mad coyotes it was mangy, but it did not act in a vicious manner."

In an account written in 1947 in *The Cattleman* magazine entitled "Mad Coyotes in the Brush Country," O. W. Nolen quotes a South Texas rancher, M. H. Martin, Jr., of Fowlerton, about a rabies outbreak near the border that began in the late 1890s and continued through 1915:

> While the epidemic prevailed in a widely scattered area it was exceptionally bad in our locality along the north side of the Nueces River, just below the La Salle-McMullen county line, and along the Guadalupe and Spring Branch creeks where the then open flats were an ideal habitat and rendezvous for coyotes.
>
> The coyotes afflicted with rabies were so numerous it was a common occurrence to find one walking around with its jaws locked open, or maybe had gotten to where it couldn't walk and would be lying down and snapping at a clump of prickly pear. When they had reached that stage where their jaws became locked they were usually so disabled as to be harmless, practically indifferent to one's approach, and could be easily killed with a club.

Dobie included his own interview with Martin in his classic book on coyotes:

> This was many years ago. The death of a boy from being dragged by a horse had drawn a number of men to the Fitzpatric Ranch in McMullen County. The house was built on a slope and the rear of it was several feet above the ground. The sleeping place for the ranch dogs—and there were always plenty of dogs—was under the floor. After dark, bedlam broke out among them. We soon discovered that a mad coyote was attacking them. They would stay under the floor and not push the fight when the coyote retreated, but when it came

back to attack, they fought furiously. The only gun on the ranch was in a servant house several hundred yards away. Nobody wanted to get out in the dark to bring it, but finally Jay Martin and I made the run. Then, while he held a lighted lantern over my head, I picked out the coyote under the house and shot it. Before daylight, bedlam broke out again. This time it was the mother of a litter of pups that was mad, and we had to shoot her. After a mix-up of this kind the only thing to do with dogs was to kill all that might have been bitten or keep them tied up for watching. During the epidemic we lost many cattle bitten by mad coyotes. When a cow brute went mad, it would make the most mournful and distressing kind of bawling imaginable. It would turn vicious and charge a man on horseback with its horns. I saw a ranch Mexican who had been bitten by a mad coyote die screaming in that same horrifying way that made cattle scream. This was before there were any Pasteur institutes.

Funding Raises Another Dispute

Meanwhile, the feud between Rupprecht and Clark had exploded. The cause for the explosion seemed minor within the context of the multi-million dollar project, but it was agreed by both sides that it was in fact the case. In the initial discussions over the project, shortly after the initial $350,000 in seed money had been received from the APHIS contingency fund, Rupprecht and Clark had agreed that CDC would get fifty thousand for its part in the challenge studies.

"The agreement was that they at CDC had to modify their existing dog runs over there before their lab animal care committee would let them accept a big fearsome animal like a coyote. They had the idea they were like an overgrown timberwolf or something," Clark said. "To do that, they needed about fifty thousand worth of repairs and modifications, which we agreed to. They did the modifications, and we said, 'Where do we send the money?' And they said, 'Whoa! We have a procedural rule here that says we can't accept money from states.' I talked with brother Chuck and with his boss, Jim Olson, and said: 'Look, you ought to be able to go to your bosses—this is not a law, its just CDC policy—and get an exception to the policy.'

At about that same time we had Chuck and Jean Smith come over here to talk to our Diseases in Nature group. We were going to

---

pay their way. That's when we found out about the deal that they couldn't accept money from states. So I asked Jim Olson and he said, "Don't worry about it." Maybe about that time it was casually mentioned that maybe we could buy them some supplies. I said, "I'm not sure about the legality of that. We can give you the money, but I'm not sure about the legality of supplies because that's not just my group. That involves our purchasing department, and the laws of the state of Texas are a little different about giving it away." They didn't seem particularly concerned at that time. So I didn't pursue it. I never asked for permission to do it. Then, after it was too late, after the buying deadlines were past, they sent us a request for X number of dollars worth of supplies. And there was no way it could be done.

Rupprecht adds his take on the dispute:

When we first began, it was discussed that in order to proceed, Texas would provide certain resources to expedite the project because we didn't have coyotes. Our Animal Care and Use Committee minimally wanted to shore up our standards as not to let loose rabid coyotes in Lawrenceville suburbia (Rupprecht, like Baer before him, maintained a rabies research facility in Lawrenceville, a suburb of Atlanta). Let's just say a lot of things fell flat. We went out on a limb for already being into a budget year and spending resources we didn't have, with the promise of remuneration that never came to pass. That's fine, because as I felt then and do now, this facility should have had the ability to respond to any state. But the fact of the matter was, it was agreed by all parties that in order to provide what we could, as expeditiously as we could, we would do it on a gentlemen's agreement for resources that never surfaced— either from the state or from industry. Obviously that inflicted very hard feelings, while all we were trying to do was our job.

Clark acknowledges that Texas spent the money on their end of the project. "On the other hand, if they [the CDC] did spend fifty thousand dollars on this project, I don't see a whole lot wrong with that, because at the same time they were spending fifty thousand dollars on Cape Cod to evaluate the effectiveness of a [vaccine] barrier keeping raccoon rabies off the Cape— which was not even threatened at that time. I don't mean to disparage their efforts, because if they hadn't been working on it we wouldn't be where we are. But I can't believe that the fifty thousand dollars is the whole story."

Getting the Baits Ready

The Texans' order for 850,000 baits—placed by Clark before he knew he could pay for them, before he had any results from Fearneyhough's experiments that would convince the USDA to approve the trial—sent Rhone Merieux's production line into overdrive. Despite the acquisition of a $100,000 machine that could inject vaccine into small plastic sachets, those sachets still had to be placed into baits and sealed by hand with lard and wax. Rhone's North American headquarters are located in a pleasantly wooded industrial park in Athens, Georgia, about an hour's drive north of Atlanta. With a severe deadline looming over the project, Rhone moved bait assembly to nearby warehouse space and offered overtime to employees to work on the Texas order after they completed their regular shifts. "They got burned out pretty quickly," said Don Steindl, head of production for Rhone.

So the company put out a call for volunteers. "We took every person we could find, asked for their relatives, brothers, sisters—we even had mothers here," Steindl says. "Hundreds of people. We had shifts set up running seven days a week to get the Texas work done on time. We knew the deadline and what they needed, because of the fire ant problem and everything, we just worked backwards from there. We basically calculated how many baits we could do a day, and we ran shifts that were eighteen hours a day, seven days a week, and just kept plugging away."

Of course, Rhone couldn't release the baits and vaccine to the Texans until USDA approved the project, and that approval came almost at the last minute. Rhone Merieux produces a variety of biologics at its Athens facility, including traditional rabies vaccines. "One of the problems we ran into logistically was there was so much volume that we ran out of cooler space," Steindl says. "We had to double-stack things all around until we could get permission from USDA to ship it out."

USDA granted V-RG conditional approval for use in raccoons only in April 1995. Rhone had sought full licensure from USDA, which required a controlled efficacy experiment as a final step. The experiment called for the company's scientists to feed V-RG in baits to caged raccoons. Success would mean the vaccine protected at least 89 percent of vaccinated animals against a rabies challenge that would kill 80 percent of unvaccinated raccoons.

"The firm was not able to attain that goal," Robert Miller with the USDA said. "They got fairly close. But there were some reasons for that, we felt. You don't really get a measured dose with an oral vaccine. We did require it be presented to the animals in a bait, and not just placed in their mouth, because that's the way it was administered in the field."

The results were close enough that the USDA granted V-RG conditional licensure based on results of the Cape May, New Jersey, trials. The one-year conditional license, which was renewed for a second year in April 1996, requires that the vaccine be sold only to governmental agencies, and that those agencies gather more data on its use in the field, particularly in regards to human exposures. "Most of these are smaller trials, but the firm is going to have to monitor these, and make sure the people doing the work are providing adequate monitoring. They'll have to document as much human exposure as they can, particularly if there's any adverse reaction."

Rhone officials feel that once the vaccine receives full licensure there will be more interest from governments—particularly communities—in using it. "Right now as a conditional license it has to have state approval," said Jack Berg, vice president of operations with Rhone Merieux. "What we're hoping is once the product is licensed that won't be necessary. There are a lot of counties that would like to at least bait their local area—parks, places that people frequent. We're really talking about a lot of small-scale projects."

The World Perspective

Many, however, believed the real market for oral rabies vaccine may well be in developing countries—particularly Africa and Asia—where the vast majority of the more than thirty-three thousand human deaths occur each year. Most of those deaths are from exposure to rabid dogs through bites or scratches. As in the United States, the disease is expensive even when it does not kill. In 1992, the World Health Organization estimated that 6.5 million people were vaccinated after exposure to suspected rabid dogs. Of those, five million were in China, and half a million were in India. Another 200,000 in African countries were vaccinated, and 175,000 in Europe.

Latin America reported some success in rabies control through traditional means. The Pan American Health Organization, an arm of WHO, promoted dog vaccination drives, administering 13.9 million doses in sixteen countries—some 58 percent of the dog population in risk areas—in 1995. While Costa Rica, Guyana, Panama, Suriname, Uruguay, Chile, and the English-speaking Caribbean were free of canine rabies that year, Columbia and Guatemala saw increases of both human and dog cases—a result, PAHO officials said, of lax monitoring and declining dog vaccination coverage.

The WHO in 1995 launched initial field trials of oral vaccination of dogs. WHO had spearheaded Europe's successful fox baiting campaign. Now the organization would look at extending the technology to the millions of free-roaming dogs around the world that cannot easily be vaccinated by traditional injection. While oral vaccination is expensive, the organization said, it is cost-effective if it can reduce the cost of postexposure treatments.

"The extension of this approach to dogs is a major advance in the war against canine rabies, which is in turn the biggest risk of the disease in humans," said Dr. Franáois-Xavier Meslin, Chief of the WHO Veterinary Public Health Unit in Geneva, in a June 1994 press release. "Our long-term aim is the elimination of rabies in dogs through a combination of injectable and oral immunization campaigns in a number of countries."

Baiting studies had already been conducted. "The recipe for success is a combination of bait and vaccine which dogs will take when they are given it or encounter it, and which pose minimum risk to other animals or to humans," another WHO report concluded. "Apart from their taste, the size, color, shape, odor, and texture of the baits are important ingredients. The locations where the baits are distributed—for example, waste disposal sites, rural roadsides or clusters of 'feeding spots'—are also of key importance."

Strategy for the campaign was developed at a meeting at WHO headquarters in Geneva in 1994. Rabies experts attended from Canada, Egypt, France, Germany, India, Israel, Kenya, Morocco, Philippines, South Africa, Switzerland, Tanzania, Tunisia, Turkey, and the United States. The following year, they launched small field trials in Tunisia and Turkey, where dog populations had been studied previously and WHO experts had good relationships with veterinarians.

V-RG Studies in the North

While Texas continued working on its massive distribution of V-RG, smaller field trials were taking place along the East Coast, where the raccoon rabies epizootic had swept through. Raccoon rabies hit New York State with a vengeance in 1990 after its long trek up the East Coast. The previous year, state health officials had recorded only fifty-four rabies cases, all in bats. By 1992, New York had 1,392 rabid animals, nearly all of them raccoons. By 1993, that number had jumped 70 percent, to 2,369—the most of any state. By early 1996, more than six thousand rabid raccoons had been recorded. The disease had washed through the dense raccoon populations living in the rugged and beautiful Adirondacks, pressing on towards the Canadian border.

The toll in health costs and public fear was considerable. The number of postexposure treatments given to humans in New York rose from eighty-four in 1989, to more than a thousand in 1992. In Albany County alone, of more than one thousand raccoons either trapped or killed by dogs or autos and submitted for testing in 1993, 71 percent were rabid. As the epizootic front moved through, the numbers of positive cases declined, but state health officials expected that drop to be a temporary one. "A majority of the population was killed, a relative die-off," Cathleen Hanlon explains. "But they repopulate pretty darn fast, raccoons."

Hanlon, who had been a major part of Rupprecht's rabies group at Wistar —and later at Thomas Jefferson University—joined the New York State Department of Health in 1993 when Rupprecht left for CDC. New York's health department had had a long history of oral rabies vaccine research extending back to Jack Debbie's collaboration with George Baer. Hanlon soon began planning for a V-RG trial in New York. Since rabies had already swept through much of the state, the only areas that were rabies free were Long Island and the area near Niagara, at the New York-Canada border.

Most of the work with V-RG had been to erect a vaccine barrier, and Hanlon considered such a trial at Long Island. Two counties, Nassau and Suffolk, together had 2.6 million residents—about 15 percent of the state's population—with a fairly narrow geographic gateway from New York City. A barrier study there would be relatively inexpensive. Hanlon could make a convincing economic argument: in counties untouched by raccoon rabies, the cost of control measures—largely from bat exposures—was twenty-three cents per person. When raccoon rabies moved in, the cost was between seventy-nine cents and ninety cents. Once raccoon rabies entered Long Island, local costs would exceed two million dollars a year.

Hanlon proposed distributing baits along a fifteen-mile-wide zone from Long Island Sound to the Atlantic Ocean, and from the Queens County border to the Seaford Oyster Bay Parkway. Because of the dense urban settlement, most of the baits would be hand-distributed on foot, with helicopters used to drop in less accessible areas such as tidal marshes. As in New Jersey, the baits would be placed on the sides of roads and streams, at railroads and culverts—routes that raccoons would be likely to travel. In addition, parks, shopping centers, and university campuses would also be baited. In residential neighborhoods, residents could be asked for permission to drop baits, since the raccoons lived and thrived there too.

"If we only do green areas and state expressways that have a little bit of edge to them, we may be able to slow the spread, but I don't think we're going to make a solid wall," Hanlon said. "We're going to have to go into areas like this where they have small detached garages, they've got trees suitable for denning, and they've got an edge row between the houses that raccoons can easily travel at night safely and without being seen." Of course with greater numbers of humans and domestic animals would come more opportunities for exposure to the baits. "We will have more dogs and cats eating them, and people handling them," Hanlon said in early 1995 in an interview in her office in Albany. But that's not a health concern. It will subtract from the number available for raccoons."

A year and a half later, she sounded a more cautious note about the Long Island study, which still had not commenced. "What one constantly has to keep in mind when you're putting out a new biologic that's capable of self-replication that no matter what the track record of that biologic, it needs to be done responsibly. From a human perspective, safety is the ultimate. And in the right host in the right dose at the right inoculation, any self-replicating biologic has the potential for causing disease."

By this time, Rupprecht and Hanlon—who had built the foundation for oral rabies vaccination in the United States—were now calling for caution regarding V-RG trials, particularly in the collaborations between the Texans and the Canadians, and the Canadians and Laura Bigler at Cornell. Some felt Rupprecht was doing an about-face in regards to V-RG because he increasingly had lost control over the vaccine. Hanlon disagreed: "I'm in really a kind of awkward position because initially—Chuck first, and then myself—we were the strongest advocates of the vaccine. And now our roles seem almost to be the brakes on the system. It's very bizarre how the pendulum swings like that. At first it was viewed with such suspicion. And now it's viewed as if it's water. I guess that's why we're such wet blankets on the whole issue of caution."

Although the vaccine was very safe, it was not totally safe, they argued. Particularly, they were concerned if someone whose immune system was weakened—a young child or an AIDS patient, for instance—became exposed to the vaccine. It was a slight risk, but still a risk. But would Hanlon still like to try V-RG in heavily populated Long Island? "I would," she said, adding her worry came down to "the fact that the vaccine has never been tested in humans. Personally, I don't want to be responsible for putting it out in the environment in a package that might be attractive to humans, and have that inadvertent experiment happen unless I felt I'd done everything I could to prevent it."

But the trial Hanlon did launch was perhaps more important from a research standpoint: dropping V-RG in a region near Albany where raccoon rabies had already moved in and taken root. The target was a 225-square-mile area in the southern portions of Albany and Rensselaer counties, an area surrounded by the Hudson River, the Helderberg Mountains, and the Taconic Range, which together form some geographic barriers to contain the enzootic. In October 1994, over thirty-one thousand baits were distributed in the area. By 1996, four baitings had been accomplished.

"We've effectively suppressed rabies in the vaccination area," Hanlon said. "It's expensive. But you can either live with raccoon rabies, as the South has done for fifty years, or you can entertain these methods and ultimately see there will be a payback. The question is, how soon?" As of late 1996, Hanlon was looking at another V-RG trial, erecting a vaccine barrier along Lake Champlain to prevent the outbreak from moving into Plattsburg, "one of the few population centers left unaffected with raccoon rabies on the eastern side of the Adirondacks."

Meanwhile, Bigler, working with the Canadians, distributed 180,000 baits in October 1995—half in Niagara County, the rest north of Watertown. Bigler is testing the Canadian bait filled with V-RG. Results of that trial are pending.

While the studies in New York were getting under way, Massachusetts state health authorities were launching another barrier trial to prevent raccoon rabies from reaching scenic Cape Cod. In May 1994, thirty-two thousand baits were distributed along both sides of the Cape Cod Canal. Tufts University researchers headed the project, with the participation of the CDC and several state agencies. Dr. Michael McGuill, a veterinarian and epidemiologist with the Massachusetts Department of Public Health, told the Boston Globe the idea had first come up in 1992, when officials considered erecting a vaccine barrier all along the Massachusetts border with Connecticut.

"But there wasn't much public interest and no funding could be found. The first case in Massachusetts hadn't been reported then, although we in the field knew it was inevitable." The first case of raccoon rabies in Massachusetts was reported in September 1992, and state lawmakers appropriated $120,000 for the Cape Cod project in 1993. Organizers of the effort credited a coalition of animal welfare, wildlife, and control officers, who formed a group called the Rabies Information Group, with lobbying for the oral vaccination effort.

V-RG in St. Petersburg

Although Hanlon never launched her Long Island study, the first true urban application of V-RG in the United States took place in St. Petersburg, Florida, in 1995. Pinellas County, a narrow, twenty-eight-mile-long peninsula, is home to nearly a million people. Prior to 1995, the county had been relatively free of rabies, with only two cases in domestic animals recorded during the previous twenty-five years. However in late 1994, raccoon rabies outbreaks popped up in two adjacent counties, Pasco and Hillsborough. State health officials placed those neighboring counties under quarantine and gave permission to Pinellas to look into launching a V-RG field trial. Kenny Mitchell, who headed the county's veterinary services, had followed the development of V-RG, and had contacted both Rupprecht and Rhone Merieux. "We're surrounded by Tampa Bay on one side and the Gulf of Mexico on the other," says Billy Howard, a veterinarian and operations manager for the county's animal services. "With that situation, it lent itself for us to be able to distribute the oral vaccine, and hopefully control the spread of rabies."

The original idea was to create a vaccine barrier to prevent rabies from entering Pinellas from adjacent counties. But the rabies outbreak was too fast for them. In July 1994, a rabid cat was reported in the East Lake area of the county. In January 1995, a raccoon and a horse also were confirmed with rabies inside Pinellas. The horse had tried to attack its handlers, and succeeded in mutilating itself. From that time, the number of cases rose quickly. Health officials suspected several of the cases were because of people relocating wildlife from adjacent quarantine areas. Organizers of the V-RG trial regrouped, and changed the goal to achieving a 50 percent reduction in cases based on the previous year's total, and to limit further spread of the disease. Low-cost pet vaccination clinics were quickly organized, and trapping begun to pick up stray pets and reduce the raccoon population.

The county ordered one hundred thousand of the baits—which had received conditional licensure from USDA around that time—and began distributing them by helicopter May 3 in the Oldsmar and East Lake areas. "The first place they dropped it was on the northern end of the peninsula, so if there were any raccoons coming in that way, hopefully they would get vaccinated before they get down into the county," Howard said. Within Pinellas, 130 square miles—just under half the county—were placed under quarantine, and the initial distribution focused on that zone. In highly populated areas, the baits were dropped in grid lines two hundred meters apart, at a rate of one per acre. "We don't put it on private property," Howard said. "We won't put it in someone's yard, but we'll put it along waterways, where raccoons would be, and in the parks and tree lines." The rest of the county was spot treated. The helicopter dropped 78,720 baits, with an additional 720 baits distributed by hand along the Pinellas Trail. When the helicopter had to be redeployed to perform its usual duties of spraying for mosquitoes, another 5,460 baits were dropped by hand in county parks and residential areas where residents had asked for treatment because of high raccoon densities. A "raccoon hot-line" had been set up for people to call and request baits.

The trial was relatively free of problems. One minor, if somewhat humorous, incident occurred when Charles Rupprecht, who flew in to assist the project, was stopped and questioned by police late at night on a section of beach, where he was distributing baits, dressed in casual garb. The officers apparently believed he was a vagrant. But the greatest concern of organizers, that people in the densely populated area would have contact with the baits, never occurred. "We have stamped on the baits that it's an oral rabies vaccine, and if there's any human or animal exposure to call the health department." One vaccinated dog ate two baits with no adverse effects. Raccoons trapped and bled after three months showed only one in ten with rabies-neutralizing antibodies. By the end of the year, Pinellas had recorded thirty rabies cases, which included twenty raccoons, seven cats, two otters, and a horse. Publicity about the outbreak prompted more people to vaccinate their pets—from 100,000 animals in 1994, to 154,000 in 1995, and 145 people underwent postexposure treatment.

In January 1996, county officials launched the second drop. The helicopter dropped eighty thousand baits, ground crews dropped an additional thirty-five thousand, and five thousand were held in reserve. Despite the low raccoon blood antibody levels, the program appeared to have achieved its stated goals as of May. During the first five months of 1996, only nine positive cases were reported, compared with eighteen during the same period the previous year. "We went from April to August [1996] without any cases, so that was real encouraging," Howard says. The Board of County Commissioners approved continued funding for the program in 1997. "We have it funded for one more year. We're going to get 150,000 baits and put them out—probably put out 140,000, and keep 10,000 in reserve. The way we've been doing it is if we have a positive case turn up, then we'll distribute some more baits in that area."

CHAPTER TEN

The Bats

Less than ten minutes north of the San Antonio city limits lies the greatest concentration of warm-blooded animals in the entire world. Bracken Cave is only about the size of a football field, but between March and November it houses between twenty million to forty million *Tadarida brasiliensis,* or Mexican free-tail bats. The pockmarked limestone walls make ideal roosting surfaces for the bats, whose body temperatures can warm the cave to around 100°F. Bracken Cave is shared only by dermestid beetles, who feed on nutrients in the guano, and on the occasional baby bat unlucky enough to fall to the ground (a company called Gardenville purchases the guano for fertilizer, scraping it up when the bats return to Mexico each winter). The beetles produce an ammonia so powerful that humans cannot survive in parts of the cave without special protective gear.

Each evening around dusk, during the months they are in residence, the bats emerge to feed. It is a remarkable sight. The almond-shaped entrance is cut from one side of a deep, almost perfect basin in the earth. As the sun begins to set, the mouth of the cave is black. The first sign of life is a rapid swirling suddenly visible in the darkness, like a fast-moving school of fish in murky water. Suddenly one daring bat emerges and hundreds follow, like a plume of smoke. They circle counterclockwise inside the basin for a few laps, then take off in a column—usually to the southeast, but sometimes to the north—climbing quickly to an altitude of a couple of thousand feet. A few red-tailed hawks sometimes hover in the vicinity; also watchful inside the basin are rat snakes, coach whips, a few raccoons—all hoping for a meal. "Everybody wants to get lucky," says Janet Tyburec, assistant director of conservation and education with Bat Conservation International (BCI).

Again the swirling, the emergence, the circling, and flight—this time a larger plume. The ballet is repeated over and over, for hours, until the cave has emptied of bats. Bracken is a maternity cave, containing only mothers and offspring; fathers roost in cooler places such as bridges, barns, and attics. The free-tails breed in Mexico and return to Texas in late winter or early spring to give birth. Like many other bat species in the United States, the free-tail mothers roost separately from their young, with the babies preferring the warmer, moist air near the cave's dome. "We used to think for the longest time that with twenty million mothers and twenty million babies, they just all herd nursed, because there's no way a mother could find her own." Biologists recently discovered that was not the case, that 90 percent of the time the mother located and nursed her own. "Only when other babies were trying to steal a drink as she was looking for her young, she ended up inadvertently nursing someone else."

The nightly exodus is so great and so dense that it appears on Doppler weather radar. Four U.S. Air Force bases call San Antonio home; early on they asked the landowners to seal the cave because the bats interfered with their pilots' maneuvers. The landowners, who for generations harvested the guano from the cave (it is now owned by BCI), refused, telling the Air Force instead to move their maneuvers. They did. The San Antonio International Airport also diverts air traffic during feeding time.

The bats fly up to one hundred square miles each night, consuming over a quarter-million pounds of insects, mostly migratory moths that fly at about ten thousand feet. The moth larvae are agricultural pests, and BCI is quick to remind people how much damage would result if the bats were to somehow disappear. This is not an irrational concern. Eagle Creek Cave in Arizona used to house more bats than Bracken—somewhere between twenty-five million and fifty million—but its census fell dramatically. The reason, BCI officials say, is because of mass destruction of bat habitat in Mexico, where vampire bats have caused millions of dollars in agricultural damage.

"Because vampires occur in Mexico, there's a lot of misinformation, a lot of suspicion," Tyburec said. "A lot of these caves are dynamited shut. They pile old tires in the entrances and burn them." BCI, which has not always had good relations with Mexican officials, has managed to survey ten bat caves just within the interior of Mexico. Over half had lost up to 90 percent of their populations from human intervention.

Beginning with the first burst of cold air in October or November, the bats leave Bracken and ride the front somewhere into Mexico—no one knows where—at speeds of up to sixty miles per hour. "As soon as they cross the border into Mexico, we're powerless to detect them," Tyburec said. "We've formed a lot of good alliances with some of the new regime with the Mexican Fish and Wildlife Services. They have a good initiative to survey caves and educate the community about the importance of these bats." In Mexico, "we don't know where they go. We don't know if they stick together as a big group, or if they split up into smaller groups. We don't know if they're all going to a single region with many caves, or if they're splitting up to different regions."

A Suspicious Death

In Bowie County, on the northeasternmost corner of Texas, family members became worried when an eighty-two-year-old farmer began having trouble swallowing, speaking, and walking. They checked him into an Arkansas hospital on November 4, 1993, and told doctors he had been perfectly healthy until the previous week, when he had become increasingly forgetful and confused. Once in the hospital, he lapsed frequently into hallucinations. Someone was standing on his feet, he complained. People were crawling out of the television set.

Doctors found he had a slight temperature, poor reflexes, tremors, and a stiffened tone in his arms and legs. A CT-scan showed widespread brain damage. They diagnosed him initially as having suffered a stroke, but by the second day they began to consider a range of other illnesses including tetanus and rabies. The family swore the farmer had not traveled to any rabies-endemic area, and hadn't been bitten by an animal.

His condition quickly deteriorated, and he was placed on mechanical support. On November 9, he was removed from a respirator and died. The Arkansas State Laboratory found a brain sample positive for rabies through fluorescent antibody testing; additional tests by the Texas Department of Health and the CDC isolated a virus linked to the silver-haired bat, *Lasionycteris noctivagans.*

His relatives were questioned again. The only suspicious incident they could recall was a cow that had died from unknown causes three months before the man's death. Health officials inspected his house and found no bats. However, there were plenty of openings into the attic and even living areas through which bats could have entered.

The farmer had a large family. Of twenty-seven members counseled about their risk, fifteen elected to receive postexposure treatment, including two who had been exposed to the dead cow. In addition, two morticians and fifty-five of the 110 Arkansas medical personnel who cared for the man were given treatment. The total cost of postexposure rabies shots exceeded $50,000.

The Context for Bat Rabies

By the time fourteen-year-old Rolando Bazan died in 1994, four Texans were dead from rabies since the canine epizootic began in 1988. Two of those deaths were from the canine strain, which was described as the most dangerous rabies outbreak in decades. A state of emergency had been declared in Texas, and a multimillion dollar campaign of eradication had been launched to stop canine rabies from sweeping further through the state. At the same time, an equal number of people were dead from bat strains of rabies.

In fact, between 1990 and 1996, thirteen of the fifteen human rabies deaths in the United States (in which exposure in a foreign country was ruled out) were from bat strains. Only one, Manuel Riojas, the Mercedes phlebotomist, knew for certain he was bitten by a bat. In three other cases, a bat or bats were found in a room of the house, but no bite or other exposure was apparent. In four others there was slight physical contact, but no apparent bite. In five there was no known exposure at all. Across the country in 1994, bats represented the third largest group of rabid animals, with 7.7 percent of all cases. Texas had the second highest number of rabid bats, second only to California.

In 1995, the CDC changed its recommendations for postexposure treatment regarding bats: "In situations in which a bat is physically present and the person(s) cannot exclude the possibility of a bite, postexposure treatment should be considered unless prompt testing of the bat has ruled out rabies infection." Those changes came after a couple of well-publicized rabies deaths, including eleven-year-old Kelly Ahrendt of Mamakating, New York. The strain of rabies that killed the child was confirmed as bat, but the family had no knowledge she had been bitten. On further investigation, it was learned a dead bat had been found in the family's home before she became ill.

Some are skeptical of the new guidelines. Bat Conservation International, the nation's largest advocacy group for bats, moved its headquarters in 1986 from Milwaukee to Austin, in part because of the Congress Avenue Bridge, where 750,000 Mexican free-tailed bats reside from spring through fall—the largest known urban bat colony. "Hundreds of people in this city have a bat in their house every day, and they open the window and let it out," says Barbara French, conservation information coordinator with BCI. "Or they put a box over it and catch it and let it go. I think it depends on where you live. If you live somewhere where there aren't very many bats, they can do that [give routine postexposure treatment]. You couldn't possibly do that here. They're everywhere. And interestingly enough, no one has ever gotten rabies here."

The risk of human infection from bat rabies is small, French argues, and overstating that risk only makes people more afraid of a beneficial animal that has gotten a lot of bad press over the centuries.

> *A bat in the public mind is a mysterious, mythical animal with all kinds of negative connotations to begin with. Then you associate it with some horrendous disease like rabies, and what happens is, you lose all sense of what really happens there. It's perfect sensationalized reporting material. It gets made into a very big deal.*
>
> *We never minimize the potential of rabies transmission from bat to human. That's a big deal for this organization. As far as we're concerned, you can't conserve an animal that you don't educate people about. This is wildlife. You don't interact with wildlife. We stress repeatedly two things: You don't handle grounded bats. The people who care for bats have had preexposure rabies vaccination. And the second thing, which is a common problem in Texas, is to get domestic pets vaccinated.*

In his book, *America's Neighborhood Bats,* BCI founder Merlin Tuttle notes the relatively small number of human deaths from bat rabies: "Placed in perspective, this means that the odds of anyone dying of a disease from a bat are much less than one in a million. In contrast, in the United States alone more than 10 people die annually from dog attacks, not to mention dog- and cat-transmitted diseases, honey bee stings, or food poisoning contracted at picnics. For people who simply do not handle bats, there is little cause for worry."

French says many people who die from bat rabies claiming not to have any exposure are later found to have handled bats after all. A twenty-four-year-old Alabama woman who died in 1994 removed dead or dying bats from her workplace. A forty-one-year-old West Virginia man, infected in 1994, shot a bat and picked it up to examine it, running his fingers along its teeth. A seventy-four-year-old California man who died in 1995 occasionally caught bats. "If you get bitten by a raccoon, what are you going to do? You're going to run to the doctor to get it treated. You get bitten by a bat, you may just go, 'Oh, that's nothing.' I've been bitten by bats lots of time. You know you've been bitten, but what's there to look at? It's nothing."

A Short History of Bat Rabies

Five humans in the United States are known to have died of rabies from exposure to Mexican free-tailed bats. Two of those deaths were blamed on exposure to aerosolized material they encountered while exploring Frio Cave, another large maternity colony west of San Antonio, in the 1950s. Some are skeptical of the claim, saying the two could easily have been bitten instead. Research, however, has shown that caged animals can contract rabies from aerosolized virus in bat caves. Still, with untold millions of bats filling the South and Central Texas skies each night, there have been remarkably few human exposures. In 1995, the rabies laboratory at the San Antonio Metropolitan Health District, which tests suspicious animals from its immediate county as well as surrounding ones, received nearly a thousand animal heads. Of those, sixty-one were positive—seventeen of them bats. This despite more than 20 million bats filling the skies each night during much of the year. Of course, 1995 was an unusual year for San Antonio, squeezed by the canine epizootic from the south, and the fox epizootic from the north.

In all, twenty-eight U.S. residents are known to have died of bat rabies. The first report of a human exposed by a rabid bat was in 1953 in Florida, when a seven-year-old boy was bitten on the chest while searching for a lost ball. The bat was tested for rabies at the urging of a ranch owner who employed the boy's father and had knowledge of rabies in vampire bats. The boy lived. It wasn't until five years later that a California woman, bitten on the finger by a silver-haired bat, became the first reported human fatality from bat rabies. However, a retrospective case was later uncovered— a Texas woman who died in 1951 after a bite on the arm by a bat.

Danny Brass, in his book, *Rabies in Bats: Natural History and Public Health Implications,* argues that rabid bats were probably present in the United States long before those initial reports. The Pima Indians feared bats, claiming that if bitten by one, a person "will go crazy and die." Since those initial reports in the 1950s, rabid bats have been reported in each of the forty-eight contiguous states.

The prevalence of rabies in bats remains cloudy. Although efforts have been made to sample bat populations, some experts argue it is the sick bats that often are easiest to capture from roosts to test. Denny Constantine, a former CDC researcher who still studies rabies in bats, found the overall prevalence among all bats low. "Most of the survey work that's been done, where people will go in and collect a large number of bats and test them all for rabies, indicates that with the exception of rabies in free-tail bats in the Southwest, about one in every thousand will be infected. In free-tailed bats, in Texas and New Mexico where I've done survey work, about one out of every two hundred has rabies. The same species in California, it's about one in a thousand. This contrasts with the bats that generally get into health departments, which will be sick bats or dead ones. Usually the cat brings them home. In that case it's about one out of every ten."

Health department statistics regarding rabies in bats are often based on those submitted for laboratory testing, a population extremely likely to be rabid. "Health department people frequently say, 70 percent of the bats in my city have rabies," French said. "Well, what it boils down to is 70 percent of the bats that were submitted to the health department for testing had rabies." Research looking at the Mexican free-tail, captured as they emerge from caves, is considered among the most reliable—finding less than 1 percent of apparently healthy bats rabid and rising to between 2 percent and 3 percent during migration, when the animals are stressed. At one time, some believed rabies in free-tails was the same virus as in vampire bats, since the two species can cross paths when the free-tails migrate to Mexico. But monoclonal antibody testing has proven this is not the case; the two strains are quite distinct.

The Vampire Bat

Vampire bats, or *Desmodus rotundus,* are found only in Latin America—from northern Mexico to northern Argentina. The vampire is the only bat species that feeds on the blood of other animals, although many people fail to distinguish this unpleasant trait among bat species. "I get calls from as far away as Wisconsin—where there will *never* be a vampire bat—saying, 'I think there was a vampire bat in my barn last night,'" says Barbara French. Vampire bats caused little harm for generations, French says, feeding mainly on tropical birds instead of livestock. "What happened was when you had a clearing of the rainforest and the land, and movement of cattle ranches, you provided this ready food supply," she says.

"The problem with the vampire bats is they're very destructive because there's a lot of risk of disease transmission—not just rabies. There's screwworm transmission. Multiple bats will feed from one bite. Vampires feed on animals along the perimeter of herds, so the same animals get bitten. The cost to cattle ranchers is millions, maybe even billions, of dollars in losses, and rabies is one of the diseases transmitted." Not only are cattle lost to rabies, but occasionally humans. Despite the myth, vampire bats tend to bite humans on the big toe, rather than the neck.

As the problem grew, ranchers and others began destroying bats by the thousands. "Unfortunately there was a misconception—which there commonly is—that a bat is a bat." Nonvampire bats were destroyed by indiscriminate eradication drives. In Brazil, eight thousand caves were poisoned or sealed with dynamite. BCI has launched an education drive throughout Latin America teaching ways to distinguish between vampire bats and other species important to agricultural interests such as the free-tailed, and fruiteating bats who disperse seeds through their droppings, maintaining the life cycle of the tropical forests.

A videotape distributed by the organization demonstrates two methods to kill vampire bats selectively. One involves spreading an anticoagulant paste on cattle. Only those bats that feed on cattle are killed. The other involves erecting nets that snare the bats when they drop to feed. The anticoagulant paste is then applied to the bats themselves, which are released. They fly back to their colony, where they groom one another, taking up the paste. This kills in larger numbers.

In 1995, Margot Martinez, the veterinarian in charge of the Texas Department of Health's Rabies Center of Excellence in Laredo, received a telephone call that a rabid vampire bat had been found near the Texas-Mexico border—much farther north than any previous report. Martinez was dismayed; with South Texas under siege by canine rabies, now they had to worry about rabid vampire bats? Fortunately, the caller proved to be wrong.

The Silver-haired Bat

Of the twenty-eight human deaths from bat rabies in this country, sixteen—or 58 percent—have been from a relatively uncommon species, the silver-haired bat. One of those, a thirty-seven-year-old woman, was infected by a corneal transplant from a donor with rabies (five other such corneal transplant infections have been recorded worldwide; the cornea can contain a large quantity of rabies virus). The silver-haired are tree-dwelling bats, typically shunning manmade environments in favor of crevices in tree bark, cliffsides, wood piles, and similar habitats. That makes their role in the transmission of rabies to people somewhat of a mystery. "The silver-haired is a fairly obscure bat," says Canada's Charles MacInnes. "So how come the majority of human deaths are the result of this one rather obscure animal? There's something about the strain of rabies in silver-haired bats, or something about silver-haired bats, which make them more dangerous to humans."

As the CDC's Jean Smith explains: "We don't really know why this particular variant is showing up disproportionately in our human cases. One of the explanations that's come forward is that, because this is a fairly reclusive bat species, when one is rabid it doesn't seek an appropriate place to roost, but tends to hide in a place where you'd not expect to see it—like a brush pile or behind a pile of wood. If you've had contact, you're not going to know it. And that's the story we get over and over with these particular cases, that the contact is superficial, that usually people don't know that they've had bat contact." BCI's French adds: "It's kind of a mystery."

Much remains unknown about these creatures, whose name is derived from the shock of silvery fur behind their black ears. They are found throughout North America, although they are less common in the South and Southwest. They are migratory, but appear to separate by sex—with only males found in southern states during the summer. They dine on a wide range of insects.

"It may be that just because we move to the suburbs that our contact with these silver-haired bats is increasing," Smith says. Biologists can't even be certain of their numbers, she adds. "A solitary tree-living bat is more difficult to assess in terms of population. You're just not going to find them. If you want to go out and look for house bats, you're going to find them everywhere."

Constantine believes cats play a big role in human bat exposures, whether its silver-haired or some other species. "If it weren't for cats, we wouldn't see many rabid bats, since they [the cats] generally bring them home." Not only are cats dropping them where people would be more likely to pick them up, Constantine said, but they may be harboring virus in their mouths. "If they happen to bite somebody or lick them on a mucosal surface, or in an open wound, they may be getting them infected that way. And the cat may not even die of rabies. They may just be a mechanical carrier in that case."

The Distinctive Nature of Bat Rabies

All bats, like any warm-blooded animal, can contract rabies. About forty species reside in the United States, but only three or four are commonly diagnosed with the disease. Those typically are the colonial bats, particularly the Mexican free-tail and big brown bat, *Eptesicus fuscus,* which congregate in large numbers, often near humans. Solitary bats, like the silver-haired or hoary bat, *Lasiurus cinereus,* have a higher positivity rate—probably because people are more likely to stumble upon a sick one. "While the free-tailed bat, and the big brown and myotis are submitted in large numbers to state health departments, you rarely get a silver-haired bat," Smith says. "It's a solitary, tree-living bat. It's not going to come in contact with humans under ordinary circumstances in a way that would be submitted to testing like a house bat would.

While very few rabies strains exist among land animals like foxes and skunks and raccoons, many of the bat species have their own distinct strain. "Bats tend to find their niche and remain distinct from other bats," Smith says. "They don't have a lot of contact with other species. So their little cluster of viruses becomes really tight. Like for the free-tailed bat, there's minimal [genetic] substitutions in isolates from free-tailed bats taken from California to Florida to Texas. It's the same population. We don't have samples from down into Latin America, but we would assume over the whole migratory range of this particular bat, they're circulating the same virus."

Vaccinating Bats

Not surprisingly, as the technology of oral rabies vaccination has moved forward in terrestrial animals, some have considered whether the idea might have merit in bats. Some are highly skeptical. A group of researchers at Rhone Merieux, which manufactures V-RG, laughed when the issue was raised. "Don [Hildebrand, president of the company] has been thinking a lot about how to insert a [vaccine] sachet into an insect," one says. Bats were not among the long list of mammals tested with V-RG, since they were unlikely to eat one of the baits distributed for raccoons. One researcher reported some success using a different recombinant vaccine in bats—but only in warm temperatures, not the cooler conditions that would be found during hibernation. Since hibernating bats would make a convenient target, some have suggested using an aerosolized vaccine within caves or similar habitat. Still others say an insect-borne vaccine is possible, although certainly a difficult technological challenge. Still, with the rapid advances in gene manipulation, and the success of efforts like the international screw-worm eradication effort—in which sterilized flies were released by the millions, successfully eliminating a major agricultural pest—it is not impossible to imagine.

The World Health Organization's Expert Committee on Rabies has suggested moving ahead with research into mass immunization of bats. But the idea is controversial. Brass writes: "With the exception of the special case of vampire bats in Latin America, modern scientific evidence is overwhelming in its support of the belief that the public-health hazards posed by bat rabies are extremely small. Even so, the public may not readily relinquish long-held fears. By functioning in a prophylactic capacity, such an immunization program might prove useful in helping to defuse public fears. Of course, the essentially preventive nature of this type of program would have to be stressed, lest bat rabies be mistakenly emphasized to the public. Such a program is certainly preferable to decimation of bat populations, which has been suggested by some."

And that was the real difference between bat rabies and canine rabies. Between the beginning of 1991 and May 1994 in South Texas, 1,149 people had required postexposure treatment at a cost of $492,314. Only a tiny percentage of those numbers were for exposure to bats, health officials said. Since human deaths from rabies are rare in the United States, public health officials have pointed to the high cost of postexposure treatment to justify wildlife rabies initiatives. While a significant percentage of the small number of human deaths were from bat strains, the economic impact of bat rabies was relatively small.

Mankind is gradually understanding the important role bats play in maintaining ecologic systems: eating insects such as mosquitoes; pollinating flowers and dispersing seeds in the rain forests. Still, they remain shrouded in fear and myth. Bats are small and night flying, difficult to see, linked forever with legends of vampires and Halloween. Despite popular belief, they aren't blind, and they don't get tangled in hair. Their large colonies make them targets for vandalism; nearly 40 percent of U.S. bat species are endangered, or nearly so. This negative image is not universal: in parts of the South

Pacific, the so-called flying foxes are tourist attractions and highly prized. Constantine said that public health workers often have been guilty of needlessly scaring people about the disease risk from bats. "We're all human. Most people like a good story, and often embellish on it a bit. The feeling among public health workers is not much different from the general public: they all know that bats are evil, associated with Halloween." In recent years, however, Constantine has noticed a shift in perceptions. "Now these days the attitudes have changed a lot, since they don't have money to make out of the deal like the folks in pest control. I tell them, I'm still working with bats, and frequently I'll hear, 'You're not hurting them, are you?'"

Pest control companies are another matter. Some claim to get rid of bats in homes or businesses, but actually increase the risk to people, French said. "One of the unfortunate things that happens is that someone will call an exterminator, who will come and spray poison. Well, you've created a big problem, because bats don't just die. They get sick inside the house. You can't eradicate a bat. They go up into tiny tiny crevices. Anyone who tells you, I can go in and exterminate those bats is pulling the wool over your eyes."

The greatest risk to humans is from handling bats, and the advice from experts is not to. "We provide educational materials for kids, and one of the most important things we say is, if you can walk up to and get close to a wild animal—a bat, a raccoon, anything—then something is wrong with that animal. You should never touch it," French says.

BCI offers brochures and advice on eliminating bats from dwellings without harming them. (BCI's address is P.O. Box 162603, Austin, Texas 78716-2603. They also have a World Wide Web site at http://www.batcon.org/). French says many times, the best advice may be just to leave them alone. "If you have bats living in a school, where you are likely to have unsupervised children, it makes sense to exclude bats from those buildings. The average person who had a couple of bats in the attic probably will never know it."

Bats that enter houses often are lost young animals, who may leave on their own if a window or door to the outside is left open. They can be caught with a net, or captured in a coffee can after landing on a wall (cover the opening with a piece of cardboard), and released outdoors. Never handle a bat with bare hands; use leather work gloves to avoid being bitten.

To prevent bats from roosting in a house or building, BCI recommends covering chimneys and vents with half-inch hardware cloth, and sealing other access routes. If bats already are roosting, suggests waiting until winter out-migration before sealing entrances. Such methods should not be used when young bats, still unable to fly, may be present (usually from May through August), or during sudden cold snaps when the bats don't leave nightly to feed. Trapped bats, BCI notes, can generate some fairly unpleasant odors. If bats must be evicted during the summer, the organization recommends attaching lightweight netting, hung at the top of bat openings with duct tape or staples "so the bat can drop down and get out, but they can't get back in," French says. "It's like a one-way valve. And its left like that for a few nights to make sure they've all gotten out, then you can seal it off. Unlike a rodent, a bat doesn't have the strength to chew something open. You also have to seal off any alternative openings at the same time, or they might just go around to the other side of a building and start going up another hole."

Even proper exclusion methods have led to unnecessary fears, French says. "People call and say, 'We excluded the bats from the building like you said. Now they're flying around in the daytime. Our public health people say that's abnormal behavior. They could be dangerous.' Well, they've just been excluded. They can't get back in. They're going to fly around for a while. That's where they've been roosting for a long time. That's not abnormal bat behavior."

CHAPTER ELEVEN

Exporting a Plague

It might almost have gone unnoticed, even in the open brush of this Starr County ranch—a half-rusted, blue-and-white Ford pickup, the kind you see everywhere in South Texas, almost disappearing into the vast and dusty landscape. But the large chicken-wire cage mounted to the bed of the truck piqued Sam Patten's curiosity, and so he drove closer to investigate. Patten, forty-nine, had just completed a bachelor's degree in wildlife biology from Texas A&M University at Kingsville, having returned to school at midlife to pursue a new career. He was wrapping up a research project he had begun as an undergraduate, working for the university's Kleberg Wildlife Research Institute, measuring white-tailed deer population densities, studying supplemental feeding, counting tracks. Deer hunting was a major part of the economy down here, and so the ranchers welcomed the researchers onto their land.

As he came closer, he saw a rail-thin Anglo, about thirty, wearing a dirty shirt and cap, and working with a thin wire snare. Patten was familiar with the snares. Ranchers and even Animal Damage Control used them along fence lines, attaching them at coyote "slides," where the animals would crawl beneath the fence. The snare would catch them around the throat and strangle them. But these snares had a stop on them, designed to capture coyotes without killing them. Patten had used similar devices in studies of mountain lions and black bears. In the back of the truck, Patten saw a heap of coyote fur, the half-dead animals piled together—at least a dozen, maybe more. Patten tried to speak to the trapper, but the man appeared nervous and started to leave.

"I've got to go," the trapper said. "These coyotes are getting hot. I've got to put some water on them."

Patten was familiar with the Animal Damage Control trappers; this wasn't one of them. He checked with the owner and found the man had obtained permission to take the coyotes. The ranch owner was delighted to see anyone removing coyotes from his property, resulting in a few less natural threats to the precious white-tailed deer. But the live trapping confused Patten, who couldn't imagine who would want to buy the animals. "You couldn't sell a live coyote on the street corner for a dollar. I thought, this is bullshit. They're going somewhere. And I started calling people."

The first person he called was Scott Henke, his former professor at A&M–Kingsville and an expert in wildlife diseases. Henke had done the baiting studies for the Texas Department of Health and was as knowledgeable about coyotes as anyone. They decided the coyotes were going out of state; in Texas they were too just plentiful to be worth anything, and almost uniformly considered pests. If that were the case, then the South Texas rabies epizootic could be making some major leaps in geography. Henke brought up the Florida raccoon epizootic, in which hunters were blamed for causing rabies to jump from Florida and Georgia up to West Virginia and Virginia after infected raccoons were shipped to restock hunting preserves in the mid-1970s.

Patten did some further checking, and what he found was alarming. That leap had already occurred, and health officials in Texas, Alabama, Florida, and at the Centers for Disease Control and Prevention in Atlanta were faced with a grim new threat. The South Texas canine epizootic was no longer contained to South Texas, and no vaccine barrier could be expected to keep the outbreak from spreading when human beings were physically moving rabid coyotes to other parts of the country.

The Coyote Black Market

Fox hunting, that sport of English nobility, has retained an amazing popularity among the less gentrified of the southeastern United States. The hunters, however, ride in pickups these days rather than on horseback; red and black riding outfits have been replaced by T-shirts and steel-toed boots; and the open, rolling English countryside is now enormous fenced coursing pens, stocked with foxes. And increasingly, even the foxes are being re-placed.

"The foxes can't hold up," says Bill Johnston, a veterinarian with the Alabama Public Health Department. "You put that many dogs on them in a place they can't get out of, they don't last long. The stress just kills them. But coyotes do." Coyotes will actually turn and fight when cornered, a trait that adds to the hunters' enjoyment of the sport. "Foxhounds are not good fighters. They're good smellers and howlers, but they're really kind of wimpy when they get something cornered that turns back on them," Johnston says.

In the final days of 1993, Johnston received a report of a rabid seven-month-old puppy in rural Alabama. It was the last case of rabies in the state that year, and as he investigated, he found the puppy was one of three that had died in a 250-acre coursing pen. The puppies had been showing rabies-like symptoms, prompting the owner to have one tested. When the test came back positive, a sample was sent on to the CDC for subtyping. The word came back: Mexican Urban Dog, the first case found outside South Texas and Mexico.

Health officials learned that the owner of the pen had been importing coyotes from South Texas, although he strongly denied it. They were told a tractor-trailer load of coyotes had traveled east on Interstate 10 to Marianna, Florida, which is a few miles from a junction where Georgia, Alabama, and Florida intersect. The truck had dropped off coyotes that were distributed to each of the three states. All of the coyotes brought into Alabama were placed in the one pen where rabies had been found.

"We quarantined it, pretty much put the guy out of business," Johnston says. "He agreed to depopulate it on his own, get rid of everything in there. And he did. He killed every coyote and fox and raccoon and every other carnivore in there."

But the incident left officials understandably nervous, particularly from the idea that the explosion of canine rabies in South Texas might be jump-started the same way in Alabama. "We've got beaucoups of coyotes—way too many," Johnston says. "Animal damage control is constantly trying to trap and move coyotes. I got a call yesterday from within the city limits of Mobile, in a large development, coyotes got into a garage trying to get into the dog food. They're just as adaptable here. They'll eat watermelons. They'll eat anything.

"Yeah, that scared us," Johnston says. "Because all we really have right now is rabies in our raccoons, and some sporadic bats. We had not had any canine rabies in a long time. The thing about coyotes is, dogs will go out and try to interbreed with them. They'll hunt with them. And when dogs get infected, people are going to get exposed more."

Johnston launched a survey of the fox hunting business. There were forty such coursing pens in Alabama—the largest one close to 1,100 acres—mostly located in the southern part of the state. "They pay maybe five dollars a dog to go in there, turn them lose. There may be ten or twelve good ol' boys who go in there with twenty, twenty-five dogs, and listen to them run." But what worried him most was the degree to which wild animals were being imported into the state. "We went through some health certificates over at the Department of Agriculture for one year, 1992. From North Dakota alone, there were over 1,700 red foxes shipped into Alabama legally on health certificates. I didn't look at any more years, any more states after that. We knew we had a problem."

State law prohibited the importation of coyotes, but it was clear they were being imported anyway. "In the survey we did, we found they would generally pay about seventy-five dollars for a coyote. If you could trap a lot of them, you could certainly ship them cheaply. You could sell several dozen and do okay, I guess."

The Florida Connection

The coyotes delivered to Florida created the potential for a much larger disaster. According to the CDC's Morbidity and Mortality Weekly Report, a Walker hound used for fox hunting escaped from an Alachua County, Florida, kennel on November 21, 1995. When it was caught, the animal was unusually aggressive and bit the kennel owner. It tested positive for rabies, and county health officials quarantined a twenty-square-mile area, finding 102 dogs and ten cats potentially exposed to the rabid hound. More than two-dozen people required postexposure treatment. On further investigation, it was found that two dogs from the same kennel had died on November 10 and 18, respectively. Neither had been tested for rabies. But over the next few days, four more dogs died, three from the same kennel and one from an affiliated facility. The CDC confirmed the strain as Mexican Urban Dog.

None of the dogs that had died were vaccinated. All had been in Florida for at least the past seven months. But most had hunted coyotes, health officials discovered (one that had not hunted had been housed with two of the rabid dogs). The kennel owners maintained a 320-acre fenced fox pen eighteen miles from the kennel. Between twenty and twenty-five coyotes that the owners said had been captured in Florida that February were placed in the enclosure along with gray foxes and raccoons.

Most alarmingly, four of the dogs had participated in a mass hunt with some four hundred other hunting dogs in late October. A massive investigation found none of those other dogs were known to have died of rabies. The Florida Game and Fresh Water Fish Commission began exterminating the animals within the fox pen, concluding that thirty-two coyotes, two gray foxes, two bobcats, and a domestic cat were at risk for exposure. None of those animals tested positive for rabies.

Citing the raccoon translocation, the CDC warned that "a recent surge in popularity of coyote hunting in the southeastern United States has resulted in an increase in sales of wild canids for fox pens; although coyotes are indigenous to that region, some of these animals may have been imported illegally. Intensified surveillance for this rabies variant is warranted in those states where residents participate in coyote hunting in enclosures."

A Quarantine Is Imposed

On January 13, 1995, the Texas Board of Health met in Austin to consider a request from Zoonosis Control to use its emergency powers to enact a statewide rabies quarantine. The idea initially had been to quarantine only South Texas. But state health officials had learned that one trapper, in anticipation of the quarantine, was planning to move his operation to another part of the state, and so they decided to make it statewide. The new rules made it a misdemeanor offense to transport any high-risk animal within or outside of Texas. High-risk animals included coyotes, foxes, raccoons, skunks, and bats. The same rules applied to any dog or cat over three months of age without a current rabies vaccination certificate, as well as hybrid animals such as domestic dog-wolf crossbreeds. "We know that South Texas coyotes have been shipped out of state to stock hunting clubs," said David Smith, the state's health commissioner. In addition, Smith said, they had learned that week that two of four foxes shipped by a trapper from West Texas to Montana had been positive for rabies. The same trapper had shipped animals as far away as the Netherlands. "This is a dangerous situation—one which can spread rabies beyond the point of our ability to control it," Smith said.

Privately, health officials acknowledged the rules held little bite, since

---

the offense was a Class C misdemeanor, similar to a traffic ticket, carrying a maximum fine of five hundred dollars. Law enforcement officials, too, were unlikely to waste much time citing offenders. At best, the rules would raise awareness among pet owners. At worst, it would drive the wild animal traffickers underground. Smith noted that state law already required owners to vaccinate pets over age three months. Including unvaccinated dogs and cats in the quarantine, he said, "really does reinforce the message that everyone needs to get their domestic animals immunized.

Ned Lammers, director of animal control for the San Antonio Metropolitan Health District, questioned the quarantine, saying it was unlikely to prompt an increase in pet vaccinations. "The problem I see in our community is we still have just as much apathy as we had before, as far as pet owners go." He predicted the new rules would make it harder for people to bring even properly vaccinated pets overseas, which could prove an impact on Texas' many military families.

Initially, the health department said the rules were temporary, and could be lifted when the threat of rabies had passed. They acknowledged that they had been reluctant to impose such action in the past because under state law, once a quarantine was declared, it would remain in effect until the quarantined area—in this case, the state—was completely free of any animal rabies for 180 days. It was unlikely, they allowed, that would ever happen.

With that in mind, on April 21, the Board of Health made the quarantine permanent. The rules were amended to exempt zoos (only accredited members of the American Association of Zoological Parks and Aquariums) and government employees such as animal control officers. Finally, bowing to pressure from animal welfare groups, the rules were amended to allow wildlife rehabilitators licensed by Texas Parks and Wildlife Department to continue caring for injured raccoons, if the animals were transported by employees or contractors with city or county animal control agencies, if the animals were vaccinated with rabies vaccine approved for raccoons and kept for thirty days after vaccination, and if the animals are released within ten miles of where they were captured.

Trappers or no trappers, the quarantine made sense in light of the forthcoming bait drop, Smith said. "Specifically, we're concerned that when we drop baits we have a containment area. and what the quarantine needs to do is make sure that these wild animals, specifically, stay where they are now."

Raising Awareness Nationwide

Keith Clark, the head of Zoonosis Control, had no love for coyotes. An avid outdoorsman, Clark had no problem with the idea of South Texas trappers getting the sixty-five dollars to seventy-five dollars each they were reportedly making off the live coyotes. "I think it would be great if we could somehow have South Texas coyotes be a cash crop for the ranchers," he says. It was only the threat of rabies that made the ban necessary. Clark had spent years trying to figure out why gray fox rabies had moved from east to west across Texas beginning in the 1940s, and then, inexplicably, had died out in East Texas in the 1960s. That was unusual for rabies, which typically spreads as an epizootic, then remains behind in an enzootic form, with the disease maintaining its presence in some level, with cyclic increases and declines. Clark had theorized the disease had gone away as the density of foxes had dropped—a result of higher fur prices and the gradual decline of small farms as a food source.

The risk of the South Texas canine strain spreading to other states was a point Clark hammered on again and again, particularly in lobbying for federal funds. Coyotes are found in every corner of North America, surviving on rabbits in the brush, stalking chickens and goats from the hedgerows of farms, and overturning garbage cans in alleys in the middle of cities as sprawling as Los Angeles and New York. "I said, you folks can ignore us if you want to, but remember—raccoon rabies was once confined to a small area of Florida. Coyote rabies seems to move at about twice the rate as raccoon rabies. Coyotes have a bigger home range. They're longer legged, can move over greater areas."

Enforcement

His encounter with the trapper still worrying him, Patten began his letter-writing campaign. He fired off letters to the Texas Department of Health, Gov. Ann Richards, U.S. Sen. Kay Bailey Hutchison, U.S. Rep. Solomon Ortiz, and others. Most sent him a polite letter back thanking him for his interest and forwarded his letter to state health officials. Some of the area legislators he wrote followed up more aggressively.

That summer, the Texas Legislature codified the health department's emergency rules. House Bill 721, written by Rep. Eddie de la Garza of Edinburg, increased the penalty for transporting high-risk wild animals, including coyotes, to a Class A misdemeanor, giving the quarantine considerably more clout. Now a violation could result in jail time. The bill deliberately excluded transportation of unvaccinated pets from the Class A category, but did increase the penalty for pet owners with a second or subsequent conviction to a Class B—punishable by a two thousand dollar fine and up to six months in jail. The law also gave veterinarians more power in local quarantine of animals they suspected might be rabid.

When the quarantine notices were posted at gas stations and convenience stores throughout South Texas, Sam Patten asked one store owner if he could have one. He tacked it to a door in his home, where it remains today. The notice warns:

> *The Texas Board of Health has determined that this area is effected or potentially affected by rabies, and has declared an area quarantine for the state of Texas.*

It went on to specify which animals are included under the quarantine and the penalties for improperly transporting them. Despite his role in enacting it, Patten—who currently is a wildlife biologist for the Texas Parks and Wildlife Department, stationed in Rio Hondo east of Harlingen—is skeptical.

"It's really a paper tiger law because its almost unenforceable. How are you going to enforce it? You can't stop every pickup truck crossing into Louisiana, and you can't guard every road that leads out of a county in South Texas. The federal and state law enforcement really aren't tuned into the regulation either. If they see a coyote in a cage in the back of a pick up it doesn't interest them at all. I don't know if the law is going to do any good. It will make the honest trappers quarantine their animals, and it will make the dishonest ones laugh."

But the entire problem of translocated animals, dramatically highlighted by the rabies cases in Alabama and Florida, had definitely captured the attention of state officials, particularly officials in the Southeast, says Buddy Baker, a state wildlife biologist in South Carolina. "Most southeastern states have now closed their border to the importation of canids for restocking purposes, and it's all tied into the fact that Alabama and Florida inadvertently brought the rabies in through their fox hounds. We've brought other diseases into South Carolina and North Carolina through the same means. It's an area of high concern for us."

In South Carolina, red foxes imported to restock hunting pens were infected with a type of tapeworm found only in north-central states, Baker says. That prompted the state to vigorously begin enforcement of statutes banning such animal imports—laws that had been on the books for many years. "It's not new legislation. We've always had the legislation in place, but our enforcement of those statutes has become more rigorous over the past few years because of the reports of these diseases being moved throughout the country. We've had a couple of really significant covert [law enforcement] operations that resulted in what we think is better compliance with our statutes than we had in the past. Our agency achieved a number of convictions and publicized them quite well, and I think it has served as quite a deterrent. I wouldn't be so bold as to say we have shut down our borders totally to importation, but I think we've curtailed that activity significantly."

Among the cases brought to light in South Carolina's sting operations was a shipment of coyotes, Baker says. "We made a case in the past year for a fox pen owner who had stocked coyotes that came from out of state." Asked whether the coyotes came from Texas, Baker declines to say. "I don't know. They [the law enforcement officers] say they've got some evidence, but without being able to confirm it, they don't want to implicate anybody or any state." The main thing, Baker says, is that these particular coyotes were free of rabies.

CHAPTER TWELVE

The Drop

The big day was not shaping up well for Gayne Fearneyhough. A thick fog had settled like a blanket over much of South and Central Texas, including the Pleasanton airstrip they had chosen as the headquarters for the airdrop. Two taxi-yellow Twin Otters, leased from the Ontario Ministry of Natural Resources, were grounded in Austin, along with another plane carrying U.S. Rep. Kika de la Garza and Health Commissioner David Smith. An 11 A.M. press conference had been delayed indefinitely, and a flock of reporters that included crews from CNN and CBS was starting to get fidgety. Two refrigerated trailers containing the baits sat at the end of the airstrip, while TDH veterinarians who had been gathered from field offices across the state milled around, along with Animal Damage Control people, a San Antonio unit of the Texas National Guard, an official or two from USDA, and two observers from Mexico.

Inside the control tower, which was really more of a shed on blocks (a severe storm would destroy it a few months later), technicians passed the time by going over the computerized tracking system that would guide the planes, with the assistance of global positioning satellites, on the zigzag routes they would take. Despite the seriousness of the threat that canine rabies would reach San Antonio and beyond, it was also an experiment—a fact that was reflected by the maps. The 14,400-square-mile drop zone, which stretched from one end of the state to the other, was divided into five zones. The dog-food baits would be dropped at densities of fifty and seventy baits per square mile; as would the fishmeal baits. Dog-food baits

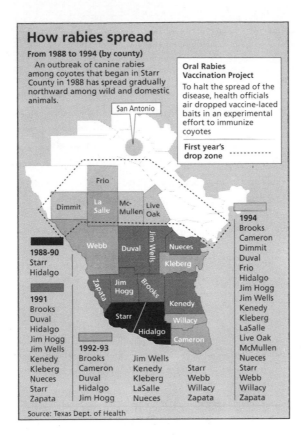

How rabies spread

From 1988 to 1994 (by county)

An outbreak of canine rabies among coyotes that began in Starr County in 1988 has spread gradually northward among wild and domestic animals.

San Antonio

Oral Rabies Vaccination Project

To halt the spread of the disease, health officials air dropped vaccine-laced baits in an experimental effort to immunize coyotes

First year's drop zone

Frio

Dimmit | La Salle | Mc-Mullen | Live Oak

1988-90
Starr
Hidalgo

Webb | Duval | Jim Wells | Nueces
Kleberg

Zapata | Jim Hogg | Brooks
Kenedy

1991
Brooks
Duval
Hidalgo
Jim Hogg
Jim Wells
Kenedy
Kleberg
Nueces
Starr
Zapata

Starr | Willacy
Hidalgo | Cameron

1992-93
Brooks
Cameron
Duval
Hidalgo
Jim Hogg

Jim Wells
Kenedy
Kleberg
LaSalle
Nueces

Starr
Webb
Willacy
Zapata

1994
Brooks
Cameron
Dimmit
Duval
Frio
Hidalgo
Jim Hogg
Jim Wells
Kenedy
Kleberg
LaSalle
Live Oak
McMullen
Nueces
Starr
Webb
Willacy
Zapata

Source: Texas Dept. of Health

An outbreak of canine rabies among coyotes that began in Starr County in 1988 has spread gradually northward among wild and domestic animals. Courtesy Texas Department of Health, graphic by Felipe Soto, San Antonio Express-News

alone would also be dropped at sixty baits per mile. Later, health officials would analyze which bait and bait density was most effective. The main barrier would be forty miles wide, from the Rio Grande north of Laredo, stretching in an arc into southern Bexar County (which contains San Antonio) down to the Gulf of Mexico north of Corpus Christi. The barrier would widen to sixty miles deep south of San Antonio. Some 830,000 baits in total would be dropped. Fearneyhough planned to hold back a few thousand in case they needed to bait any hot spots that arose later.

From September 1988, when the first rabid coyote entered Monte and Sue Smith's yard, to this foggy Wednesday, February 15, 1995, more than five hundred animals in eighteen counties had been infected with the canine strain of rabies, including 266 coyotes, 213 dogs, and forty-three other wild and domestic animals. Of course, the actual number of rabid coyotes was certainly much higher than the reported number of cases. In a forty-month period between January 1991 and May 1994, 1,321 people had received postexposure treatment, at a cost of $619,594. By the time of the first drop, the number of people treated was closer to fifteen hundred. Those figures did not include, officials noted, adjuvant medical costs, lost wages and productivity, the impact on tourism, or the costs to agriculture from livestock lost to rabies. It did not include the human suffering the rabies epizootic had caused. And it did not attempt to place a value on the two people who had died from the canine rabies strain.

As the afternoon began, and the fog refused to abate, the reporters were told the day appeared to be a washout and that, with luck, the airdrop would begin the following day. Most returned to San Antonio, an hour to the north. But in the late afternoon the fog began to break, and the Twin Otters were able to take off from Austin, touching down in Pleasanton about 3:15 P.M. The planes were quickly loaded for two short runs before dark, if for nothing else to give the Texans a quick feel for their responsibilities. Those included the careful loading of the baits onto special conveyor belts inside the airplanes.

"We're up," an obviously relieved Fearneyhough said in a brief telephone interview late that afternoon. Later, he admitted, it nearly broke his heart not to be onboard the first plane to take off that day, but fog-related delays and duties on the ground made that impossible. Still, there were plenty of opportunities ahead to ride along. The entire drop was expected to take nearly two weeks. "We had estimated about two weeks. The Canadians are telling me now they feel the efficiency is good enough we may be taking less than that—possibly ten days," Fearneyhough said.

Despite the enormity of the undertaking—the millions of dollars in direct and indirect costs, the manpower and the months of planning, the politicking, and praying—most of those involved continued to emphasize one critical point: that no one, really, knew for sure whether it would work. Rabies was forty miles south of San Antonio; if the epizootic reached there, it could sweep through that city's vast unvaccinated domestic dog population. If it passed San Antonio and moved out of Texas, it might be impossible to stop and, potentially, a national catastrophe. The stakes were huge. And yet, everyone from the Texans to the USDA to Rupprecht stressed that

Karen McDonald and Justin Henefey with the Texas Department of Health arrange
baits in rows on a conveyor during flight over South Texas.
Courtesy Jerry Lara, San Antonio Express-News

it was an experiment, albeit a large one. The bait zone health officials planned to erect from one end of the state to the other would contain two different baits and several baiting densities; they would later analyze which combination proved the most effective.

"This is an experimental program," Fearneyhough said. "It's a very large experimental program. I will be honest with you and say we hope we will have control impact, and will be able to stop this thing from moving. But the thing that's driving us right now is that it's confined to South Texas, and if we miss this year, it's probably going to be geographically too large to drop any baits." In a telephone interview at the time, Rupprecht struck a diplomatic tone: "It was only this time last year we talked about trying to do this in coyotes. It's hopeful, it's novel, it's exciting. But people shouldn't get too excited and expect too much."

The Bait Drop Begins

The real work of dropping baits began the following day, with crews rotating through the grueling three-hour flights. In each plane, a Canadian pilot and a Texas navigator sat in front, while a Canadian technician monitored two Texans loading baits onto the elaborate conveyor mechanism. More than one of the Texas volunteers required the use of air sickness bags stashed throughout the cabin. An extra seat in the back of the plane was occupied by observers, mostly reporters the first day or two, but other VIPs later on. Cruising at about five hundred feet, the planes flew over mile after mile of brush and small farms, interrupted occasionally by a few cows, a surprising number of white-tailed deer, and a farmer or two plowing fields. The navigator, who controlled the speed of the conveyor to maintain the desired density of baits, also had an emergency shutoff to avoid hitting the occasional human, or when flying over the small towns such as Poteet, Jourdanton, Beeville, and Cotulla which dotted the bait-drop maps.

Only the pilot and the navigator—and the observer, if one was aboard—had time to appreciate the view, or lack of one. The crew in the back of the plane was constantly busy, removing trays of the matchbox-sized baits from large Rubbermaid tubs and laying them carefully onto the conveyor belt, which was divided by long stainless steel tracks separating six rows of baits.

Texas Department of Health personnel load crates of vaccine-laden baits onto a Twin Otter to airdrop over South Texas. Courtesy Jerry Lara, San Antonio Express-News

At the end of the conveyor belt, prongs attached to a rotating metal drum caught the baits one at a time and rolled them into a chute that opened at the bottom of the plane. Between ten thousand and fifteen thousand baits per flight were dropped at intervals of about one each second. Through the observer's bubble window, the small baits could be seen dropping to earth in a steady stream.

"If a coyote hears a plane, will it start to run?" asked Gary Stewart, a Canadian pilot, apparently puzzled by the lack of coyotes visible in the brush. He described flying over vast herds of caribou, which would scatter as the planes flew low overhead on missions to vaccinate arctic fox in Ontario.

"They might run, or they might hide under a bush," replied Mike White, a Texas Department of Health veterinarian from Tyler, acting as navigator.

No one really expected to see coyotes, which prefer the cover of dusk and darkness. Still, one ADC official said, there's not much doubt they were out there, their brush-colored coats blending with the dusty landscape of South Texas.

The last of the 830,000 baits were dropped late in the day Tuesday, February 28, after 180 hours of flight. At the end of their mapped route, a few thousand baits were left over, and Fearneyhough decided to drop them around Laredo, a city of about 130,000 people on the border. About twenty thousand baits were being held back to treat any subsequent outbreaks within the drop zone. "It went really well," Keith Clark said. "The real proof will be nine or ten months from now, when we see what the incidence has been inside the zone, and on both sides of it."

Back in Austin, the Canadians were honored in a brief ceremony by state lawmakers and the Secretary of State's Office. They flew home on Thursday.

Checking the Results

Beginning thirty days after the end of the air drop, Animal Damage Control captured 446 coyotes from the five bait zones. Dave Johnston, who was no longer with the Ontario Ministry of Natural Resources, had agreed to examine teeth and bones for the presence of tetracycline to determine overall bait acceptance. On paper, the results did not appear encouraging. Initially testing was done in 230 of the 446 coyotes captured. In the three zones where dog-food baits were dropped, bait acceptance was evident only in a disappointing 14 to 22 percent of coyotes sampled. That percentage rose slightly to between 17 and 22 percent of younger animals whose bone metabolism would make them more likely to absorb the tetracycline. Even in the heaviest-baited areas of seventy baits per square mile, tetracycline was found in only 14 percent of all animals, and in 22 percent of younger animals between one and three years of age.

The two fishmeal zones fared better. In the lowest density of fifty baits per mile, acceptance was 31 percent for all animals and 41 percent for young animals. And in the higher density, the fishmeal baits were eaten by 69 percent of the young animals. Apparently the fishy smell was easier for the coyotes to find. The following year, the state would switch to all fishmeal baits. And a wide range of additional animal species had also swallowed baits, including armadillo, badger, bobcat, feral hog, gray fox, javelina, opossum, raccoon, and skunk.

But did the low percentages in many of the zones mean the baiting was unsuccessful? Clark and Fearneyhough argued it did not. "What we found was that Texas has an older coyote population than most places. We didn't know that before," Clark says. More than half of their sample of coyotes were three years of age or older. That was a larger percentage of older coyotes than had been found in other states—for instance, 25 percent in Iowa and 38 percent in Minnesota. Since tetracycline was harder to detect in older animals, the exact percentage of animals that ate the baits was impossible to determine, they argued—and in this they were backed by Dave Johnston, who had more experience at this than anyone. Among those coyotes that did have proof of tetracycline, one bit of good news emerged. The average number of baits—determined in bone the way rings in a tree indicate lifespan—eaten by the coyotes ranged between 2.1 and 2.6 for fishmeal and 2.4 for dog-food within the highest baited density. Their earlier research had shown the more baits eaten, the better the chance of successful immunization.

But that, too, was hard to prove, at least through blood tests. Of the young coyotes that showed traces of tetracycline in their teeth, indicating they had eaten one or more baits, only 40.3 percent had evidence of rabies neutralizing antibodies in their blood. Those percentages ranged from 25.9 percent to 42.9 percent for fishmeal, and 37.5 percent, 42.9 percent, and 100 percent for dog food (the 100 percent was within the zone with the lowest density of dog food, resulting in the poorest tetracycline results). Several of the animals that did not show evidence of tetracycline had rabies neutralizing antibodies, but most did not. In all, only 41 of 230 coyotes captured and tested had rabies titer levels.

So what did that mean for the hope of erecting a barrier of vaccinated coyotes, to prevent the incursion of rabies, when only 17 percent of coyotes have evidence of rabies neutralizing antibodies? We don't know, admitted Clark and Fearneyhough. But they warned against reading too much into blood antibody levels either. The vaccine, they argued, may have produced more cell-mediated, rather than humoral—or blood-circulating—immunity against rabies, which would not be detected by simple titer measure. The real test becomes San Antonio. The real proof is whether the vaccine barrier holds.

Rupprecht's Thoughts on the Texas Drop

The Texas distribution of V-RG was by far the largest and most complicated to date on American soil. It was also the first that wasn't attended by Charles Rupprecht, the man most responsible for the vaccine's development. "He wasn't invited," Fearneyhough said bluntly in Pleasanton during the airdrop. A few months later, in a lengthy and wide-ranging interview at his office at the Centers for Disease Control and Prevention, Rupprecht was at times philosophical, at times humorous, at times angry with the Texans, the Canadians, and their vast experiment in South Texas.

"We haven't been invited to visit Texas. I guess you'd have to ask the Texans [why]. Texas is the only field site per se that CDC hasn't been invited to have access to and participate in. Since our priorities are national, we continue to focus on surveillance issues beyond Texas—since Texas appears clearly to have this issue in hand without CDC's direct participation beyond that first phase."

Rupprecht was plainly bothered by the way he perceived the Texas campaign had been sold to the lawmakers, the regulators, and the public. "There was a difference in perception from the start. Ours was that it was an experiment, not a control program. You didn't have the empirical data to suggest that it would work. It should have been sold on that basis, and not that this is a control program. After more than a decade of work with raccoons, we still don't have a control program for raccoons."

Although he wasn't present in Texas, his involvement in the effort was clear.

> You wouldn't have had the Texas drop without direct CDC participation. We did all the basic groundwork that asked the question: Was this vaccine safe and efficacious in coyotes, delivered in a bait or not? If you didn't have that work, you wouldn't have had

*your field trial. We not only continue to work on surveillance issue
in the coyote (rabies) variant, but also rabies vaccinology orally,
and coyote bait development directly.*

*Any state is free to do what it wants to as long as it doesn't
endanger the public health. In which case we only participate on a
state-invited basis. We walk a very fine line with our constituents.
There's been problems in the past where the agency raises a flag too
much, and there's always a little tension between the state and
CDC—as there always is, almost laughably, in any TV sitcom between the feds and the locals. Look at the* X-Files *(a television program about federal agents investigating paranormal mysteries) or
at any of the* Die Hard *movies as to who are the antagonists and
protagonists.*

As for the partnership with the Canadians: "As far as our Canadian
colleagues are concerned, they're not doing this for free. They're even charging
for things that I feel that, as spelled out in our national mission statement,
we don't have the ability to charge for—and that's people's salaries. It's not
as if it's just fuel that's being paid for. Nobody's to say it's not a good deal,
but it's not free. One would hope with traditional American entrepreneur-
ial spirit, that the service being provided by the Canadians would someday
be provided by the U.S. to solve its own problem."

The CDC was continuing to look for a better oral vaccine, one that
would work better and safer. Although V-RG was very safe, Rupprecht
says, it was not without any risk. The vaccinia could theoretically cause
illness in immune-compromised humans. "The whole vaccinia concept is
almost passé, in the sense that it was the first-generation recombinant." He
is vague about what type of vaccine his group is working on, saying now a
better approach would be to go with an "Nth-generation recombinant, or
to an inactivated vaccine, or to a conventional attenuated," or possibly
microencapsulated—presumably to bypass the stomach acids and be absorbed in the gut. "Hopefully a new approach will be able to address some
of those concerns."

He would be skeptical of the Texas campaign's results, even if the outbreak were to be stopped. "If we haven't seen further spread, then certainly
it could be a temporally related outcome of the project," Rupprecht allows.
On the other hand, he adds, if Baer and his colleagues had gone ahead with
oral vaccination of foxes three decades earlier, they might have been cred-

ited with stopping the fox rabies outbreak in northern states, even though fox rabies died out on its own. "We don't have an explanation for that. I can't think of a reason why that would be going on in Texas, but in lieu of more rigorous scientific peer review and analysis of those data, you have to keep an open mind."

Some Get Through the Barrier

On May 30, an Atascosa County sheriff's deputy spotted a coyote and chased it through a peanut field and subdivision west of Pleasanton, not far from the airfield that served as headquarters for the airdrop. The deputy shot and killed the animal. Two weeks later, near Jourdanton, also in Atascosa, a coyote attacked four dogs. The dogs killed the coyote. Both animals tested positive for rabies.

Those positive cases were well inside the barrier. Clark and Fearneyhough waited to see if the two cases were isolated, but on July 28, a third rabid coyote was reported in Atascosa, inside the Poteet city limits. In that case, a coyote tried to attack a man through a fence. The man shot the coyote, which later proved rabid.

"This is of concern, but it is by no means a disaster or unexpected," Clark said. In fact, they had held back twenty-five thousand baits for just such a hot spot. On August 14, Fearneyhough and a couple of other TDH veterinarians, along with an Animal Damage Control pilot, flew over a 250-square mile area of central Atascosa in a small ADC helicopter, dropping the baits by hand over three days. "The pilot is experienced in wildlife movement, so what we've told him is, you fly like you're looking for coyotes, and we'll drop baits along that terrain," Fearneyhough said. "A coyote moving from point A to point B is going to choose the easiest way to get there." That becomes important, Fearneyhough said, because coyotes are less hungry in the summer months, and tend not to move as far. They also eat less meat and more vegetation, including watermelon and cactus.

State health officials acknowledged that the hot summer months were exactly the wrong time to drop baits. "Because of the hot weather, the coyotes aren't moving as much," Clark said. "They have quite a bit to eat right now, and the fire ants are pretty active" to compete for the bait. In subsequent weeks, two additional rabid coyotes were reported, but by the end of the year, it appeared the outbreak had fizzled.

Meanwhile, some local health officials, particularly Ned Lammers in San Antonio, were frustrated by the delay in getting preliminary results of the airdrop. Rabies was at his back door, and Lammers, who had done as much as he could to be ready for the outbreak, wanted as much information as possible. The outbreak in Atascosa, along Bexar County's southern border, was particularly worrisome. "It's not just a little cluster," Lammers said, "it's the extension of this epizootic continuing to move northward. I honestly believe we're going to have a rabid coyote in Bexar County by the first of February."

Clark denied officials were delaying release of the results from the drop, saying that as of August, only about 20 percent of the data had been analyzed by Dave Johnston. The final report probably would not be completed until the end of the year when the next drop was scheduled. However, an interim report would be presented in October to the USDA, which funded the initial drop. The USDA had already made it clear there would be no more money coming from their contingency fund. But Clark had managed to leverage the highly publicized first-year campaign, along with the continuing threat of rabies, to obtain funds from the Texas Legislature for the second and third years of the project (Texas budgets are written for a biennium). The remainder for the second year's drop would be scavenged from the Texas Department of Health's own budget. For the third and subsequent years—well, Clark had been flying by the seat of his pants so far. He would solve that problem when he came to it.

The Debate Rages

Between October 24 and 27, the Seventh Annual International Meeting on Research Advances and Rabies Control in the Americas was held in Merida, Mexico. All the leading rabies researchers in the hemisphere shared their latest findings, successes, failures, and speculations with their colleagues. Rupprecht led off a section on oral vaccination. To be fully successful in the Americas, Rupprecht said, a number of questions have to be answered: What is the relationship between the density of baits and the density of the animals being vaccinated? What percentage of immunization is required to eliminate the disease, rather than merely limit its incidence? Is aerial distribution or handbaiting better? Baiting in a random grid, or targeting animal habitat? What is the likelihood of long-term, sustainable funding to allow regional cooperation in such programs? And perhaps most importantly, what is the cost of rabies itself, compared to the cost of eliminating it—in terms of the biology, the ethics, the economics? Until those questions are answered, he said, it is unlikely that oral vaccination programs will ever be widespread—much less extended to the far more severe and deadly rabies problem in developing countries.

But subsequent speakers made it clear that the oral vaccination strategy and technology was moving forward. Sam Linhart, a biologist with the Southeastern Cooperative Wildlife Disease Study—and Jean Smith's husband—told of a collaboration to study which vaccine bait worked best in Israeli red foxes and Egyptian dogs. Researchers from the laboratory established by George Baer in Mexico also discussed ongoing work in orally vaccinating dogs. Texas, Ontario, and New York researchers discussed their programs. And Hilary Koprowski's program at Thomas Jefferson University unveiled a new vaccine strategy, one that used another part of the rabies virus, the ribonucleocapsid, spliced to bacteria and viruses that can infect edible plants. The first approach was to grow tomato plants bearing the rabies gene; so far, they had yet to achieve a plant with potent enough immunogenicity to protect animals. Still, the strategy, they said, was a promising one.

An Official Assessment of the Texas Effort

By the end of the year, Texas health officials were confident the barrier had slowed, if not stopped, the northward progression of the canine rabies epizootic. The front of the outbreak had been moving north at about fifty miles per year. That movement had more or less ceased since the baits had been dropped in February. At that time, the northernmost canine rabies case had been in Atascosa County (months before the so-called hot spot that resulted in the additional baits being distributed), about forty miles southwest of San Antonio. At the rate it had been progressing, canine rabies would have entered San Antonio by the end of 1995, with the risk increasing during the last four months of the year when adolescent coyotes break away from their packs and search for new home ranges.

In fact, based on previous years' observations, had the airdrop not taken place, they would have expected a canine rabies case rate of 19.7 per ten thousand square miles within the 15,000-square-mile drop zone between April 15 (when coyotes which had eaten the baits would have had time to develop rabies-neutralizing antibodies) and August. Instead, the case rate was 5.2. This was the epidemiological evidence Clark and Fearneyhough pointed to as they prepared for the second year of the program.

"It appears to be having a good effect in controlling that outbreak," said Robert Miller of the USDA. "The downside of that study is you don't have any positive control area to say, here's what happens if you don't vaccinate and here's what happens if you do. But if they are successful in pushing rabies down to the Rio Grande area, if they can clear out that Central-South Texas area, I would say it shows the vaccine can be effectively used in coyotes as well as raccoons. The first year results look very nice."

Round Two

January 6, 1996, was like a recurring nightmare to the Texans. Arriving at Cotulla for the launch of the second year's bait drop—an effort that would be twice as large as the previous years, and bigger than anything even the Canadians had attempted—they were once again grounded by pea-soup fog that covered the entire region. This time, three Twin Otters had flown in from Ontario, along with MacInnes, Dave Johnston, and the crews; even Laura Bigler from Cornell would drop by later for a visit. But no one from the CDC. Occasionally the skies would clear a little, and one of the planes would take off, only to return quickly. "One of the pilots from Ontario called it a sucker hole," Fearneyhough said. "You think it's clear, but once you get up its foggy all around."

The first year's barrier had held. This year, a far larger area of South Texas, some eighteen thousand square miles, would be baited—1.3 million baits at a density of seventy baits per square mile. The new bait zone was mostly in a pyramid shape, with the tip resting just south of San Antonio—plus the addition of a thirty-mile-wide strip across the border from Laredo to the Gulf of Mexico. Clark and Fearneyhough had originally proposed a seven-year plan that would gradually push back rabies to the border; now they were saying the outbreak could be eliminated by the end of the decade, in only three or four more years. If they moved the northern boundary of the drop zone a little bit south, it was theoretically possible to drop baits over all of South Texas. It would be a huge logistical effort, but it could be done.

Things had gone well enough so far that Clark, that consummate salesman, might be able to convince lawmakers to pay for it. For this year, he had secured four million dollars—half of it emergency funds appropriated from the legislature, and the rest from internal Texas Department of Health operating funds. Health Commissioner David Smith explains, "One bait costs about $1.50. It costs more than one thousand dollars to treat someone whose been exposed to rabies and more than thirty thousand dollars to treat someone who gets rabies before they die, which they will. And of

Texas and Canadian crews pose for a group photo in Cotulla during the 1996 airdrop.
Courtesy Texas Department of Health

course the dollar value of a human life is incalculable. We're not doing this for coyotes. We're doing it for people."

As it was, they had gotten the money to launch a second field trial of V-RG in gray foxes in Central Texas. More than three decades after George Baer first began studying the problem of vaccinating foxes against rabies in the United States, the Texans were finally going to do it. The fox bait drop, which would be almost as large as the coyote drop at 1.2 million baits, was a giant C-shaped barrier that began at the Rio Grande above the Big Bend, extended well into North Texas, and back down to the northern tip of San Antonio—a city that had seen a record year for rabid foxes in 1995, with twenty-four positives.

Despite the scope of the fox project, there was reason for uncertainty. Dave Johnston had done some radio tracking of foxes for the Texans, placing transmitters in baits and waiting to see if they were picked up. Of the baits he rigged, only one was disturbed by a fox—and that one cached the bait away for a later meal. But the USDA was allowing them to go ahead with the trial. In Robert Miller's mind, the safety questions about V-RG were largely answered. If there was even a reasonable expectation of success, he said, it was worth a try.

The Scope of the Problem

Of course, even if it worked—if V-RG eliminated both canine and fox rabies in Texas—bat rabies would still exist. And so would rabies in skunks.

That was true across the country as well. Each December, in its annual report on rabies published in the *Journal of the American Veterinary Medical Association,* the CDC produces a map showing the distribution of animal rabies in the United States. To look at it, one might think skunk rabies to be the nation's biggest rabies problem. Three separate viral variants in striped skunks (*Mephitis mephitis*) are found in California, the north central states and the south central states. The two enzootics in the central United States meet in the middle near the border between Kansas and Nebraska, resulting in a sea of skunk rabies extending across the northern states from Montana to Pennsylvania, and across the southern states from Arizona to Louisiana. Skunks were the leading species for rabies in the United States from 1961 until 1989, when they were displaced by raccoons, due to the fierce intensity of that epizootic across the East Coast. In 1994, 17.6 percent of all rabid animals in the country were skunks.

But people and pets labor to avoid skunks under most circumstances, and so the public health threat from skunk rabies may be the least of all major vectors in the United States. Whereas a rabid skunk might attack, the malodorous tip-off that the animal is close usually provides ample opportunity to flee. And while a dog might attack a rabid fox—or a cat might drag home a rabid bat—all tend to give skunks a wide birth. In Texas, with perhaps the most complex rabies problem of any state, skunk rabies has declined steadily since a peak of 857 cases in 1979, and in 1994 they were supplanted by foxes as the state's leading rabies vector.

Foxes, which some virologists describe as the species most susceptible to rabies, became the most commonly reported rabid animal in Texas in 1994 as a result of the gray fox rabies epizootic in Central and West Texas. The number of fox rabies cases jumped that year to 264 cases, from fifty-three the previous year. Across the United States, foxes were the fourth leading rabies vector, making up 6.5 percent of all rabies cases. But that percentage, too, was rising, with four separate pockets of fox rabies in Alaska, Southeastern Arizona, Texas, and along the borders between Canada and New York, Vermont, New Hampshire, and Maine. Gray foxes carried the disease in Texas and Arizona, while it was red and arctic foxes in Alaska and New England. And as with raccoon rabies on the East Coast, fox rabies tended to put domestic cats at highest risk for crossover infection. Between raccoon and fox rabies, cats were the domestic animal most often reported rabid in the United States (267 cases in 1994, compared to 153 dogs and eleven cows). Texas was third among states in the number of rabid cats, behind New York and Pennsylvania.

The Numbers Are In

Because of the success of the fishmeal baits, fishmeal was the only bait selected for coyotes. However, a smaller, sweeter version of the dog-food bait had been developed for the foxes. Scott Henke at Texas A&M–Kingsville had tested them for palatability. And in a growing sign of the program's success, a commercial firm had jumped in this year. Hills Food Company, which manufactured the Science Diet line of pet food, had provided a special flavor-enhancing secret sauce they had developed for their medicinal dog foods. The Texans had agreed to treat a portion of the baits with the sauce in a double-blinded study to see if uptake was improved. Fearneyhough had given executives of the company a briefing at their Topeka, Kansas, laboratories. They had also discussed a microencapsulation process Hills had developed that looked promising as a potential future replacement for the plastic vaccine sachets used inside the V-RG baits.

The South Texas coyote baiting took two weeks. This time, the team had purchased a trailer to house the computer mapping and tracking operations. As South Texas wrapped up, they left the Cotulla–La Salle County Airport in Cotulla and moved their headquarters to Fort Stockton in West Texas for a week, followed by Brownwood in North Texas, and finally, Burnet, northwest of Austin.

Between the beginning of the coyote baiting and the completion of the fox baiting, a rabid coyote was discovered near Fredericksburg in the Hill Country, well north of either the first or second year's barrier zones. The coyote, which was killed by a Gillespie County rancher, turned out to be infected with the fox strain, rather than the canine strain, meaning the barrier still hadn't been breached. A skeleton staff at zoonosis control at the Texas Department of Health didn't bother Fearneyhough with the matter. "He has enough on his mind," one colleague said.

As the entire program wrapped up, some 2.5 million baits had been dropped over thirty-five thousand miles of South and Central Texas. Nearly eighty of the state's 254 counties were included in the baiting. More than 672 rabid animals had been recorded in South Texas since the canine epizootic began in 1988. About two thousand people had undergone postexposure treatment, and two people had died from the canine strain.

On July 15, 1996, shortly before he presented a paper on the project at the annual American Veterinary Medical Association meeting, Gayne Fearneyhough sent an e-mail message to the staff at the Texas Department of Health:

> There has been a series of "good news reports" coming from the early results of the 1996 ORVP Surveillance. A brief summary is as follows:
>
> 1. The measurable immune response in coyotes collected in 1995 and 1996 has increased significantly. In 1995, only 15% of all coyotes taken from the bait drop area had a measurable immune response ("all coyotes" includes both animals which were identified by tooth analysis as having eaten a bait and those which had not; those which had not eaten a bait obviously should not be considered in the study to determine immune response). Laboratory analysis of tooth specimens revealed which had actually eaten a bait and in 1995, 42% had an immune response. In 1996, 50.8% of all coyotes now have an immune response, and when we are able to further define which animals have actually eaten a bait, the percentage of immune responders should be even better. Therefore, we already have better results than last year and that is before we identify which animals actually have taken a bait containing vaccine.
>
> 2. The mean titer or the strength of the immune response has increased from 1:13.4 in 1995 to 1:50.6 in 1996—almost a 4-fold increase. This is mostly likely due in part to an amnestic response [intensified immune response] in animals that ate a vaccine in 1995 and were boosted in 1996. We have identified animals that consumed multiple baits in 1995 and 1996, those that ate only in 1995, and some that ate only in 1996 and will compare serologic responses when all the data is in. That data will allow for some interesting information on duration of immunity.
>
> 3. The number of animals showing "biomark" or evidence of a marking agent in the teeth has increased from 42% in 1995 to 69% in 1996 (approximately 50% of the 1996 specimens have now been processed for biomark determination). We have learned that the biomark process doesn't work as well in the older animal and that greater than 90% of the younger animals are biomarked, therefore the true percentage of animals eating a bait is between 70% and

90%. Those are much better numbers than we had hoped to achieve when we started in 1994.

4. The mean number of baits eaten by each animal has increased from 2.6 in 1995 to 7.5 for the juvenile animals in 1996. The range of baits eaten is from 2 to 19 in 1996. Apparently coyotes like the baits and can follow yellow airplanes. Dr. Dave Johnston's comments were that no one in Canada, Pennsylvania, New York or New Jersey has achieved that level of success in individual bait acceptance.

5. The code has not yet been broken on which animals were from the separate "palatability product" study that involved the addition of a "secret sauce" from Hill's Food Company applied to baits dropped over a 900 square mile area. Hopefully, we will find that product enhanced acceptance and immune responses.

All the numbers are not counted yet, but it looks very promising so far. Everyone should give themselves a pat on the back. It has been a fantastic team effort, but we aren't done yet, still more to do in South and Central Texas.

As 1996 came to a close, canine rabies in South Texas appeared to be sputtering to a halt. Since March 15—roughly two months after the second distribution of baits—only four cases of rabies had been reported within previously baited areas. Health officials began their counting March 15 because the coyotes would have had time to mount an adequate immune response in that period following the second airdrop. An additional six cases were reported in unbaited areas during the same period. That compared to 142 cases of rabies in South Texas during all of 1995.

Not everyone was willing to give complete credit for the decline in cases to the Oral Rabies Vaccination Program. William Lammers, San Antonio's animal control director, noted that during 1996, South Texas had experienced its worst drought since the 1950s. Around the time of the second South Texas airdrop, San Antonio began its second-longest dry spell in history, a sixty-day rainless period that ended February 29.

"We can't ignore the fact we're in a drought situation, and a drought is sure going to have an influence on wildlife populations—affecting not only the predator, but also its food supply," Lammers said. "I'd hate to say it's one thing or another. I can't help but feel it's a combination of events."

Gayne Fearneyhough acknowledges the drought may have played a role, but says that role was unclear. Estimates of coyote populations in South Texas remain high. "White-tailed deer populations have suffered more severely than the coyotes, so the predators are doing quite well on the weakened fawns and white-tailed deer," Fearneyhough says. But the drought definitely affected coyotes. Newspapers throughout South Texas carried accounts of unusually aggressive coyotes entering urban areas and neighborhoods in search of food. Many small pets became meals for hungry coyotes, and Animal Damage Control trappers were busier than usual.

As for Lammers, he had cause for concern. While a massive pet vaccination campaign in 1995 resulted in tens of thousands of pets protected against rabies, a series of clinics in 1996 attracted little response. Perhaps people were used to living with rabies, he says; certainly there were fewer television and newspaper reports about rabies, so it wasn't a front-burner issue. One clinic October 19 drew only about 500 people. In most years, such a clinic would have attracted five times that many.

But it was also true that private-practice veterinarians, animal groups, and even pet stores had stepped in during the year, advertising low-cost rabies vaccinations and vaccination clinics, and so many people certainly took advantage of those, Lammers acknowledges. So what level of rabies protection did San Antonio have? As the canine rabies epizootic approached, Lammers had estimated fewer than a quarter of owned dogs were vaccinated; in 1995, in the wake of an intense public health drive, he guessed that percentage could have grown as high as 50 percent. But as 1996 came to a close, he admitted he didn't really have a clue.

"Unfortunately, of the animals that are reclaimed from the animal control facility, about 90 percent of the time the owners haven't had their pets vaccinated, or can't demonstrate proof of vaccination. And all they have to do to demonstrate proof is give us the name of the veterinarian and we'll call them up. Which tells me in most of those cases they're just not currently vaccinated. I feel that we have more pets vaccinated now than we had two years ago. But to put a figure on that and say, we've got X-percent vaccinated—I just don't have a good basis to do that."

The Argument for Oral Vaccination

On Saturday, December 7, 1996, exactly one month to the day before the planned launch date of the third year of the Texas Oral Rabies Vaccination Program, a select group of some eighty-five scientists, public health officials, and drug company executives converged on the campus of the University of Georgia in Athens, also the home town of Rhone Merieux. The weekend gathering was designed to focus a hard look at the progress of oral rabies vaccination to date, and to consider strategies for moving it forward, particularly in the United States. The gathering was timed to precede the annual meeting on rabies in the Americas, which would take place the following week in Atlanta.

Opening the meeting was Charles Rupprecht, who could reasonably be called the father of V-RG, but whose public remarks toward the idea of oral rabies vaccination had sounded increasingly skeptical in recent years. The problem of rabies in the United States, he began, was "one of the most complex in the world." Unlike other countries, which had perhaps one or two rabies hosts, the United States had distinct viruses in raccoons, foxes, skunks, dogs, coyotes, and a host of bat species.

Public perception of rabies would be key to the wide scale use of oral vaccine, Rupprecht said, noting that most of the pilot baiting projects in the United States to date were grassroots efforts, more or less, with local health departments and advocacy groups demonstrating the strongest support. That public perception of rabies may be out of proportion to the reality of actual risk, he said. "There's probably more mythos associated with rabies than any other disease." Although rabies probably was present in the Americas at the time of the Conquistadors, the highest number of reported human deaths from rabies in the United States—given the lack of

Charles Rupprecht (left) discusses oral rabies vaccination with an Israeli health official at the December 1996 conference in Athens, Georgia. Photo by author

diagnostic testing—occurred near the turn of the century. "A lot of people are surprised to find out that it's only about 100 or so (143, in 1890), and it's only gone down from there."

Most of the research and development toward an oral rabies vaccine had been aimed at stopping raccoon rabies. But with no known human deaths from raccoon rabies, the public health argument for oral vaccination becomes shaky, Rupprecht said. Some had posed theories for the absence of human mortality: possible differences in raccoon biting behavior, the effectiveness of public health surveillance and technology, the possibility some deaths are being missed. But no clear answers. And while human rabies deaths have declined, "greater than 80 percent of our human cases [today] have no known source of exposure." Laboratory analysis has shown that nearly 40 percent of human cases were acquired outside the United States, and the vast majority of the domestic cases were caused by bats. "And peculiarly, the vast majority of those are ascribed to a single, relatively rare variant we believe associated with silver-haired bats." With all of these unknowns, how strong an argument could be made for oral vaccination?

The real driver of oral vaccination may well be based on the enormous costs associated with the disease, Rupprecht said. But what are those costs? Hard figures were scarce. There were the costs of postexposure treatment, perhaps forty thousand treatments each year. "We have to think about domestic animal involvement, not just primary but booster vaccinations, the loss of loved pets to euthanasia, diagnostic overload and the costs associated with that—forty, fifty, sometimes one hundred dollars per submission, and they rise with the invasion of a new virus. And the programmatic expenditures for investigations of such cases."

But that is only part of the economic model, Rupprecht said. Most cost-effectiveness studies involving oral rabies vaccination have been conducted by veterinarians and public health officials. The CDC assigned one of its economists, Martin Meltzer, to the problem, and his study was presented during the Atlanta rabies meeting later that week. Using a theoretical model of raccoon rabies elimination, in which rabies baits were distributed in a circle and pushed outward in expanding rings over a twenty-year period until the virus was eliminated over a thirteen thousand-square-mile area, Meltzer found that oral vaccination would fail to save society money, compared to simply living with the disease, unless pets and other domestic animals could be vaccinated less often than they are today.

Cathy Hanlon, who had left the New York State Department of Health in 1996 to work with her mentor, Charles Rupprecht, provided the first estimate of what it would cost to eliminate raccoon rabies along the East Coast by oral vaccination: a stunning six hundred million dollars. That would pay for four applications, at one hundred baits per square kilometer. Those kinds of figures, Rupprecht pointed out, are greater than the entire budget for the National Center for Infectious Diseases.

A Word from Texas

The Texans, who could claim by far the largest effort to date on U.S. soil, were a major part of the Athens meeting. They had successfully built a large-scale oral vaccination program, something no one else had been able to do. In two years, some 2.3 million baits had been dropped over South and Central Texas, with a third distribution planned for January 7, 1997. Keith Clark's address to the group struck a philosophical tone. The head of zoonosis control for the Texas Department of Health left most of the details of the Texas program to Gayne Fearneyhough, who spoke next. Clark had been out on leave most of the year; a viral infection had damaged his heart, and he was stepping down from his administrative position and considering retiring altogether. "I want to take the prerogative of one who is nearly retired—if not retired—from the field, to pontificate a little," he said. Sounding a bit defiant, Clark began: "I want to start off by emphasizing the Texas Oral Rabies Vaccination Program is not an experiment. It is a public health measure, and one which was deemed to be a public health emergency." It was undertaken in response to the threat of canine rabies, vectored by coyotes, moving northward toward San Antonio and beyond.

Clark offered a series of practical suggestions to anyone wishing to build an oral vaccination program: First of all, "you need to be lucky." An example of their good fortune was the change in leadership at the Texas Department of Health with the arrival of Commissioner David Smith. What Clark didn't mention was that a few months earlier, Smith had announced his retirement from the state health department to become the president of the Texas Tech University Health Sciences Center in Lubbock. The decision was a family matter, Smith had said. His wife, also a physician, had found it difficult attaining suitable employment in Austin, where her husband's state job made many offers a potential conflict of interest. Before Smith left, he made certain the Oral Rabies Vaccination Program would have adequate funds for a third year, together with the last of two year's funding provided by the state legislature.

Beyond 1997, with rabies cases plummeting, with Clark and Smith gone, and a new commissioner yet to be appointed, the future of the program was anyone's guess. Fearneyhough, who continued as head of the Texas Oral Rabies Vaccination Program, was hopeful. Still, in his remarks to the group, he discussed the possibility of reducing the bait density even further, to lower the cost of the program, about four million dollars a year. But they were far enough along, Fearneyhough said, that for the first time they could begin thinking about how to keep canine rabies out of Texas once it was pushed south, back into Mexico. There were two strategies: one would maintain some sort of vaccine barrier along the Rio Grande; the other would increase surveillance for new rabies cases along the border, so that any new outbreaks could be spot treated quickly with vaccine in order to contain them. The latter option, which would be far less expensive, seemed to be the more attractive. For that to work, however, the state would have to switch from a passive system of detecting rabies, which relied on someone stumbling across a rabid animal, to an active system that would continuously search for rabies. That would require the creation of some sort of rapid response team.

Rupprecht's Report on SAG-2

Keith Clark and Gayne Fearneyhough were curious as they sat down in the CDC auditorium on the second day of the conference, to hear Charles Rupprecht's paper on a new oral vaccine for coyotes. They had heard rumors he had been working on a new oral vaccine based on a canary pox, a generation improved over V-RG. Instead, Rupprecht presented some early results on studies of SAG-2, a live, weakened vaccine that had been used widely in Europe. It was an advance over what the Canadians were using, but it was still a live rabies virus. In a laboratory study of a handful of coyotes, SAG-2 protected the animals against rabies with one bait, as opposed to the three baits containing V-RG. The Texans were surprised, given Rupprecht's stated concerns about the relative safety of V-RG. SAG-2 was manufactured by a European company called Virbac, which had an office in Fort Worth, Texas. Robert Miller with the USDA said he had recently had informal contact with someone about what it would take to approve SAG-2 as an oral rabies vaccine in the United States. Miller explained the process would be similar to that undertaken for V-RG. As for the Texans, they weren't particularly interested. "We're not going to change horses in the middle of the stream," Fearneyhough said.

The Third Drop

It was becoming a tradition, or perhaps a curse. The third airdrop was scheduled to commence January 7, 1997, but was postponed a day because of severe weather. Over the next six weeks, 2.6 million baits were dropped by three Canadian Twin Otters over forty-one thousand square miles, including parts of seventy-seven Texas counties—similar in scope to the previous year's project, with somewhat different geographic boundaries. In 1997, 1.5 million baits targeted for the canine epizootic were airdropped over most of South Texas—except for a notch along the Gulf Coast and Cameron, Texas' southernmost county, which had been largely rabies-free all along— and another 1.1 million baits dropped in a long band encircling much of West and Central Texas, for fox rabies. And although it was still too early to know for sure, the number of fox rabies cases appeared to be declining as a result of the drop. In 1995, 244 cases were reported; while in the first eleven months of 1996, only ninety-eight cases came to light. Again, health officials weren't willing to rule out the possibility that the drought may have been a factor.

Full Circle

As for Sue and Monte Smith, whose farm was the scene of the first recorded rabies case of the South Texas canine epizootic in 1988, they were later revisited by the epizootic. More than five years after that first encounter with the rabid coyote, in late 1993, they were summoned outside by the sound of excited barking. Once again, they found their dogs [by this time, Sheiba had died of old age, though Buckwheat was still around] locked in battle with an angry coyote. Monte shot the intruder. "He then turned to his beloved puppies and felt on their faces for damage," Sue Smith recalled. "And I'm standing there going, 'Monte!' And their little faces were soaked with coyote saliva. He just looked at me and went, 'Oh no.' Of course, a farmer's hands are cracked. I made him go to the doctor. Our dogs again had recently been vaccinated, so we knew we were okay. The vets did give them a booster. My husband then had to take the rabies series. We had to pay for it out of our pocket, where everybody else in the county who had to take them got them for free. Because we had insurance. But because the vaccine was provided by the state of Texas, our insurance wouldn't pay for it." The cost of the shots was $657, plus doctor's fees.

Rabies Recommendations

Recommendations regarding humans exposed to potentially rabid animals call for prompt cleansing of the wound with soap and water, then disinfecting with alcohol, iodine, or other antiseptics. After any bite or attack, the size, kind, and color of the animal should be noted, as well as the location the exposure occurred. Children should be taught to seek the help of an adult—a policeman or school guard, for instance. A decision to begin postexposure treatment can be made by a physician or public health official, but usually is based on several factors, including the type of exposure. The World Health Organization lists three categories of rabies exposure:

Category	Type of contact with suspect animal*	Recommended treatment
I	Touching or feeding of animals. Licks on intact skin.	None, if reliable case history is available.
II	Nibbling of uncovered skin. Minor scratches or abrasions without bleeding. Licks on broken skin.	Administer vaccine immediately, and stop if ten-day observation or laboratory techniques confirm suspect animal to be rabies negative.**
III	Single or multiple transdermal bites or scratches.	Administer rabies immunoglobulin and

Category	Type of contact with suspect animal*	Recommended treatment
III cont.	Contamination of mucous membrane with saliva.	vaccine immediately, and stop if suspect animal confirmed as rabies negative.***

* Exposure to rodents, rabbits, and hares seldom, if ever, requires specific antirabies treatment.

** If an apparently healthy dog or cat in or from a low risk area is under observation, the situation may warrant delaying the initiation of treatment.

*** Observation period only applies to dogs and cats. Other domestic and wild animals (except threatened or endangered species) suspected as rabid should be killed humanely and their tissue examined using appropriate laboratory techniques.

What the Vets Say

Each year, the National Association of State Public Health Veterinarians publishes its annual recommendations for rabies control. The recommendations are then published by the Centers for Disease Control and Prevention. In 1996, the association recommended that only vaccines with three-year efficacy be used to vaccinate dogs and cats. Some states continued to require the older one-year vaccines. Dogs and cats should be vaccinated against rabies annually starting at three months of age. Because more rabies cases are reported in cats than dogs in the United States, vaccination of cats should be required—again, something not all states have done.

A healthy, vaccinated dog or cat that bites a person should be confined and observed for ten days. Rabies vaccination should not be given during that period, and the animal should be evaluated by a veterinarian—and the health department notified—at the first sign of illness. If rabies symptoms develop, the animal should be euthanized, and its head sent under refrigeration for testing. Stray or unwanted dogs or cats that bite people may be euthanized immediately and tested. Other biting animals that might have exposed a person to rabies and should be reported to the health department immediately.

Unvaccinated dogs and cats exposed to a rabid animal should be euthanized immediately. If the owner is unwilling to have this done, the animal should be placed in strict isolation for six months and vaccinated one month before being released. Animals with expired vaccinations should be evaluated on a case-by-case basis. Currently vaccinated dogs and cats should be revaccinated, kept under the owner's control and observed for forty-five days.

As for wildlife, the association recommended against the use of any traditional parenteral rabies vaccine in wild animals, since efficacy has not been established, and because virus-shedding periods are unknown. "The use of licensed oral vaccines for the mass immunization of wildlife should be considered in selected situations, with the approval of the state agency responsible for animal rabies control." Wild or exotic carnivores and bats should not be kept as pets. Because of the rabies risk in such animals, the association, along with the American Veterinary Medical Association and the Council of State and Territorial Epidemiologists "strongly recommend the enactment of state laws prohibiting the importation, distribution, relocation, or keeping of wild animals and wild animals that are crossbred to domestic dogs and cats as pets." The guidelines continue:

> *The public should be warned not to handle wildlife. Wild mammals (as well as the offspring of wild species crossbred with domestic dogs and cats) that bite or otherwise expose people, pets, or livestock should be considered for euthanasia and rabies examination. A person bitten by any wild mammal should immediately report the incident to a physician who can evaluate the need for antirabies treatment.*
>
> *1. Terrestrial Mammals. Continuous and persistent government-funded programs for trapping or poisoning wildlife are not cost effective in reducing wildlife rabies reservoirs on a statewide basis. However, limited control in high-contact areas (e.g., picnic grounds, camps, or suburban areas) might be indicated for the removal of selected high-risk species of wildlife. The state wildlife agency and state health department should be consulted for coordination of any proposed vaccination or population-reduction programs.*
>
> *2. Bats. Indigenous rabid bats have been reported from every state except Alaska and Hawaii and have caused rabies in at least 22 humans in the United States. However, it is neither feasible nor desirable to control rabies in bats by programs to reduce bat populations. Bats should be excluded from houses and surrounding structures to prevent direct association with humans. Such structures should then be made bat-proof by sealing entrances used by bats.*

For further information or assistance, contact local or state health departments, state veterinary associations, or your local veterinarian.

BIBLIOGRAPHY

Baer, George M., ed. *The Natural History of Rabies.* New York: Academic Press, 1975; Boca Raton, Fla.: CRC Press, 1991.

Brass, Danny A. *Rabies in Bats: Natural History and Public Health Implications.* Ridgefield, Conn.: Livia Press, 1994.

Cadieux, Charles L. *Coyotes: Predators & Survivors.* New York: Stone Wall Press, 1983.

Dobie, J. Frank. *The Voice of the Coyote.* Boston: Little, Brown and Company, 1949.

Doughty, Robin W. *Wildlife and Man in Texas.* College Station: Texas A&M University Press, 1983.

Grady, Wayne. *The World of the Coyote.* San Francisco: Sierra Club Books, 1994.

Hoeprich, Paul D., M. Colin Jordan, and Allan R. Ronald. *Infectious Diseases.* Philadelphia: J. B. Lippincott Co., 1994.

Kaplan, Colin. *Rabies: The Facts.* London: Oxford University Press, 1986.

Keirle, Nathaniel Garland. *Studies in Rabies.* Baltimore: Lord Baltimore Press, 1909.

Leydet, Francois. *The Coyote: Defiant Songdog of the West.* Norman: University of Oklahoma Press, 1988.

MacDonald, David W. *Rabies and Wildlife; a Biologist's Perspective.* London: Oxford University Press, 1980.

Tizard, Ian R. *An Introduction to Veterinary Immunology.* Philadelphia: W. B. Saunders Co., 1977.

Tuttle, Merlin D. *America's Neighborhood Bats.* Austin: University of Texas Press, 1988.

INDEX